# POLES IN ILLINOIS

# POLES IN ILLINOIS

JOHN RADZILOWSKI
ANN HETZEL GUNKEL

Southern Illinois University Press
*Carbondale*

Southern Illinois University Press
www.siupress.com

Copyright © 2020 by the Board of Trustees,
Southern Illinois University
All rights reserved
Printed in the United States of America

23  22  21  20    4  3  2  1

Library of Congress Cataloging-in-Publication Data
Names: Radzilowski, John, 1965– author. | Gunkel, Ann Hetzel, 1963– author.
Title: Poles in Illinois / John Radzilowski, Ann Hetzel Gunkel.
Description: Carbondale, IL : Southern Illinois University Press, 2020. | Includes bibliographical references and index. | Summary: "This short, clear, and comprehensive history of Poles in the state of Illinois from 1818 to the present shows a rich story of diversity and the changing nature of Polish ethnicity in the state over the past 200 years"—Provided by publisher.
Identifiers: LCCN 2019023354 (print) | LCCN 2019023355 (ebook) | ISBN 9780809337231 (paperback) | ISBN 9780809337248 (ebook)
Subjects: LCSH: Polish Americans—Illinois—History. | Polish Americans—Illinois—Chicago—History. | Polish Americans—Illinois—Social life and customs. | Polish people—Illinois—History. | Immigrants—Illinois—History. | Illinois—Emigration and immigration—History. | Immigrants—Illinois—Chicago—Social conditions. | Chicago (Ill.)—Ethnic relations—History.
Classification: LCC F550.P7 R33 2020  (print) | LCC F550.P7 (ebook) | DDC 977.3/0049185—dc23
LC record available at https://lccn.loc.gov/2019023354
LC ebook record available at https://lccn.loc.gov/2019023355

# CONTENTS

# TABLES AND FIGURES

# PREFACE

The present book is the first attempt at a historical overview of Poles and Polish Americans in the state of Illinois. Chicago is the most prominent Polish community in the United States, and while there have been many fine books and articles written on various aspects of Polish American history in the Windy City, no modern, comprehensive work has ever been attempted. Even less has been written about the histories of the many smaller Polish settlements in the rest of the state of Illinois.

*Poles in Illinois* has been written for a broad audience: for the general public interested in an overlooked aspect of Illinois history, for those interested in one facet of the state's tremendous cultural diversity, and for the nearly one million people of Polish ancestry who make their home here. The book focuses on the lived experiences of Polish Americans in Illinois rather than on historiographic interpretations of Polish American history.

This book contains notes and references as well as a guide for further reading, and it draws heavily on the research of American and Polish scholars who have explored aspects of the history and culture of Polish Americans in Chicago ranging from the earliest settlement in the mid-nineteenth century to the creation of institutions as diverse as fraternal societies, churches, hospitals, and publishing companies. Despite this impressive range of scholarship, many gaps remain in the historical record that an overview history such as this simply cannot fill. For example, the history of Polish American communities in the decades after World War II is not well understood aside from a few noteworthy works on smaller waves of immigrants who came in those decades.

In approaching such a large and diverse topic, the authors chose to emphasize the lived experiences of ordinary Polish Americans in Illinois rather than biographies of "famous people" or the histories of organizations as important as some of these are. While scholars and journalists have often focused on the experiences of individuals and small groups whose histories diverge markedly from the normative experience, *Poles in Illinois* also seeks to bring back into focus the lives of "ordinary" men and women whose stories appear too rarely in history books. This is done through the use of letters, oral interviews, and contemporary newspaper articles. The authors were blessed with an abundance of resources in this effort. Through archival collections, such as the Chicago Foreign Language Press Survey and the Oral History Archives of Chicago Polonia, and published selections of letters, such as the recently issued *Letters from Readers in the Polish American Press, 1902–1969*, the authors have attempted to let the Poles of Illinois speak for themselves as much as possible.[1]

Illinois's large and diverse Polish American community awaits and deserves further research and appreciation as an important element of the state's history. This is a task for scholars but also for the educated public on whose shoulders also rests the responsibility for preserving, understanding, and interpreting the state's past. *Poles in Illinois* represents a small step in that direction.

# ACKNOWLEDGMENTS

This project was made possible by many colleagues, friends, and mentors over the years, particularly those in the Polish American Historical Association (PAHA) and the Polish Institute of Arts and Sciences of America (PIASA). The presidents, boards, and membership of both organizations have given me a Polish-American home in academia. For their camaraderie, solidarity, and expertise, I thank the women scholars who have bolstered my work on Polonia, especially Dr. Mary P. Erdmans, Dr. Anna D. Jaroszyńska-Kirchmann, Dr. Grazyna J. Kozaczka, Dr. Karen Majewski, Dr. Anna Mazurkiewicz, Dr. Dorota Praszałowicz, Dr. Agnieszka Stasiewicz-Bieńkowska, Dr. Pien Versteegh, Dr. Joanna Wojdon, and Dr. Małgorzata Zachara. I'm particularly grateful for warm encouragement of my work in Polish American studies from the late Dr. Stanislaus A. Blejwas, the late Dr. Thaddeus Radzilowski, Dr. Thomas J. Napierkowski, and Dr. John Bukowczyk, gentlemen and scholars all. A great debt is owed to my wonderful colleagues in Cultural Studies at Columbia College Chicago. For their friendship and collegial warmth, I thank especially Dr. Jaafar Aksikas, Dr. Sean Johnson Andrews, and Dr. Carmelo Esterrich. I thank all my students at Columbia College Chicago for their energy and passion.

My work would not exist at all if not for my profoundly influential high school teacher, Sr. Mary Jerome Rompala, C.R., and my university mentors, Dr. David H. Krause, Dr. David Ferrell Krell, Dr. Michael Naas, and Dr. John Sallis.

My sincere appreciation is extended to Dr. Jeff Hancks. I am in debt to the entire staff of the library at the Polish Museum of America for their assistance, and to our editor Kristine Priddy. This project was supported with Summer Project Completion and Subvention Grants from Columbia College Chicago.

I'm deeply grateful for the expertise and dedication of my coauthor Dr. John Radzilowski, who brought this project to fruition.

For their love and many warm memories of Polish holidays, I thank the Aylward, Dankowski, Dolata, Hetzel, Gunkel, and Uzdańska families.

The project wouldn't have been possible without persistent love, support, coffee, and cake from my family: my husband, Dr. David J. Gunkel, my son, Stanisław J. Gunkel, and our faithful dog Maki. They are truly my most beloved Poles in Illinois.

*Ann Hetzel Gunkel, PhD*
*Chicago, Illinois*

\* \* \*

This work builds on a foundation of scholarship created over many years by many hands and many minds. The Polish American Historical Association deserves special thanks for fostering that scholarship since its inception in the late 1940s. A particular debt of gratitude is owed to the late Mieczysław Haiman, the late archivist and scholar Sabina Logisz, scholars Stan Blejwas, John Bukowczyk, Mary P. Erdmans, William Galush, Anna D. Jaroszyńska-Kirchmann, Tom Napierkowski, Dominic Pacyga, and James S. Pula, to name but a few. My father, the late Dr. Thaddeus Radzilowski, was a constant source of new ideas and a sounding board for large parts of this work. His insights into important but still largely overlooked aspects of Polish American social history continue to inspire me. My friend and mentor Dr. Joseph Amato also deserves thanks for teaching me to look at the past through the lens of the Annals School and to better understand the *mentalities* of our ancestors.

Research on this book could not have been completed without the kind help of many people. In particular, I thank the archivists and librarians of the Polish Museum of America in Chicago, especially Julita Siegel, Małgorzata Kot, Iwona Bozek, and Jan Lorys. Sister Lea Stefancova, FSJB, archivist of the Diocese of Peoria, and Sister Mary Fran Flynn SSND, archivist of the Diocese of Belleville, provided access to sources and answered questions about Poles in downstate Illinois. Mr. John Krolak of Peru, Illinois, provided additional sources and access to family photographs. Professor Mary Cygan who was one of the guiding spirits behind the creation of the Chicago Oral History Archives in the 1970s, also deserves a word of thanks. The project she helped to oversee greatly enriched this book.

Dr. Jeff Hancks encouraged and fostered this project. Editor Kristine Priddy and the staff of Southern Illinois University Press saw it through many ups and downs to final completion. The University of Alaska Southeast provided professional development funds to help with travel and research.

Coauthor Dr. Ann Gunkel deserves great thanks for countless contributions to the project. Her good humor and patience with the many starts and stops of the publishing process was of inestimable value.

Any errors and omissions in the present work are entirely my own.

*John Radzilowski, PhD*
*Ketchikan, Alaska*

Poles in Illinois

# INTRODUCTION

"Chicago," Sophie Nadrowska explained in a letter to her parents in Poland in 1890, "is Poland in perfection." For generations of Polish immigrants and their descendants, Illinois has been a place to call home: perhaps not always perfect, yet still welcoming. Since the early nineteenth century, Poles have made the state their home, and in turn they have shaped the history and character of Illinois. They settled in the industrial neighborhoods of Chicago and its environs, in Joliet and Rockford, in the coal-mining towns of south-central Illinois, and on farms across the state. In 2010, an estimated 1 million Polish Americans lived in Illinois, making up 8 percent of all state residents.[1]

Polish immigrants have made Illinois home for almost two centuries. Chicago has been home to one of the densest urban concentrations of Poles anywhere outside of Poland. There is a saying that Chicago is the second largest Polish city in the world, after Warsaw, Poland's capital. Although this is not entirely correct (at least as of this writing), the popularity of this "fact" is a reminder of the outsized role played by Illinois in the consciousness of Poles and Polish Americans. Many of the most prominent Polish American organizations are headquartered in Chicago. In Poland itself, "Czikago" is, as much as "Nowy Jork," synonymous with America.

With such a long and storied background, one would imagine a small shelf of books surveying the history Poles in Illinois or even covering the contributions of Poles to Chicago. Yet, the present volume is the first effort at writing such a history. There are many excellent specialized studies on aspects of the Polish experience in Chicago but no overall history aside from a memorial book produced for city's centennial in 1937 and a popular history/cookbook.

For Polish communities beyond Chicago, aside from parish jubilee books, there is virtually nothing. Standard histories of the state make only passing mention of the Polish presence. Although Poles played an outsized role in shaping Chicago's physical and cultural history, standard histories of the Windy City again provide little detail other than to note the size of the Polish population and its role in heavy industry.

But perhaps this is not as surprising as it seems. The Polish presence in Illinois and in the state's leading city is so large and so integral to the identity of the state and of Chicago that it has become invisible and taken for granted. Moreover, there is no single "Polish community" encompassing Illinois or even Chicago. Polish immigrants created many distinct communities in the state that were often so complete and intensive in their development that they sought and needed little input from other Polish communities, let alone their neighbors of different backgrounds. The inward focus of so many of the Illinois communities created by Polish immigrants in the late nineteenth and early twentieth centuries made it hard for them mobilize politically and elect their members to public office. The later arrival of waves of more politically conscious Polish refugees in the second half of the twentieth century did little to change that. Despite the massive Polish presence in Chicago since the 1880s, and much to the frustration of those who sought to be leaders of Polonia (the Polish community in America), the city never had a Polish mayor and probably never will. That inward focus, however, created a dense and rich world of institutions—banks and restaurants, hospitals and orphanages, churches and schools, publishing houses and recording studios, artistic societies and sports leagues, unions and social service agencies. Poles shaped the physical environment of the state from modest working-class neighborhoods to factories to massive neo-Gothic churches whose splendor rivals those of the Old World.

The world created by Polish immigrants exists like a kind of parallel universe to the more familiar history of Illinois. Its history is little known outside of interested historians and history enthusiasts. Sadly, it is often little known by those whose forebears built it and breathed it into life. The task of this book is to begin to tell this story and provide a window into a rich and important but overlooked part of the state's history.

* * *

Poles who have settled in Illinois came in several distinct waves from a Poland that was at the heart of modern Europe's fiercest political convulsions. Poland is situated in the geographical center of Europe, between the southern coast of the Baltic Sea and the Carpathian Mountains. Poles speak a Slavic dialect—a western branch of the largest ethnolinguistic family in Europe. This ethnolinguistic core mixed freely with a host of ancient and modern peoples in central Europe—including Germans to the west and other Slavic groups to the south and east such as Slovaks, Czechs, Ukrainians, and Ruthenians. Poles had close and sometimes fractious historical links to Lithuanians. At one time, the country was a haven for the world's largest Jewish populations and one of the world's most northerly Muslim communities. Poland's location made it a crossroads for peoples, cultures, and ideas from across Eurasia. Its culture and its predominant Roman Catholic faith tied it to the West, but throughout much of its history, Poland gazed East.

Walter's Tavern on West 47th Street in Chicago, circa 1930s. Operated by immigrants Walter and Mary Zielinski, it was one of the few bars in its day that served customers of all races and ethnicities. Chicago History Museum, ICHi-059450, copyright © Chicago Historical Society, published on or before 2013, all rights reserved.

A Polish monarchy emerged by the middle of the tenth century and expanded to include much of what is now modern Poland by the early eleventh century. Thereafter, a long period of feudal fragmentation and external invasion ensured that the country remained politically divided. Under the reigns of Władysław Elbow-high (1261–1333) and his son Casimir the Great (1310–70), the Polish monarchy revived and its boundaries expanded, becoming an important regional power. In 1386, Poland entered a dynastic union with the neighboring Grand Duchy of Lithuania, creating the largest single country in Europe, stretching from the shores of the Baltic to the Black Sea. By the early 1500s, the Polish-Lithuanian Commonwealth had developed a unique form of constitutional monarchy with limited royal power, an elective king, and a strong parliament made up of a large and diverse class of service gentry who constituted 10 to 15 percent of the population. The limited powers of the monarch ensured that in an age when kings sought to impose religious uniformity on their lands, Poland remained a place of relative toleration and provided a haven for numerous dissenter groups. While Moscow was still a provincial backwater, Polish kings, bishops, and nobles made cities like Kraków, Warsaw, Wilno, and Lwów centers for the northern Renaissance, sponsoring learning, art, literature, and architecture that combined Italian and eastern European influences. Cities such as Gdańsk became centers for trade, with links to England, Holland, and beyond. Poland's relatively small but battle-tested armies repelled invasions from her powerful neighbors and played the critical role in saving Vienna in 1683, defeating a major Turkish invasion of central Europe.

By the late 1600s, the internal tensions and external threats weakened the commonwealth. A small strata of powerful and wealthy nobles, known as "magnates," expanded their powers at the expense of the majority of lesser nobles, as well as to the detriment of cities and the peasantry. Poland's neighbors developed autocratic monarchies with a taste for territorial expansion and were increasingly able to use their money to influence Polish politics and buy candidates for the throne. As the commonwealth declined, it grew increasingly impoverished and fell under the control of a Russian empire led by tsars such as Peter the Great and Catherine the Great. By the mid-1700s, Polish reformers, influenced by new political winds, sought to revitalize the government but were blocked by foreign interests and their local supporters. In 1772, Russia, Austria, and Prussia annexed pieces of the commonwealth, but this did not halt the reformers. During this period many Poles went into political exile to escape the decline at home or avoid problems with pro-Russian foes. Many journeyed to France and some to America, where soldiers like Kazimierz Pułaski (1745–79) and Tadeusz Kościuszko (1746–1817) aided the American colonists in their struggle for independence. In 1791, the Polish parliament enacted Europe's first democratic constitution, modeled on American efforts, transforming the country into a true constitutional monarchy. This proved a direct threat to Poland's autocratic neighbors. With an eye on revolutionary events in France, Russia and Prussia seized large swaths of Poland, reducing the country to a mere shadow of its former self and ending the experiment in democracy. A revolt in 1794 led by Kościuszko sought to restore Poland's independence. Despite some initial victories, it was defeated by Russian armies, and Poland lost her independence.

For the next 123 years, Poland remained under Russian, Prussian (German), and Austrian occupation. Although Polish patriots staged periodic revolts to regain their lost freedom, none succeeded. Only with the end of World War I and the defeat of Germany and the collapse of the Austro-Hungarian and Russian empires would Poland finally break free of foreign domination. This loss of freedom and the desire to regain it profoundly shaped Polish consciousness. The "Polish Cause" would occupy the minds and hearts of generations of Poles. The tragic loss of independence, the suffering and repression that accompanied it, and the hope of Poland's restoration would be a key piece of the cultural legacy that Polish immigrants brought to America.

Emigration from Poland began in earnest during this "long nineteenth century" of subjugation. Polish political exiles often ended up in France or Switzerland, though small cells of these emigrants could be found throughout the world. In the years after the American Revolution, few Poles chose to come to the United States, but that began to change in the early 1830s following the unsuccessful November Insurrection in Poland. A few hundred Polish émigrés came to America in the 1830s, some of whom would find their way to the Illinois frontier.

There were several main waves of Polish immigration to the United States. Although some of the earliest and best-known Polish immigrants were political exiles, the vast majority of Poles who came to the United States—and Illinois—came for economic reasons.

Mass Polish immigration began in the 1850s. The first identifiable Polish community was founded by a group of Silesians on the Texas Gulf Coast in 1854. The majority of early arrivals, however, chose to settle in the Midwest and Great Lakes states. Between the 1850s and the 1880s, most Polish immigrants came from areas of western Poland under Prussian (later German) rule. They followed their German and Czech neighbors as part of a European-wide wave of migration sparked by the economic and cultural changes brought on by industrialization and the modernization of agriculture. Traditional farm holdings were often converted to cash rents, impelling rural families to seek out opportunities for wage-labor jobs on larger estates or in Europe's growing cities. America, with its abundant farmland and growing industry, attracted more and more of these migrants. Wages in the New World outpaced those in Europe, and hard-working immigrants could earn good money. Immigrants came to support their families, sometimes saving their wages to return home to Poland to buy a small piece of land or build a better house.

These earliest immigrants were often "settler immigrants"—they came as family groups seeking to settle in the New World, often in rural areas. Poles from the German partition area enjoyed a somewhat higher standard of living than their counterparts under Austrian or Russian rule, so the first Poles coming to Illinois included some people with education and craft skills. While most Poles came from rural villages, over 85 percent of immigrants before World War I would make their homes in industrial cities like Chicago or in mining districts like central Illinois.

Although the earliest Polish communities were founded by settler immigrants, their numbers were soon dwarfed by masses of "labor immigrants." These immigrants came as young men (and, as time went on, women) to take wage-labor jobs. Their sojourn in America was often viewed as temporary, and as many as 30 to 40 percent would ultimately return to Europe after working in the New World.

By the 1880s and 1890s, labor immigrants dominated the Polish immigrant flow. In addition, more and more immigrants began to arrive from the Austrian-controlled portion of Poland, especially from impoverished villages in the Carpathian Mountains. Immigrants from the Russian zone also began to arrive, although it was illegal to leave Russia until 1891. By the turn of the century, immigrants from Austria and Russia dominated the migration of Poles to the United States, which grew into a torrent during the first decade of the twentieth century. By 1910, an estimated three million Poles had come to the United States. Only the outbreak of World War I put a halt to immigration from Poland as well as most of the rest of Europe. These American Polish communities became collectively known as "Polonia."

The overwhelming majority of these Polish immigrants was Roman Catholic. Although a very large number of Jews from historic Polish lands also came to America's shores during this same period, Jews and Poles in America adopted different identities, unlike in Europe where a portion of Jews identified as "Poles of the Mosaic faith." Catholic Poles identified as Polish Americans and Jewish Poles as Jewish Americans, though they often settled in close proximity to each other, especially in large cities like Chicago. The same was true of other immigrants from historic Old Poland: Lithuanians, Ukrainians, and Rusyns (or Ruthenians), though some of these immigrants who joined Polish parishes in America did adopt a Polish identity.

Kilinski's Ice Cream Parlor on Milwaukee Avenue, Chicago, circa 1913. Pelagia Kilinski, who worked at the family business, stands in the doorway while customers Janina and Irma Ulatowska look out through the window. Courtesy of Polish Museum of America Archives.

Amid the chaos of war and revolution in 1918, Poland regained her independence. The end of the war brought a brief renewal of emigration from Poland, as well as some returns from America by those hoping to rebuild their mother country. In 1924, amid a growing wave of nativism, the U.S. government placed sharp restrictions on immigration from Poland and other countries in eastern and southern Europe, effectively halting the arrival of more Poles.

Poland's independence lasted a mere twenty-one years. On September 1, 1939, Nazi dictator Adolf Hitler launched German armies against Poland, which were joined seventeen days later by Soviet dictator Joseph Stalin's communist forces from the east in support of their Nazi allies. In spite of desperate resistance, Poland was again partitioned. From 1939 to 1945, Poland was ravaged by the forces of Europe's most genocidal dictators. Under German rule, Poland's ancient Jewish population was nearly annihilated. Both the Soviets and the Nazis sought to destroy the Polish nation, murdering millions and deporting millions more to concentration and death camps. Nearly 3 million Polish Jews died under Nazi rule between 1939 and 1945, along with about 2.5 million Polish Christians, leaving aside at least an another 150,000 murdered by the communists and an estimated 100,000 killed by Ukrainian nationalists.[2] Nearly a quarter of Poland's population perished. Despite the sacrifice and valor of Poland's armies, which fought alongside the Americans and British throughout the war, Poland was given to Soviet dictator Stalin in 1945, who imposed a murderous program of subjugation on the exhausted and traumatized Poles, resulting in the murder of between 30,000 and 50,000 more people.

The war resulted in one of the greatest refugee problems in modern history, as millions of people were displaced or deported from their homes. Huge numbers of Poles found themselves as stateless refugees in camps throughout Germany, and many did not want to return home to the brutality and poverty of Soviet-ruled Poland. Hundreds of thousands of refugees—many former slave laborers and concentration camp victims—were joined by veterans of the Polish armed forces whose service alongside the Americans and British marked them as enemies of the Soviet-imposed communist regime. Many of these refugees made their way to America in the late 1940s and early 1950s, creating a new wave of Polish immigrants. These newcomers were quite distinct from the earlier waves of Polish immigration to the United States. They were deeply affected by their experiences in Europe, and many were well educated, patriotic, and motivated on behalf of the Polish cause.

Following the death of Stalin, a trickle of emigrants was able to leave communist Poland in the 1960s and 1970s. Despite some efforts at economic liberalization during this period, Poland was wracked by periodic crises and protests caused by government malfeasance and repression. Despite this, the communist regime in Warsaw backed by the Soviet Union and its vast military resources remained in control. In October 1978, however, that situation changed forever. A little-known Polish cardinal, Karol Wojtyła, was elected as the first non-Italian pontiff of the Roman Catholic Church in centuries. Pope John Paul II's intelligence, wit, and evident personal holiness inspired his compatriots to peacefully challenge communist rule. Following the pope's visit to Poland in 1979, the communists' tools of fear and coercion began to fail. In 1980, Solidarity, the first independent trade union in the communist bloc, arose in Poland, setting off nationwide strikes that paralyzed the regime and captivated the attention of the world. In December 1981, the regime cracked down with force on the nonviolent Solidarity movement with targeted killings, beatings, and mass arrests of its leaders. In May of that year, Pope John Paul II barely survived an assassination attempt engineered by the Soviet KGB.

As in previous periods of repression, many Poles were forced to flee abroad. Imprisoned Solidarity activists were offered one-way visas to the West. Many, knowing that they and their children would face a lifetime of discrimination in jobs and schools, took the offer. The largest number of these "Solidarity émigrés" came to the United States, creating yet another wave of Polish immigration. Like their post–World War II counterparts, many of these immigrants were educated, often with families and children.

The violent response of Poland's communist rulers, however, proved futile to stop the march of freedom unleashed by Pope John Paul II and Solidarity. Moreover, other communist satellite regimes began to unravel as well, as their people joined their Polish neighbors. In 1989, following protracted negotiations, Poland's communists agreed to national elections. While not entirely free, Polish voters overwhelmingly rejected Communist Party candidates. The Communist Party collapsed, and with it the edifice of communist rule began to crumble and a new democratic Poland began to emerge from the rubble.

The economic legacy of communism did not, however, disappear quickly. Throughout the 1990s and 2000s, large numbers of Poles migrated to Western Europe and the United States to look for work, to reunite families, or to seek education, creating the most recent wave of Polish immigrants. With Poland's accession to the European Union in 2004, the flow of Poles to America slowed once again as Polish migrants chose closer destinations in Europe.

Poland's tumultuous history over the past two hundred years sparked successive waves of Polish immigrants to the New World. Their experience of emigration or exile shaped their outlook, colored their perspectives on America, and passed on in some form to their American children, grandchildren, and great-grandchildren. The Poles who settled in Illinois brought an ancient culture and experiences of home lost and found once more, discovering a place there that offered opportunity and hardship in equal measures. The heritage they carried with them and the experiences they found in the New World would form the building blocks of Illinois's Polish American communities.

Polish survivors of German and Soviet concentration camps marching in the Constitution Day parade, May 2000. Photo by Zbigniew Bzdak; copyright © 2000.

# 1

# NA POCZĄTKU: SETTLING IN ILLINOIS

### Early Polish Settlers, 1818–50

The first Polish settlers in Illinois came as early as 1818, the year the state was admitted to the Union. Limited records, poor spelling of names in early documents, and a tangle of tall tales and stories make it hard for scholars to penetrate the fog of the past. The first Polish names found in Illinois were John and Killon Sandusky (Sądowski) who settled in Franklin County in southern Illinois in 1818 or shortly thereafter.[1] Several members of the extended Sandusky family were among the first Poles in the state. All were probably descendants of Antoni Sądowski, a Polish nobleman who came to America in 1704 via Great Britain. He settled in frontier Pennsylvania where he learned local native languages and served as an interpreter for colonial officials. Sądowski married an Englishwoman, and his descendants married into English or Scots families, so that by the beginning of the nineteenth century the Sanduskys fully assimilated into the frontier society of the middle border region, though they were well aware of their Polish origin. Isaac Sandusky, Antoni's great-grandson, moved with his extended family from Kentucky in 1827 and settled in Vermilion County, Illinois, near the Indiana state line. According to an early county history, Isaac "brought in the first drove of good cattle from Kentucky to Illinois. . . . He also brought in the first flock of sheep which ever graced the prairies of Vermilion County, driving them from the Blue Grass regions in the fall of 1827."[2]

A larger group of Polish immigrants came to the state in the 1830s in the wake of the failed November Insurrection against Russia. The plight of these political émigrés and their struggle against Russian oppression made them minor celebrities in an America where the memory of the Revolution was still fairly fresh.

In November 1833, 234 Poles were expelled from Austria and put on ships bound for the United States. Their arrival created a sensation in America, and the question of what was to be done with the nearly destitute immigrants became a matter of public debate in the press as well as in the U.S. Congress.[3]

On arriving in New York, the exiles formed a committee and publicly requested a grant of land from the U.S. government to form a Polish settlement to be called "New Poland." Sympathetic senators introduced a bill to Congress in 1834 to give the Poles land in either Ohio or Illinois. Illinois senator Elias Kane objected to the Poles being sent to his state. After heated debate and much amending, a bill was passed, and President Andrew Jackson signed it into law. The act allowed Polish exiles to purchase land in northwest Illinois in the Rock River Valley for about $1.25 per acre, but only after they had worked on it for ten years. Since this was about the rate that anyone could purchase government land, all the bill did was allow for land sale to these non-citizen Poles.[4]

If the details of the act were disappointing, more trouble ensued for the exiles when the group's secretary absconded with funds collected for the exiles' support. By then, few of the exiles were in any position to take advantage of the offer of land in Illinois, and many had to work as laborers to support themselves. Nevertheless, some Illinois residents, eager to see their state grow, wrote glowing letters of welcome. Citizens of Vandalia tried to entice some of the Poles to central Illinois, writing to the group, "Noble descendants of a brave nation come to us. Heroes of freedom come to us. We greet you with a brotherly embrace. Come and share the abundant fruit of the land and of the freedom your forefathers helped us acquire."[5] About seventy-five of the exiles attempted to go to Illinois, though only a few settled there, either in Vandalia or Galena, with the remainder ending up in St. Louis or Louisville or returning to the east coast.

Austria and Prussia continued to expel Polish revolutionaries, and many, finding no welcome in Western Europe due their background and their association with radical causes, made their way to America. Americans' initial sympathy for the exiles began to evaporate, and the idea of settling large groups in Illinois lost political support. Although some Illinois towns had initially welcomed the prospect of Polish settlement, more and more land was being settled throughout the state. Exile leaders who tried to realize land claims on behalf of their compatriots found some of the land already occupied, and the residents were, unsurprisingly, hostile to the idea of being displaced.[6] By 1840, the "New Poland" plan was dead.

In spite of the failure to create a Polish colony in Illinois, the young state did attract some Polish exiles in the 1830s and 1840s. The precise number of Poles in the state prior to 1850 is a matter of conjecture due to the spotty nature of the evidence, the mobility of early residents, and the tendency of recordkeepers to spell unfamiliar Polish names in creative ways. Aside from the Sandusky family, one researcher has found a minimum of twenty Poles, about twenty-three Polish Jews, and several persons with distinctly German surnames who listed Poland as their place of birth. There were also several dozen names in the early state censuses that may be Polish but cannot be conclusively identified.[7]

Nearly all of these early Polish settlers were men, and presumably most were political émigrés. Most spoke German or French prior to arriving in the New World, so they may have made their way west by working with the more numerous German or French inhabitants. With no contacts and little money, the Poles took any jobs they could find. Many eventually worked their way into solid professions. A few were successful farmers, but more appeared to take up trades. Virtually all married American wives. Their children would be raised as English speakers, though most had some awareness of their fathers' Polish background and the struggle for Polish independence that had driven them to America.

The process of exile resulted in a somewhat random cross-section of immigrants from Poland's politically active classes. Some were well educated and hardworking, and despite having few resources and working low-paid jobs, they earned the respect of their fellow Illinoisans. One Pole, Franciszek Włodecki, went to work as a waiter in Albany's City Hotel. The hotel's owner Sidney Chapin wrote a letter in 1836 testifying to his employee's character:

> Francis Wlodecki, one of the exiled Poles, came to live with me as a waiter and porter in the early part of the summer of 1834, and has remained with me in that capacity up to the present time. His conduct has been during that time such as to entitle him to the character of an honest, sober, industrious man. He is at all times willing to work, and I cheerfully

recommend him to any person who may wish to employ him.
I should be pleased still to keep him in my employ; but it is
his own wish to leave.[8]

Several others wrote similar testimonies for Włodecki, who that
same year married a woman with the very Irish-sounding name
of Ellen O'Sullivan. The couple became respected founding members
of Waukegan's first Catholic parish.[9]

Other Poles left a different impression. Stanisław Bilanski, a
tailor and sometime saloonkeeper, settled for a time in Winne-
bago County but eventually moved to Wisconsin and then to
Minnesota Territory in 1842. Known for marrying and divorcing
wives in a summary fashion, as well as for heavy drinking and an
abusive temper, Bilanski's luck ran out in 1859 when his then-wife
Ann Evards Bilanski poisoned him with arsenic. She was later
convicted and executed for the crime.[10] Most of the Poles who
followed these exiles to Illinois would lead quieter lives.

As the initial group of Polish exiles spread out across the state,
more Poles soon came. The Revolutions of 1848 largely bypassed
Poland, but many Poles participated in revolts in Germany and
Hungary, and a few of these revolutionaries came alongside their
Magyar or German compatriots. Although Chicago would later
become the main gateway to the state for most Polish and other
immigrants, most Polish exiles traveled from France to New Or-
leans and then to St. Louis during this period. Those who arrived
in Illinois entered from the south. St. Louis was the home of the
only significant grouping of Poles in the region, and even that
numbered probably no more than a hundred men at any given
time. Chicago contained a mere handful of Poles until around
1850.[11] A few Poles from the 1848 group settled in Illinois, and
some may have participated in the creation of a Hungarian colony
in neighboring Iowa, which met a similar inglorious end as the
earlier New Poland effort.

### The Beginning of Economic Migration, 1850–70

The decade of the 1850s saw a continuing trickle of political émigrés from Poland, but it also witnessed the first groups of economic migrants to the United States. The first permanent Polish
settlement was founded at Panna Maria, Texas, in 1854. Prior
to that, however, individual families and small groups of Poles
came to the New World in search of land and jobs. Following the

founding of Panna Maria, Polish immigrants created communities in Michigan, Wisconsin, Minnesota, and Illinois.

Yet it was Chicago where the Polish immigrants began to flock in such large numbers beginning in the 1850s. The city's location at the south end of Lake Michigan at the closest point between the Great Lakes and the Mississippi River made it the ideal site for commerce and industry and the access point for the growing states of the Upper Midwest. The city's growth demanded labor, and that demand brought migrants and immigrants. Immigrants arriving on the east coast in the 1850s were increasingly funneled via canals and lakes to Chicago, where many dispersed to the farmlands of the Midwest but where just as many stayed.[12]

The initial group of Poles to come for economic reasons rather than political exile would be attracted to Chicago more than to any other single location. Among the first was Antoni Smagorzewski (known as Sherman-Smarzewski), who settled in Chicago in 1851 with his wife and two children.[13] According to historian Dominic Pacyga, "He was not the first Pole to settle in Chicago, but his family did establish the core around which the West Town settlement developed. . . . Thirteen years later some 500 of his countrymen also lived in the city, the great majority from the German partition."[14]

The coming of the Civil War drew more people and more Poles to the state. The exact number of Poles who served in Illinois

Kasper and Stanisława Krolak and their American-born children, Anna and John, Peru, Illinois, circa 1890s. Courtesy of John Krolak, Peru, Illinois.

regiments during the Civil War is unclear, since some registered under Anglicized or Germanized names. The 24th Illinois Volunteer Infantry made up of many German and Hungarian exiles appears to have contained some, as did the 9th Illinois Cavalry. Battery L of the 2nd Illinois Light Artillery was commanded by a Polish officer, Tadeusz Hulanicki, at the end of war, but it is unclear whether other Poles served in this unit.[15] Bernard Stąpowski (Stampofski), a veteran of the Seminole and Mexican Wars, described by one Chicago history as an "old and respected resident of the city," commanded Company F, 9th Illinois Cavalry, in 1861 but was cashiered after disputes with fellow officers.[16]

Although the number of Poles serving was small, some of them would have an important impact on the development of Polish communities in Illinois. Piotr Kiolbassa arrived with his family to the Polish farming community in Texas in 1855. When the war broke out, he enlisted as a private in the 24th Texas Cavalry. He was captured by Union forces and later switched sides, enlisting in the 16th Illinois Cavalry, rising to the rank of sergeant and serving alongside his brother Ignacy. In January 1865, Kiolbassa was commissioned an officer and placed in command of an African American unit as a captain in 6th U.S. Colored Cavalry.[17] In between his military assignments, Kiolbassa would help to found the first Polish organization in Illinois, the Society of St. Stanislaus Kostka, which would become the nucleus of the first Polish church.

By 1860, there were at least a few Poles living in most parts of the state, though many were listed as coming from Prussia (their place of birth). Later waves of Polish immigrants would often consist of unskilled or semiskilled laborers, but these first Poles appear to have been skilled workers. They were usually in their mid-thirties, and quite a few were married to women of other backgrounds. In Chicago, John Petrowski was a thirty-five-year-old gilder (an artisan who applied gold leaf to objects). He and his Irish-born wife Hannah had two children. Yet another Polish gilder lived in a neighboring ward. Stanisław Rockowski was thirty-five and lived with his Polish wife Jadwiga (age twenty-seven) and two young children. Tailor Samuel Witkowski, thirty-eight, and his wife had come to Chicago from New York where one of the couple's young children had been born.[18]

The number of Poles arriving in Illinois grew steadily thereafter. A few were veterans of the unsuccessful January Insurrection against Russia in 1863, but most appear to have come from the German-ruled area of western Poland, the provinces of West Prussia, Poznań, and Pomerania. They intermingled with an even larger wave of ethnic Germans as well as quite a few Jewish immigrants from those same regions. In Chicago, the Poles had begun to form the state's first Polish community in what was then Ward 15, located west of the North Branch of the Chicago River (table 1.1).

Antoni Smagorzewski renamed himself "Anthony Sherman" but settled in what would become the heart of Chicago's first Polish neighborhood, opening a saloon and "travel agency" at the intersection of Noble and Bradley Streets. Over the next thirty years, his establishment served as a kind of commercial gateway and informal bank for Poles traveling from Europe. Sherman arranged tickets and documents for relatives of his compatriots seeking to come to Chicago and transferred money from immigrants in America to families in Europe.[19]

Prior to the Civil War, Poles in Chicago were scattered individuals and families forming no coherent community. Between the war's end and 1870, a community coalesced around what would become known as the "Polish downtown" on the near Northwest Side, which contained a few businesses—mainly saloons—and, most important, a Polish Catholic parish, St. Stanislaus Kostka. The area was increasingly inhabited by Poles from western Poland, mainly young families, though there were still many Irish, Germans, and Scandinavians in the neighborhood. The men worked as laborers, though quite a few held skilled positions, especially as tailors in the area's growing garment industry. Women usually kept

Table 1.1. Growth of Chicago's Northwest Side Polish Community

| Year | No. of Families (est.) |
|------|------------------------|
| 1864 | 30 |
| 1867 | 150 |
| 1869 | 235 |
| 1870 | 500 |
| 1871 | 600 |

Source: Karol Wachtel, *Dzieje Zjednoczenia Polsko Rzym-Kat. w Ameryce* (Chicago: L. J. Winiecki, 1913), 53–57.

house, though a number of them took in boarders. Judging from the birthplaces of their children, about half of the families had arrived in the United States within the previous few years. Other families, however, appear to have arrived prior to 1860, though they do not appear in the earlier Chicago census, suggesting that the new Polish community was also drawing in Polish immigrants from other parts of the state or perhaps from other communities in neighboring states. By this time as well, a number of young Polish women could be found working as domestic servants in other parts of the city. Eighteen-year-old Anna Chuppa (Czupa) lived with a large family of a well-off German clothier and his wife, helping to keep house and care for the couple's children.[20]

## Mass Migration, 1870–1914

In the four and a half decades following the formation of the state's first real Polish community, Poles flooded into Illinois in massive numbers, becoming one of the state's most significant

Balloon seller and a group of boys in front of St. Stanislaus Kostka Catholic Church, **1911.** Chicago Sun-Times/Chicago Daily News collection, Chicago History Museum, DN-0006537, copyright © Sun-Times Media, LLC, all rights reserved.

immigrant groups. By 1920, one in ten Chicago residents was Polish. This growth was driven by the state's rapid industrialization and near unquenchable demand for labor. Chicago with its steel mills, packinghouses, and a myriad of smaller industries easily absorbed the greatest number of the Polish newcomers. Yet, Poles also went to smaller manufacturing towns like Peoria, Joliet, Lamont, and East St. Louis. The coal boom in central Illinois drew many Poles as well, both directly from Poland and from other coal-mining states such as Pennsylvania.

The state's demand for labor coincided with growing labor surplus in east central Europe sparked by major economic and social changes. Land reform in Austria-Hungary and later Russia fundamentally altered long-standing patterns of subsistence farming, converting peasant labor obligations into cash rents. This in turn spurred many rural Poles to begin to migrate in search of wage labor in nearby towns and on large estates. Growing populations and land-tenure patterns served to fragment small peasant holdings, making it difficult to maintain standards of living or pass land onto the younger generation. Slow but steady industrialization and better transportation and communications brought the outside world closer to remote villages, opening up the possibility of traveling further in search of better wages. Polish peasants began to perceive their family economies as more than a zero-sum game, one that could be expanded in limited increments. The wages from work could be used to buy livestock or improve one's home and barn. The American experience of the small group of early immigrants was conveyed back to Europe through returning travelers and letters, encouraging yet more immigration. Like a snowball rolling down a mountain, it would become an avalanche.

For Poles coming to Illinois, the journey itself was both high adventure and high risk. Despite the growth of railroads on both sides of the ocean and the expansion of steamship routes, immigrants had to negotiate a world of unfamiliar languages, sights, and experiences. Many had never before left their home villages, and few spoke a language other than Polish. Years later, one Illinois woman remembered her first train:

> I went with my brother to Grajewo and that was [the] border of Prussia. . . . But [until] that time I never saw a train. I saw such a big train and tracks. And I said "What is that?" And he said to me, my brother, "You gonna ride on one like this

and maybe a couple hours. You gonna find out what they are. They make lotta noise and ring the bells and whistles." And I did . . .[21]

As immigration shifted from family groups to single men and women traveling alone or in the company of a few acquaintances, dangers and risks increased. Thieves and human traffickers sought to prey on immigrants who were usually carrying at least some cash. Young women were vulnerable to sexual assault, particularly in the crowded steerage sections of steamships—by fellow travelers or by the ship's crew.[22] Many Polish American newspapers of this period contained columns of inquiries by readers seeking information on friends or relatives who had failed to arrive at their destinations. Yet if there was danger, immigrants also found help and support. Angela Mischke traveled from Poland as a child in 1913 with her mother and brothers to join her father in Chicago. Along the way they encountered young men leaving Europe to escape conscription into the military: "Three such young men traveled with us and were of immense help to mother. They helped with the baggage, played and amused us children."[23]

In coming to the New World, immigrants were not wholly without resources or information. Letters home to Poland often contained detailed instructions on how to get to America. In 1891, John Chmielewski of South Chicago Heights wrote home to his family with instructions for his brother-in-law's travel:

> From home to Berlin . . . [he] must travel on his own money. Only from Berlin will the agency deliver on that steamship ticket to South Chicago, that is, to me. And especially remember when you are traveling on the steamship ticket do not pay anything, because they will demand money from you; and even if you should have it, do not pay anywhere. Say that you do not have it, and they will not do anything about that. They must transport you because the steamship ticket is prepaid.[24]

John Lubieński wrote from Chicago to his parents near Toruń, Poland, with information for his brother Ignatius: "Do not let Ignatius leave home until you receive a confirmation from the agent in Berlin. All kinds of tickets will be sent to you, so let Ignatius take those tickets with him, and let him take his birth certificate." Lubieński went on: "When you get the information from the agent as to when he is to leave from home, then quickly write so that we will know when we are to go meet him at the depot. Now, let father prepare him well for the trip because father knows better than we as to how he is to behave on the journey."[25] Sadly, Lubieński's letter never reached his parents. It was confiscated by Russian censors. Emigration from Russia was illegal at that time, and the Russian government tried to stop the flow of information from America.

Yet it was more than practical instructions that brought Poles to Illinois. Immigration meant a new life, not simply in terms of economic betterment—though that was essential—but of being able to become someone more: a person of standing, a person of honor. One young woman who later settled in Chicago recalled receiving a letter while still in Europe from a much poorer friend who had already made the journey to America. Along with the letter came a photograph in which her friend "looked as pretty as a countess." She decided that she would work no more on a farm: "I came to this America because I wanted to send back a photograph to show that I am also such a lady."[26]

Families often came in stages due to the cost of travel and the need to maintain farms and take care of family in Poland. Catherine Kozik's father came to Chicago in 1902. "He was about 10 years here, before we arrived. My father came here first, then about 7 or 8 years later, my mother sent up the two boys, because they were hard to handle. . . . Then three years later after the boys came mother and the rest of us children."[27]

Urban and industrial work drew the great majority of Poles to Illinois, but not all. In 1873, a Polish farming community was founded in Washington County in Southern Illinois. Radom was the first of a small cluster of Polish farming settlements in Washington and Jefferson Counties. The unlikely founder of this Polish community was Ivan Turchaninov, also known as John Basil Turchin, a former Russian general who served in the same rank in the Union Army during

The wife, name unknown, of newspaper editor Joseph Michael Sądowski. Courtesy of Polish Museum of America Archives.

the Civil War. Turchaninov, probably working as an agent for the Illinois Central Railroad, named the first settlement for the Poles "Radom" after a city in the Russian-controlled sector of Poland. Immigrants bought land from the railroad for seven to ten dollars an acre, usually in forty- or eighty-acre allotments.[28] Although it is commonly believed that the town's name came from the region of Poland where some of the early inhabitants came from, census records show that none of the Poles in Washington County came from Radom area. Some came from an area around Kórnik, south of the Polish city of Poznań, and some had first worked in Calumet, Michigan, before taking farms in Illinois. A number of the settlers were veterans of the Franco-Prussian, Danish, and Austrian Wars in Europe.[29]

A letter from Radom to the newspaper *Gazeta Polska Katolicka* in Chicago from 1876 claimed, "Three years has not yet passed when the first group of Poles purchased small areas of land, and hardly two years have passed [since] people have already built homes; Radom has grown to the extent that there are 450 people here and soon there will be up to 600 families. The church and school will soon be completed. The Illinois Central Railroad has been generous to the Poles and there is no doubt that those who purchased land from it shall not lose on it."[30] The colonists remained grateful to the Russian general who had helped them find homes in America, and when Turchaninov became destitute in his old age, the colonists of Radom supported him with contributions.

The pattern of Polish settlement is mostly easily tracked by the founding of Polish ethnic parishes. In most cases, parishes were founded when a critical mass of Poles already existed in a given locale. Depending on the intensity of settlement, parish formation could take place from one to several years after the arrival of the first Polish residents. In Chicago during the 1880s and 1890s, some parishes grew extremely large due to peculiarities of ecclesial politics (discussed in more detail in chapter 4). After the turn of the twentieth century, however, smaller daughter parishes split off from larger parishes at a greater rate. Naturally, not all parishes were of equal size, with those in rural parts of Illinois being significantly smaller than the large urban ones in Chicago.

The graph shows the pattern of Polish settlement during the period of mass migration. The first Polish parishes in Chicago were on the near Northwest Side, but by 1885 a significant population of Poles was already filling up parts of south Chicago as they took jobs in the stockyards and slaughterhouses. Polish workers and their families also established a parish in Lemont at the southwest edge of Cook County by 1883. With massive flows of immigrants from Austrian Galicia and the Russian-controlled Congress Kingdom of Poland, the number of Polish parishes grew rapidly in the 1890s. Growth was fairly evenly divided between North and South Chicago, and new Polish parishes were founded in Cicero, Joliet, Calumet City, and Downer's Grove. After 1900, Polish parishes grew rapidly on both the North and South Sides of Chicago. This growth continued unabated through World War I, despite the curtailing of immigration from Europe due to the war. Although immigration in the 1920s was limited due to laws restricting Eastern and Southern Europeans from coming, the sheer size and relative youth of the Polish community in Illinois meant that the number of parishes continued to grow almost to the end of the decade.

In the first decade of the twentieth century, Poles also came in increasing numbers to the coal mines and smaller factory towns of central and southern Illinois. The first Poles settled in East St. Louis by 1896. They attended the Polish parish across the Missouri River until 1904 when they had enough members to form

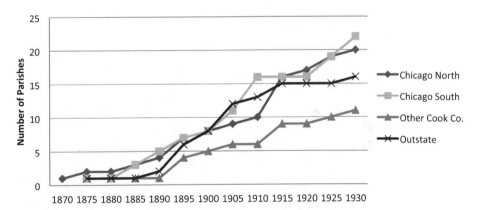

Polish Catholic parishes in Illinois, by location, 1870–1930. From Archdiocese of Chicago Polish Parishes online database, Polish Genealogical Society of America, www.pgsa.org; Kruszka, *History of Poles in America to 1908*; *Srebny Jubileusz parafii św. Wojciecha w East Louis, Illinois* (East St. Louis: n.p. [1929]), Golden Jubilee 1916–1966 Saint Casimir's Church, Streator, Illinois (Streator, IL: n.p., 1966), accessed online at http://www.liturgicalcenter.org/media/parish_pdf/PEO/peo-15.1.pdf; St. Charles Borromeo Church, DuBois, Illinois: Centennial 1877–1977 (DuBois, IL: n.p., 1977); Diocese of Belleville, Illinois, Papers, Central Archives of Polonia, Polish Mission, Orchard Lake Schools, Orchard Lake, Michigan; Diocese of Peoria, Illinois, Papers, Central Archives of Polonia, Polish Mission, Orchard Lake Schools, Orchard Lake, Michigan; Niklewicz, Polacy w Stanach Zjednoczonych (Green Bay, WI, 1937).

St. Adalbert Parish.[31] Polish settlement in Streator appears to have begun gradually in the late 1880s as the coal mines drew in more and more workers. It was not until 1916 that a Polish parish formed.[32]

By the 1920s, the shape of Polish settlement in Illinois had been established. A tight network of parish communities dominated the skyline of the Northwest Side of Chicago. Poles were the largest group in many areas of South Chicago, particularly Back of the Yards. Parishes in Lemont, Cicero, and the southern parts of Cook County shared some links with the South Chicago cluster but were self-contained communities. According to historian Edward Kantowicz, Chicago contained "five large Polish colonies. . . . Each was in an area of heavy industry: Polish Downtown on the northwest side, just west of the Goose Island industrial complex; the Lower West Side, adjacent to many factories on along the Burlington Railroad and the ship canal; Bridgeport and Back of the Yards, circling the Union Stock yards; and South Chicago, hard against the steel mills."[33]

Beyond Chicago itself, Polish communities had formed in North Chicago, Rockford, LaSalle, Joliet, and Kankakee. Radom

Holy Trinity Parish, one of Chicago's oldest Polish parishes, in the late 1950s or early 1960s. Courtesy of Polish Museum of America Archives.

in south central Illinois was the state's main Polish farming community, but it had spawned a number of small daughter communities as Polish farmers spread out from their initial settlement.[34] Poles in East St. Louis were closely tied to the larger Polish community in St. Louis proper, but they also had bonds to the smaller mining and farming towns of the Catholic Diocese of Belleville. Small mining and manufacturing towns in the central and southern parts of Illinois such as Madison, Kewanee, Oglesby, Peru, and Streator contained Polish populations large enough to support parishes, though Poles were often closely intermingled with other eastern and southern Europeans.

Although parish formation provides a rough outline of Polish settlement in Illinois, it does not provide a complete picture. The large size and rapid growth of Polish immigration ensured that Polish residential patterns often spilled over the practical bounds of ethnic parishes. While Polish clergy, especially in Chicago, tried hard to keep Poles in Polish parishes, their endeavors were not always successful. In addition, Polish parishes often absorbed other East-Central Europeans, especially Lithuanians and Slovaks. In South Chicago, the large influx of mountaineers (*Górale*) from Galicia in southern Poland was joined by a significant number of Slovak immigrants from the other side of the Carpathian mountain range. These immigrants came from a similar environment, arrived in the same places, and spoke a mutually intelligible dialect. In locations where there were not enough Slovaks to form institutions, they joined Polish parishes and organizations. In Argo, the Polish parish of St. Blase had a Slovak society along with its Polish ones.[35] Poles also joined Slovak community institutions. One Slovak fraternal insurance society that admitted Poles reported with satisfaction that its Polish members were learning to speak quite passable Slovak.[36] Poles also at times joined with other ethnic groups as well. In Toluca, Poles formed organizations with the more numerous Lithuanian community. At Oglesby, in central Illinois, Poles and Irish formed the parish of Sacred Heart in 1900 under the leadership of a Polish priest, while in Moline Poles joined a church founded for Belgian immigrants.[37] Many of the early Polish parishes were founded by Poles from specific regions of Poland and retained a regional identity along with an emerging Polish identity. St. Hyacinth Parish in Chicago was settled mainly by Kashubs from the Baltic coast region of Poland. The parish history proudly noted that, "having recovered his health" after a serious illness, their indefatigable pastor, Father Lange, "returned to his old parish post and began once again God's work among his very own people. He too was a Kashube [*sic*]." Lange was succeeded by yet another Kashub pastor in 1914.[38]

Poles also joined territorial parishes,[39] which were usually founded by Irish immigrants or were ethnically mixed. In some cases, older territorial parishes were gradually taken over by new-comers. The parish of St. Gall in Gage Park in South Chicago, originally attended by German and Irish Catholics, was increas-ingly made up of Poles and Czechs by 1920.[40] Polish parishes in DuBois and Sheller initially served a mix of Poles and Germans.[41] The growth of Polish settlement also meant that Poles occasion-ally took over the parishes belonging to other groups as those groups moved to new areas. On the Northwest Side of Chicago, the parish of St. Boniface was created by German immigrants in 1864, well before large-scale Polish settlement. By the beginning of twentieth century, the original German community was being displaced by the growing Polish influx, and the parish attendance dwindled. Some Poles began to attend, but nearby Polish pastors discouraged attendance at a German parish, and the remaining German members disliked worshiping with Poles. One of the German pastors even tried to learn Polish to bridge the gap. By the 1920s, St. Boniface was a territorial parish whose members were largely Polish, but which also served its remaining German members and any local English speakers.[42]

### Chicago Polonia and the Great West

William Cronon's classic history of Chicago's influence on the Upper Midwest and Great Plains, *Nature's Metropolis*, dem-onstrated how the city's railroads, canals, processing plants, and banks organized the settlement and economic life of a vast hin-terland of the United States. For Polish immigrants, Chicago was also the jumping-off point and recruitment center for rural colonization efforts that stretched as far west as Montana and Washington. Chicago-based railroads needed settlers to generate traffic on their lines and to fill the land grants they had been given in the west, and the city's growing Polish community provided a pool of potential migrants they could not ignore. In many cases they partnered with Chicago's major Polish organizations such as the Polish National Alliance (PNA) or the Polish Roman Catholic Union (PRCU) to help them recruit Poles.

In 1877, the PRCU started a Polish colony in central Nebraska. A few years later, the rival PNA started a colony in Arkansas, and when that proved disappointing, it followed up with more successful ventures in Minnesota. Polish colonization bureaus based in Illinois recruited Polish settlers from Chicago, LaSalle, Lemont, and other communities. The daughter of one such colonist claimed that her father was walking down an alley in Chicago when he was approached by a recruiter who told him that a true Pole like her father should be on his own farm, not in a city. Polish farming colonies north of Green Bay drew a large portion of their population from Chicago. In other communities, the number of ex-Chicagoans was well over 75 percent. These communities retained strong ties to Illinois, and visits back and forth each year were common—families had branches in both urban and rural communities.[43]

### Many Polonias

The term "Polonia" has long been used to describe the Polish American and Polish immigrant population in the United States as well as within individual states and cities. By the 1920s, common economic and social changes in Europe and the attraction of jobs and land in America drew Polish immigrants from diverse regions of Poland. They distributed themselves somewhat unevenly across broad swaths of Chicago and Illinois. They followed jobs,

Polish wedding party with a car, Chicago, 1919. Courtesy of Polish Museum of America Archives.

friends, acquaintances, and most of all family. Thus, it is fair to say that by the 1920s Chicago and Illinois as a whole had a large and well-established Polonia.

Yet, such a picture is at best incomplete. The sheer number of Poles, the diversity of their regional origins, the different jobs they took, and the intensive and sometimes insular ways they created American communities meant that Illinois and Chicago were home to not one Polonia but several. Bonds of language and common interests at times drew them together, but their focus remained most often on the small worlds of family, parish-community, and work.

# 2

## RODZINA: FAMILY LIFE

Family was at the heart of why Poles immigrated to the New World and why they came to Illinois. They came to support their families financially and to make it possible to live as they felt proper people ought to live. The conditions of rural Poland in the late nineteenth and early twentieth centuries seemed to increasingly threaten the life they had known, while the world of migration, with America in the distance, opened up new possibilities and the hope of living a better, fuller life. Polish immigrants operated within what is known as the "family economy," which meant that the goals and needs of the family superseded those of its individual members. This implied a complex intergenerational exchange of wealth and authority that defined what the roles of each family member were, what it meant to be a man or a woman, and what their places were within the larger community. The work of children, both as youths and young adults, was crucial to supporting the family, serving as a form of social security. The labor and wages of the young helped to support parents as they aged and took care of them when they were no longer able to work. In return, the children gradually assumed the authority, status, and inheritance of their parents.[1] The increasing subdivision of land, the threat of military conscription (which took away young men whose labor was the basis of future family prosperity), and the growth of a money-based economy in Poland made sending young people to America to work an increasingly attractive option for families that sought to maintain their way of life.

Yet at the heart of this choice was a cruel irony. The decision to migrate in order to earn wages separated children from parents, husbands from wives. While some immigrants returned home to Europe after a time in America, the majority would stay.

Migration stretched the bonds of the family to the breaking point as it offered new opportunities. Poles who came to Illinois in the period up to the 1920s left behind a close-knit world of kin—parents, grandparents, aunts, uncles, cousins. In their new homes, they would struggle to reknit the frayed fabric of their families and forge new families.

## Coming to America

The initial decision to leave Poland and come to America was not always made easily and could be the source of conflict within families. Catherine Kozik's family left behind a large extended family to join her father in Chicago: "My father's brother was a priest. He begged my mother not to leave Poland, but Mother was determined. He was a priest, and even though he was, he couldn't help. A big family like we were." Kozik's elder brothers grew unruly and hard for her mother to handle alone, so they were sent to America to join her father.[2] Sometimes children were separated so long from their fathers that they forgot what their fathers looked like. A well-known Polish song of this period recounts a father's sorrow when, on returning home to his family after a long absence in America, his children run in fear from the stranger who has suddenly appeared in their home.[3] Angela Mischke recalled, "I remember the long train ride from New York and also meeting my father at the railroad station in Chicago. It was a reunion after five years of separation. We children barely remembered dad but we recognized him immediately because he looked exactly as on the photograph mother had of him. He was tall, very erect and quite handsome. As was the fashion of the day, he sported a good-sized mustache, which even when in later years was no longer fashionable he never shaved."[4]

Immigration changed the structure of families by changing the relationships within the family. Women assumed new roles and responsibilities. When husbands left to work in America, their wives took up the task of running farms and making critical decisions for the family. Children, who had always worked in rural communities, also had new responsibilities. In her memoir, Mischke noted,

> About this long separation between mother and father I must write in some detail I'm sure they wanted to be together but mother felt it would not be wise to give up the home and the

farm they both worked so hard to preserve. Then too, she was apprehensive as to what the life in the distant and unknown America would be. Dad came to America to earn some money to pay off the mortgage on the farm. And mother, with money coming regularly from Dad did an exceedingly good job in managing the farm. For one so young, she had the three of us before her 23rd birthday, she kept an immaculate house, cooked for six, worked on the farm and looked after livestock. True, she had aunt Hanka and a hired farm hand to help but she was the boss (*gospodyni*). I recall in winter time, during the long evenings, she occupied herself by doing beautiful needlework, which later adorned our house—bedspreads, billowing pillows, tablecloths and curtains. She loved flowers and had a showy flower garden in the summer and many potted plants in the house in the winter. The decision to leave her little domain was difficult one—but leave she did! Dad, as much as he loved Poland, strongly believed that America was truly a land of opportunity for all and especially his own children, which indeed it proved to be.[5]

For married women like Mischke's mother, the decision to emigrate was often hard. Having established a family and enmeshed

The Kuflewski sisters Mary, Leona, and Lucia at play with two friends or cousins, Chicago, circa 1910. Courtesy of Polish Museum of America Archives.

themselves in kin groups that provided a support network, these women often had the most to lose by leaving home and going to an unfamiliar environment where perhaps the only adults they would know on arriving would be their husbands. Yet despite the hardships and risks, many married women also found opportunity just as their husbands had. As one Polish immigrant wrote to his wife, "I remind you that you should not listen to anyone, only come to America, because in America it is very good for women."[6]

Some women (and men) left to escape hardship at home. Bessie Leniak lived with her brother's family, and her sister-in-law treated her so cruelly that she contemplated suicide. Before she left for America, she told her sister-in-law: "'Listen . . . Sister-in-law, I'm gonna wear hats, and I'm gonna be rich someday in the United States. Maybe you beg me for something.' And that came true. . . . And when she was real old she couldn't get along with her daughter-in-law and her son. . . . She asked me for forgiveness for what she has done."[7]

For most unmarried women, the benefits of immigration were much more immediately apparent in spite of the dangers of traveling far from home alone or in the company of a few peers. By immigrating they gained greater freedom. They earned their own income working in America and made real contributions to the support of their extended families. Perhaps most important, they got far more say in choosing their own marriage partners. In rural Poland, marriages were arranged and approved by parents and other older relatives. The family of the bride often paid a dowry to the family of the groom. In America, where there were more young men than women, the situation was quite different. In 1891, a young Polish woman in Chicago, Sophie Nadrowska, wrote to her parents near Rypin in north central Poland, who had apparently informed her that her suitor in their village had asked them to pay Sophie's bride price: "Mr. Litwieński has asked you for the one hundred rubles! Let him come to me and ask me for it. I will tell him that if he has three hundred dollars, then he can get married, because in Chicago the custom is that the girl's boyfriend must even buy her a wedding dress and everything else that is needed for the house. The young lady only has to worry about getting to the wedding. Here they do not ask how much dowry she will receive, dear parents."[8] For young men, the situation was often bleaker, and more than one letter was written to Poland to entice a young woman to come and marry a lonely immigrant man. Such letters were sometimes enhanced with attempts at poetry or blandishments about nice dresses women were able to purchase in the New World. Although immigrant families in America did arrange marriages for their children when possible, the practice soon fell out of favor. Choices in marriage partners were still often dependent on the community and the social circles of the prospective brides and grooms. Joseph Wadolowski and Julianna Ogonowska came to East St. Louis from neighboring villages in Poland about a year apart. They met in America, probably thanks to mutual friends from the same villages, and married in 1914.[9]

### Separation

The freedom and opportunities offered by life in America remained in tension with the obligations that immigrants had to their families back home. Sophie Nadrowska told her parents that she was working in a tailor shop, earning two and a half dollars a week, "and will earn more. I am going to be sewing at this tailor shop until Christmas, and then I will set up my own sewing business." She went on:

> It is very gay here so that one can forget one's longing. And I cannot regret those two years even though I would have been already different but when I think about you I am a little lonely. I am, as it were, still at home. . . . When you receive this letter from me, and I receive an answer from you, I will send you my photograph; but you will probably not recognize me. Dear Mommy and dear Daddy, do not be lonesome for me, because I thank you for sending me to America. I trust in God and the Mother of God, that they condescend to hear my prayers, so that I will still take care of you until death and that you will die in my arms. . . . I close this letter happily, I kiss the hands and feet of my dear Father and Mother, and I kiss every part of their bodies a thousand times. I remain loving you always as long as you live, Sophie Nadrowska.[10]

For a young woman like Nadrowska, Chicago offered wide possibilities. She was happy, independent, and paying her own way. She even planned to start her own small business. So changed was she that her parents might not even recognize their own daughter if they saw her. And yet part of her heart remained at home, and the hope of caring for her parents as they age remained powerful.

Letters from immigrants in Illinois to their families in Poland are filled with such longing: "I, Marianna Jakubowska, your granddaughter, write this letter and greet my Grandma, if she is still living. If she is still alive, then I send regards to my dearest Grandma and I wish you good luck, good health, and whatever you, yourself, ask of God until death. And if my most beloved Grandma is dead, then may God grant her eternal rest forever and ever. And now, dear Grandma, I am going to school. I have learned enough to write at least this much to you."[11]

Establishing a home and a family was central to the lives of Polish immigrants in Illinois. Young women entered married life in communities without mothers and grandmothers. Basic things like making familiar foods for holidays were a challenge when American stores and markets contained an array of strange choices. Polish immigrant women had to improvise and choose how their families would celebrate important rites of passage and annual holidays like Christmas and Easter, which are so central to the lived cultural experience of Poles.

Family and home life was fraught with difficulties for Polish immigrants in their new Illinois home, and a lot of the burden fell on women who already undertook much of the daily chores of caring for the home and children. Immigrants lacked a support network of older relatives and neighbors who oversaw social relations and helped mitigate problems. Thus, young immigrants often turned to peers as well as to public forums like newspapers or the court system to address issues that were once handled informally. In 1916, the female editor of the women's page of Chicago's *Naród Polski* wrote,

> Every girl comes to this country with the aim of getting married at the first opportunity. She is ready to give her heart at once to any young man and go with him to the altar. Blindly she believes in him, then, after the wedding, the mask comes off the face of her lover-husband. . . . Drunkenness and abuse has no end, and she becomes the slave of her husband, living without faith and customs. She cries, complains, moans, and that grief drives her to drink. . . . Only once you can make such a mistake in your life. So you should be careful before you marry a man, investigate the life of your future husband, his bad and good habits, get information from those who know him for a long time, but this you can't do in a week or two. . . .

It is our duty to protect them from such a beast and brute in the human flesh. Our immigration accomplished good things for any of the category, notwithstanding the fact that they have done almost nothing for our immigrant girls.[12]

If marriages were a source of concern, so too was child rearing, and the two problems were closely linked. Immigrants who arrived as children and the second-generation children of immigrants adapted to the new environment far more quickly than their parents, who often struggled to learn basic English while working long hours. The result was a profound gap between the outlook and experiences of parents and children. This gap was exacerbated by the vast number of children born to Polish immigrant parents in the United States. In most Polish immigrant communities by the 1920s, half or more of the population was under the age of sixteen.[13]

Polish National Alliance group "Eagle of Freedom" dressed in Polish highlander (*Górale*) costumes for a play, *Highlander Wedding*, September 1929. Courtesy of Polish Museum of America Archives.

## Struggles for the Family

The problems of immigration caused a high rate of dysfunction among Polish immigrants as they tried to build new lives in America, resulting in problems with crime, substance abuse, and family breakup that endangered the future of Polish communities. Nowhere were these problems more noticeable than in Chicago, where they became the basis for an entire school of urban sociological research at the University of Chicago. The family and personal problems of Polish immigrants also spurred a major social reform effort by community leaders and clergy.

Couples separated by an ocean struggled to maintain their relationships by letter, and lost or stolen letters exacerbated misunderstandings. Stanisław Kłosowski wrote to his wife from South Chicago Heights in 1891 complaining that she had not responded to his previous letters and his entreaties to come and join him:

> Now my dear wife, no one can have more worry than I have with you. Dear wife, write to me as quickly as possible whether you desire to come to America or not. But tell me the truth, so that you do not let me down, so that you do not make a fool of me after I would spend the money on you and you would not come with the children. If you do not wish to come, then write to me and I will take the children myself and you can do as you wish.[14]

Immigrants wrote back to families in Europe as well discussing problem relatives. Leopold Przewoźny wrote from Chicago to inform relatives of one such instance:

> What Joseph writes to You God only knows. But may God have pity on him for his deeds and his way of life. I am ashamed of him and so is Anthony. Anthony is now being pushed around by Joseph's debtors for Joseph has run up a debt of 50 dollars. . . . I tell this story to no one else but You because You let him leave for America at such an early age. You should have kept him at home instead or at least until he was mature, and tanned his hide then maybe he would have been a better person. . . . He does not even have a cent in his pocket. He does not want to work even if it happened to be the best kind of work possible. He is only wasting his time [bumming] in the streets.[15]

Family problems were often exacerbated by poor living and working conditions. Living spaces could be cramped, and there were few activities for young people. Immigrant families took in boarders to make ends meet, often young, single males newly arrived from Europe. This put additional burdens on wives who had to care for boarders as well as their own family. Frank Kozik lived in a Chicago boardinghouse when he arrived in America along with three other boarders and the family's four children. About the woman who ran the house, he recalled, "That poor woman didn't last very long. Too much work, I guess it was for her." Another family he lived with had two children and three boarders, including himself: "They only had one little stove, so they'd heat the two rooms, and the bedrooms they had, they didn't heat. It was so cold there was frost on the blanket."[16]

Many families who took in boarders did the best they could, but in some boardinghouses there was disorder, whether due to the neglect of the owners or the bad behavior of the boarders themselves. Reformers identified boardinghouses as a major threat to Polish families in Chicago. *Naród Polski* described an incident in 1914 in which a group of male boarders living in one part of a

Polish immigrants and their children enjoying a summer picnic, about 1900. Courtesy of Polish Museum of America Archives.

boardinghouse got drunk and tried to break into a room housing a group of young women. The attackers were forcefully driven away: "In such a way do our pious and respectable girls defend their maiden honor and such a lesson they gave to those godless ones! Oh! If there were only more of this kind!" In such boardinghouses, the paper opined, "more decent neighbors [wonder] . . . at the drunken orgies of their neighbors."[17]

Unstable marriages among the younger generation of immigrants were the result, according to the Polish newspapers, of a lack of parental oversight and of children who were being raised in an American atmosphere that was overly permissive and materialistic. *Naród Polski* noted that parents should train their daughters to be good household managers, but "unfortunately our parents care little for this. The sight of a beautiful daughter, doll like, blinds them, fills them with joy. In order not to soil her daughter's nice silk dress, mother does all the work and the nice daughter likes it."[18] Chicago's *Dziennik Związkowy* placed the blame on immigrant women:

> In Poland, under three different governments, brave Polish women fight valiantly against the oppressors and bring up their children in the Polish spirit, but here many neglect their sacred duty, and allow the younger generation to become irrevocably lost to national causes. Here it is not enough to bring up a son to be a "sport," to chew tobacco, to pour down liquor, and, often, to become a bully; it is not enough to bring up a daughter to be a painted and powdered "doll," who chatters only in English, and who seeks amusements in inappropriate places. One must bring up these young sprigs in accordance with the example set by our great-grandmothers, that is, imbue them with virtue, respect for the mother tongue, and love of their homeland back in Europe, instill modesty in the girls, and noble manliness in the boys.[19]

The solution, the newspaper opined in another article, was to give girls more and better schooling:

> In many cases the mothers are to blame for allowing their daughters to acquire this passion for spending and fine clothes by constantly reminding them of their appearance. Mothers always complain about lack of money whenever anyone suggests a higher education for their daughters, but they won't

even utter a whimper when a new dress, hat, or shoes are suggested, saying that they will manage somehow or other. . . . This passion for extravagance is leading these girls and women to destruction and will continue to do so until parents insist upon a higher education, through which their children can develop character and self-respect.[20]

It was not only girls who needed a stronger parental hand and more education: "We know from experience that our American boys do not especially like to learn or go to school. But there is a cure—a well oiled switch or strap. After this medicine a desire for learning will be found."[21]

Broken families, alcoholism, crime, and delinquency were a reality for far too many Polish families in America. In the old country, extended kin networks could provide support for families in trouble, but in Chicago and other cities, Poles often turned to public agencies, the police, the courts, and even newspapers to address their problems. Of all immigrant women in Chicago, Polish women were among the most active in turning to the legal system in cases of abandonment or abuse.[22] Sometimes, they would put their case before the public through the pages of the Polish press. A notice in *Dziennik Chicagoski* from 1896 stated,

> We published an advertisement in yesterday's paper in which Mr. Robert Koszyński announced that he was not responsible for the debts of his wife Agnes, and warned everyone not to lend her any money or give any goods on credit, because she has deserted him without any cause. Mrs. Agnes Koszyńska has requested us, in the name of truth and justice, to announce that she has gone to live with her parents, that she does not intend to hide, or purchase any goods on her husband's account, and that she left her husband, who had once before deserted her, because she refuses to attend services at the "Independent" Church, and that she is a member of the Saint Hedwig Church, which her husband forbids her to attend.[23]

In spite of such problems, Poles worked hard to build stable homes and families in Illinois, and most ultimately succeeded. For every dysfunction that made the newspaper headlines, there were many acts of kindness and goodness that did not.[24] Many parents, clergy, and community leaders did their best to ensure young couples got a good start and would approach married life realistically. Roman Lapkiewicz recalled how the priest gave him advice before his wedding: "I was over there for the instruction . . . [on] how to get along with your wife. . . . [The priest said] None of those wives know everything . . . [like] how to cook. Has says you have to understand that. He said you'd better eat [what she cooks]. He said, don't make a wife disappointed. If you don't eat it your wife thinks you just don't like her cooking . . . but [if you do] you can get along better."[25]

One Polish newspaper reported that

> We see today how some couples are mismatched, to whom a joint life becomes a virtual hell and continuous suffering. On the other hand, we come across married couples that are happy, fortunate, always satisfied with their lot. In one family the head of which, a husband and father, earns less money per week than his neighbor and has more children to feed but in spite of this we see in his home neatness and order; the children are clean and neatly dressed; at home every piece of furniture is in its place; the food is nourishing, healthy, and always prepared on time; the housekeeper always joyfully greets her mate, returning home from work, and there can be seen a mutually satisfied and fortunate life.[26]

Polish immigrants on a fishing trip near Chicago, circa early 1900s. Courtesy of Polish Museum of America Archives.

## The Polish Home

The home was the center of family life, and Polish immigrants deeply valued home ownership. In rural communities like Radom, Poles generally owned farmland and built houses on it. In mining communities, housing was sometimes provided by the company, but families still sought to acquire their own home. Kantowicz noted that the land hunger that motivated Poles to come to America "was translated into the urge to buy one's own home in Chicago. While Czech immigrants made the most extensive use of building and loan associations, these cooperative institutions were significant in Polish communities as well. An association member made regular payments of fifty cents or a dollar per week for a number of years to build up a downpayment and the association supplemented this accumulation with a low-interest loan when the member actually purchased a home. By 1900, Polish building and loan societies held assets approaching one million dollars."[27]

In Chicago, Poles not only bought houses but were instrumental in developing housing stock in many Chicago neighborhoods. In the heavy Polish areas of Back of the Yards, 38 percent of residents already owned their own homes by 1890. That number increased steadily, especially after 1920. By 1939, over half of the residents in Back of the Yards were homeowners. More densely populated neighborhoods like the near Northwest Side and the "Polish Downtown" contained more multifamily dwellings and thus had lower rates of ownership. Rates were highest in neighborhoods where Poles were among the earliest residents and who had entered the real estate market "at the ground floor." Many of the Polish homes were very modest in size, but the owners modified them as circumstances allowed. Often Polish owners had duplexes or added apartments to their homes. The rental income provided a hedge against hard times and helped pay the mortgage and for improvements. This feature also kept rent money within the Polish community.[28] The home was not only the primary financial investment of the family but also its emotional and spiritual center.

It was in the home that Illinois's Polish immigrants, primarily women, began to create a new hybrid culture—a painstaking compromise between the Poland they had left behind and the America they found. This culture involved food, customs, beliefs, and relationships that blended new and old in a creative way. A key factor was the social circles that replaced the larger distant family, separated as they were by an ocean. The lack of parents and grandparents could be filled in part by neighbors and close friends as well as by those with whom they created bonds at work or in the many parish and community groups that sprouted in nearly every Polish community in Illinois like mushrooms after a rain. Faced with harsh working conditions, families under strain, and the gritty reality of life in industrial America, Polish immigrants and their children worked to transform and humanize the world around them. Marta Leszczyk recalled that her parents' door was always open, especially to new arrivals from Poland: "We used to have lots of company because they used to come from the old country, and they always stopped at our house, because we always had a big flat, and my mother . . . she just liked to help everybody. . . . My mother liked to make roasts, and chicken. . . . Naturally vegetables and Polish meal[s] had sauerkraut and sausage. . . . Pierogi . . . and well naturally they came to visit us."[29]

Perhaps the most memorable part of Polish family life was the dinners and meals, especially around the holidays. Lillian Cwik recalled her mother preparing pierogi, dumplings, "then Polish sausage, sauerkraut and then veal prepared different ways, beef . . . and beef tongue in horseradish sauce, and your different kind of soups, mushroom soup."[30] Mary Hojnacki's family converted a boiler for washing clothes to cooking for the holidays: "For Christmas and Easter . . . we had ham. We cooked . . . three hams together, we had that boiler. . . . Aunt Joey, when we took the hams out from the boiler . . . [they] were sliced up . . . [and] Aunt Joey . . . was frying like that you know. . . . [That] was good. You couldn't get anything like that."[31]

Christmas Eve was the central time for family, as the holiday most closely resembled how the birth of Jesus was celebrated in Poland. It was also the holiday that most closely brought to mind distant family in the old country. The family would gather before the evening meal and share wafers of unleavened bread (*opłatki*). The sharing of the *opłatki* symbolized family unity and the putting aside of the year's past conflicts. *Opłatki* were even sent by mail to relatives in distant places. A meatless meal followed the *opłatki*, and then the family went to midnight Mass. After the Mass, a meal with meat could be served. Christmas Day was then a time for visiting neighbors and family.

Easter, celebrating the death and resurrection of Jesus, was an equally important holiday for Polish Americans, coming after forty days of Lenten fasting. Special cakes, colored eggs, and meat dishes were prepared in advance, but they were not eaten until Easter. Mary Hojnacki recalled, "We had ham, [kiełbasa], and eggs." On Holy Saturday, the day before Easter, a basket with samples of each of the Easter foods was specially blessed for the holiday. "My pa used to bless at home, but Dorothy, she used to go [to church] with her basket. . . . [They] put it in a basket and take it to church . . . and they bless them. . . . Dorothy takes . . . her basket, Kabasa [kiełbasa] and eggs and [a] little loaf of rye bread, they used that fancy bread, you know like round one, nice. . . . I remember I had to go to the church and have the priest bless it."[32]

From the start of Polish immigration to Illinois until World War II, Polish immigrants and their second-generation children struggled to rebuild and maintain family ties stretched by immigration, the harsh conditions of urban industrial life, and the differences between parents and children. The New World offered great possibilities, but often at a high price. Obligations to family in Europe remained strong and a constant source of longing and concern. The ideal of making the circle of the family whole again after the disruption of migration could be realized, but at a cost. As a girl, Catherine Kozik watched her parents' marriage nearly fall apart and felt lifelong resentment toward her father for not reuniting the family soon after he immigrated alone to work in Chicago. Yet, years later, she was able to tell an interviewer that "Mother passed away here in 1940 while living with us. I am happy to say that she died in my bed and I was holding her head when she died."[33] The ability to purchase property in their new homeland, the hybrid culture they created, their faith, and their toil were the soil in which Polish American communities would grow.

PRCUA girl scouts (Cory Zjednoczenia) during Polish Day in Harms Park, Chicago, June 1939.
Courtesy of Polish Museum of America Archives.

# 3

# PRACA: POLES IN INDUSTRIAL ILLINOIS

The need for work drew Poles to Illinois. The massive growth of Chicago as a center for transportation, manufacturing, and processing, the expansion of downstate coal mines, and the labor requirements of smaller factory towns created an insatiable demand for workers, which brought Poles as well as other immigrants from across Europe, from many U.S. states, and from around the world. These newcomers built Illinois and its cities in the years between the Civil War and World War II. The work that Polish immigrants did was tough, poorly paid, and dangerous. They often lived in appalling conditions. Yet they persevered, fought for better working and living conditions, and transformed their neighborhoods into places they could call home.

Although Polish immigrants and their children could be found in many types of industries in Illinois, as well as in agriculture, four main industries accounted for most of the work done by Poles in the decades before World War II: garment making, meatpacking, metalworking (mainly steel), and coal mining. The clothing industry was one of the first to draw a large number of Poles to Chicago, and it was particularly important to Poles on the near Northwest Side of the city. Led by industry giant Hart, Schaffner, and Marx as well as a host of smaller firms, Chicago became a major supplier of ready-to-wear clothing by 1900. Although less physically demanding than some of the city's other industries, garment workers suffered from lung diseases and repetitive stress injuries. Workers hunched long hours over sewing tables without breaks. Both men and women found employment in clothing factories, and it was one of the few large industries in Chicago that hired a large number of Polish women. By 1890, a good worker could bring home $2.50 a week to her family.[1]

Meatpacking is associated more closely with Chicago than any other industry. Chicago's packinghouses, concentrated in South Chicago, transformed the meat business and factory labor in general by creating mechanized processing plants that compartmentalized the complex tasks of butchering into many small operations. This not only sped up the rate of processing but allowed the industry to hire large numbers of low-skill workers to do the many repetitive tasks the plants needed. By 1905, "there were over thirty classifications of men in the killing department. Included were twenty rates of pay that ranged from 50 cents to 16–1/2 cents an hour."[2] The jobs were plentiful but seasonal, since farmers shipped animals to market in fall and spring. Workers were hired at the factory gates or through contacts with friends or relatives already working in the plants. Most workers were male, with women making up a tenth of the workforce. Working conditions were harsh, and the health and safety of the workers was a secondary concern to factory owners. The wooden floors were wet and slimy, and they often became soaked with blood and water from the slaughtering process. Rooms were poorly lit and ventilated. As one historian noted, "Some of the workrooms in the interior of the building enjoyed neither daylight nor fresh air. Rank smells filled these rooms."[3] Accidents and injuries were

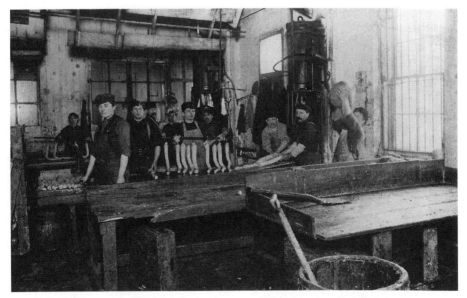

Polish workers in a sausage factory, 1902. Courtesy of Polish Museum of America Archives.

common due to the poor conditions, the problems associated with herding livestock in enclosed spaces, and the sharp knives used to perform the work.

Iron and steel factories also employed large numbers of Polish immigrants. Concentrated in South Chicago, North Chicago, Chicago Heights, Deering, Calumet City, Joliet, and in next-door Gary, Indiana, the industry thrived in the decades after the Civil War due to Chicago's transportation links to iron mines in Michigan and Minnesota and coal mines in Kentucky and southern Illinois, and due to the demand for steel rails and building and manufacturing materials.[4] Poles also worked in other metallurgy plants, including factories in southern Illinois specializing in zinc plating. Like their meatpacking counterparts, steel-making firms in the United States mechanized their processes, relying less on skilled workers and more on masses of low-skill laborers, providing a ready draw for immigrant labor. Poles and other eastern European immigrants found work in large numbers. By 1910, Poles were the largest group of workers in the South Chicago mills and made up nearly a quarter of all steelworkers in the Midwest.[5] Similar to the processes at packinghouses, much of the hiring of Polish immigrants went on at the factory gates or through the recommendation of friends and relatives who might bribe a foreman to hire their kin.

Working conditions were poor, and the constant noise, heat, and dust led to a wide variety of skin and lung ailments. Accidents in the steel mills were frequent and often horrific. "In January 1900, for example, at the Illinois Steel Foundry at 33rd Street and Ashland Avenue, three Poles were taking metal up in an elevator. Near the top the line broke and the men plummeted to the bottom of the shaft. One survived the fall but died soon afterward in the hospital." Men died or were injured in the blast furnace, around the rail lines that moved through the plant, and in many other ways.[6] For those who could endure the hardship, however, the mills provided steady employment.

Coal mining in Illinois began in the 1830s, and over the next several decades, coal seams in both southern and central Illinois were brought into production. Illinois coal was shipped to Chicago or St. Louis where it was most often used for heating, railroads, and providing power for factories. Poles began to arrive in the mines in the 1880s as the demand for coal grew, coming both from Poland itself but also from other Polish mining communities in Pennsylvania. By the standards of low-skill labor of that period, coal miners were paid better than some industrial workers, but the job was one of the most dangerous a man could perform. Fires, explosions, gas poisoning, and cave-ins were sudden and usually fatal. Any of these accidents not only killed men in the immediate area of the disaster but often trapped many others in mine shafts where they died of asphyxiation. This was brutally demonstrated in the 1909 Cherry Mine Disaster in Bureau County, Illinois, when kerosene dripping on a pile of hay caused a fire that quickly grew out of control, killing 259 men, including many Poles.[7]

### Earning a Living

What did Polish workers earn for working in such conditions? Wages for day labor in Chicago were $1.50 to $2.00 by the 1890s.[8] Chicago's Polish packinghouse workers averaged $9.34 a week in 1914, though this was higher during periods when the plants were busy.[9] Nevertheless, packinghouse work could also be uncertain, and workers often could not count on full-time work year round. In Illinois steel mills, the average blast furnace worker earned just over 15 cents an hour in 1907, though that number rose to 53 cents at the height of wartime production in World War I. Most

Polish laborers, circa 1900. Courtesy of Polish Museum of America Archives.

common laborers worked between 6 and 7 days a week, many alternating between 6- and 7-day stints. For common blast furnace workers, the average take-home pay for such a week was $13.40 (though this rose to $38 a week during the boom year of 1920).[10] For coal miners, the picture is not as clear: since miners were often paid per ton of coal mined (minus rocks), their wages often varied. Available statistics, though, suggest that by the turn of century, Illinois coal miners worked six 10-hour days underground and earned between $1.50 and $2 a day or somewhere between $9 and $12 a week in 1898 and 1899, though by 1922 this had increased to about $50 a week.[11]

Seasonal work slowdowns as well as layoffs during economic recessions were especially hard on Polish immigrants, since their jobs did not allow them to put aside much money when times were good. Injuries that kept a worker from the factory, whether temporarily or permanently, were a major crisis. Rent, food, and clothing ate up a portion of each week's pay, and often immigrants were also helping to support families in Europe. In many Polish families, money earned by the wife, even though she earned less than her husband, often made a crucial difference between poverty and getting ahead. A survey of Chicago workers in the 1920s found examples of Polish families earning between about $1,200 and $2,500 a year, with the largest number earning $1,300 to $1,500. While Poles earned less than most native-born workers, they did better than the city's newly arriving African Americans.[12] More than one in five Polish mothers with children at home found work outside the home. Of all the groups surveyed, only black women were more likely to have jobs.[13] Although jobs outside the home were the most obvious example, work inside the home was just as crucial. After rent, food and clothing were the biggest items in the budget of an immigrant family. Backyard gardens and even chicken coops were usually the province of women, and these alone could save a family a great deal of money over the course of a year, as well as improve their diet. Women also took in boarders and managed the renting of spare rooms. University of Chicago researchers noted "another Polish family in which the mother works consists of the man, his wife, and five children aged eight, six, five, three, and two years. In 1924, Mr. S—— earned $912 while the estimated budget for the family amounted to $1,678. In order to help support the children and to save a little money for a house, Mrs. S—— has done night work as a janitoress for the past three years. She now works in an office building and earns $15 a week [$780 a year]."[14] Compared to other countries in Europe where Poles migrated to find work (such as Germany), living in Chicago was less expensive, and wages went further.[15]

Angela Mischke recalled, "My father's wages in the tailor shop [$12 per week] were small and there were five of us to feed, clothe and house. It wasn't long, therefore, that mother who was very good with the needle found herself working in the same tailor shop with dad. Her job greatly helped supplement dad's earnings, especially since expenses kept mounted as we children grew older."[16] For mothers with children, though, going to work was a hard choice, since it meant the children would have to take care of themselves all day. This contributed to a host of problems, from household accidents to juvenile delinquency. In many cases, mothers returned from work and had to prepare food and take care of the household chores as well. Ideally, the older children could carry some of the burden. "Mother and father worked five and half days a week and much of the homework had to be done by Karol and me. We took turns scrubbing the floors, we helped mother with her weekly wash. . . . Karol . . . [had] to bring a supply of wood and coal from the storage room under the sidewalk. In Winter before anyone else was up, it was his job to start the fire in the stove to heat up the kitchen. He took the ashes out, washed the windows and helped with the dishes. . . . It was my duty to get the meals started and the potatoes peeled."[17] Chester Parks recalled that "after my mother went to work for the Woods Restaurant on Michigan Avenue, my brother and I became 'latchkey kids.'"[18]

While most children whose mothers worked went to school thanks to compulsory laws, when school was over and during the summer it was common to see children playing in the streets unless the weather was very poor. Women's religious orders sought to provide some relief by opening daycare centers as early as 1892. The newspaper *Dziennik Chicagowski* reported,

> Because many Polish mothers have to help their husbands earn the daily stipend, the Nazareth Sisters at 130 W. Division Street will open a home to accommodate the children of working parents. It will be called Sister Freblowska's Garden. This home will solve many wearisome problems for working mothers and will save many children from unfortunate mishaps. Beginning May 1, those children who are not of school

age will be accepted in the Garden. The children will be under the constant care of the nuns from 7:00 A.M. to 7 P.M. They will receive three meals a day: at 10 A.M. 12 noon, and 4 P.M. . . . The fee of ten cents per child, or less, will pay in return ten times the amount. Worry, accidents, waste of hours will be averted, while the children will be acquiring new playmates in a homelike atmosphere.[19]

Polish parishes and fraternal societies were the only fallback Polish workers had in hard times. In 1918, during court testimonies on conditions in the stockyards, the Polish daily *Dziennik Związkowy* reported:

One of the witnesses was Mrs. Rozalie Bobak, a young widow with a baby in her arms, whose husband was buried Saturday. The young woman testified as to the miserable life she led while her husband was still working; when he became ill, however, their poor family, consisting of the parents and three very small children, really came to know poverty. At the question by Frank Walsh, attorney for the workers, as to whether she received any aid during her husband's illness from the welfare societies maintained by the stockyards owners, Mrs. Bobak said she had not. . . . One of the last witnesses of the day was Rev. Ludwig Grudziński, pastor of St. John of God Parish (52nd and South Throop Streets), who is intimately acquainted with conditions existing among the stockyards workers' families. Among other things, the pastor described the poverty existing among the workers living in his parish. He said that his parish consists of 1800 families, ninety per cent of whom are employed in the local packing houses. In order to relieve slightly the conditions among these victims of capitalism, Father Grudzinski established a home at 46th and Gross Streets, where girls who have no parents can live at very small cost. In addition to this, the priest-friend of labor testified that his parish school is attended by 1200 to 1300 children of both sexes. Many mothers, Father Grudzinski testified further, who are forced to go to work, can leave their children at the parish shelter, where they are cared for by the nuns. The priest answered the cross-questioning of the lawyers and the judge clearly, and the catch-questions put by the shrewd Meyer, attorney for the stockyards barons, served no purpose.[20]

Yet, such centers were not universally available, and many families either could not take advantage of them or could not even afford the modest fees the sisters asked for the service. For mothers with small children, taking in boarders was also a way to earn extra money if the family had a spare room. Yet, this, too, had its drawbacks since it required additional work to cook, clean, and mend clothes for the boarders. Boarders were usually single men without families in America, and while most were decent enough, some drank heavily, and a few could even be a threat to other members of the household. In addition, landlords often raised the rent on properties where they knew families could rent rooms to boarders.[21]

Once children got old enough, they left school and went to work. Most boys left school after the sixth grade. Girls might stay in school a little longer unless needed at home to care for younger siblings while their mothers worked. Children's earnings were used to supplement those of the parents, but they were absolutely crucial in case one of the parents became ill or was injured and unable to work. Boys got jobs as errand boys or messengers but often entered the factories, packinghouses, mines, or steel mills as they got older and better able to handle physical demands of that type of work. Girls usually found employment in light industry or local shops. For boys and girls under the age of sixteen, the average weekly wage averaged between three and five dollars a week, though boys generally earned a little more.[22] Children under sixteen did work in packinghouses and other factories, though their numbers dropped steadily in the first decades of the twentieth century as public campaigns against child labor grew more effective.

Unemployment was among the worst fates that could befall a Polish immigrant. A bad accident at work, a dispute with a foreman, or a recession in the economy could turn a household with a modest if limited standard of living into one facing destitution and hunger. *Naród Polski* reported on one such case:

Frank Dombrowski, unemployed, living on Dickson St., left his home in despair to see the county agent in regard to relief for his wife and four children. In his absence his wife received a letter from him advising her he was going to commit suicide in the lake. He however, did not commit suicide and decided it would be better to die of hunger than to take his life. His wife was left destitute with the oldest child 9 years old, and the youngest nine months. Friends collected a sum of money which was turned over to her. . . . Mr. Dombrowski [went to] a small town in Indiana, 34 miles from Chicago, and received temporary work. He worked ten days and with his earnings returned to his family. He thanked all who helped his family.[23]

## In the Shadow of the Factory

Living conditions in Polish neighborhoods close to factories, stockyards, and mines were never easy. Poverty, and the Polish immigrant's need to be close to work, meant that they occupied the toughest and most run-down neighborhoods in the towns and cities where they settled. These neighborhoods rarely had city services like water, sewer, or garbage collection. (It was not until the 1920s that most towns and cities in the United States began to install water and sewer lines in the majority of their residential areas, and Polish neighborhoods were often the last to receive such services.) This resulted in communities where residents suffered overcrowding and a lack of basic amenities and often fell prey to disease.

Printing shop for the Polish newspapers *Dziennik Związkowy* and *Zgoda*, operated by the Polish National Alliance, circa 1920s. Courtesy of Polish Museum of America Archives.

Angela Mischke described her family's first home on the North-west Side of Chicago:

> 1420 W. Division Street, where Dad rented a four room, two bedroom flat. This was to be our home for the next seven years. . . . Mr. Levy, the owner was an absentee landlord. We only saw him when he came to collect his rent money, which was $8.00 a month. Dad was earning $12.00 a week as a presser in a tailor shop. Our living quarters consisted of a living room, kitchen and two bedrooms. The toilet was three flights down in the hall. The stairway was always dark and narrow passageway allowed in little daylight. We generally had to grope our way going up or down the stairs. At night a tiny gas light flickered illuminating the entrance. . . . The length of the building extended to the alley, so there was no room for even a blade of grass or a tree to grow.[24]

Although her family's home was fairly decent by the standards of the time (after all, it had an indoor toilet), it was heated in only two rooms. Mischke's parents slept in an unheated room under a thick feather tick, but she remembered her father waking up one morning with frost on his mustache due to a broken window the landlord never replaced.[25]

In many neighborhoods in industrial South Chicago, Poles were among the pioneering residents. In the early 1890s, the Back of the Yards neighborhood had a scattering of small frame houses, dirt streets, and few city services. By 1910, the community was filled with such small houses, some with a basement apartment to rent out to a single worker and provide some additional income for the family owning it.

### The Struggle for Workers' Rights

Labor conditions for Polish immigrant workers and their American-born children in late nineteenth- and early twentieth-century Illinois were often brutal, and workers had little recourse to dangerous conditions or low wages other than quitting or going on strike. Although some employers sought to treat their workers fairly, others had no compunction about mistreating their employees, seeing them as expendable cogs of industry. Hiring and firing practices were often corrupt, and foremen and mid-level supervisors could exploit their power over their workers to demand bribes, gifts, or, in the case of female workers, sexual favors. Since most hiring was done without written contracts, wages and deductions from paychecks were a source of constant misunderstanding and friction.

As a result, Poles were often drawn into labor conflicts almost as soon as they arrived in America. Historian John Bukowczyk commented on the significance of the Polish worker's identity in these conflicts: "They were not some native-born tradesmen who had acquired a reputation for protest . . . but unskilled immigrants. These men and women who so dramatically re-shaped the American working class during the mass-production years had often remained outside the American labor movement. But as their attitudes hardened and their numbers grew, immigrant workers . . . posed [a] serious challenge to America's industrial capitalist order."[26]

Strikes and protests indelibly marked the history of Poles in Illinois and other industrial states. These conflicts occurred even at the early stages of Polish settlement in the state. In 1876, the *Chicago Tribune* reported on Polish and Czech workers staging an unplanned "wildcat" strike in a south side lumberyard.[27] These conflicts were often intensely violent and, in the case of Poles, involved not only workers but their families and communities as well. Strikes and labor disputes brought Poles into conflict with powerful business interests as well as with other ethnic and racial groups, as employers habitually pitted different groups against one another in order to divide and conquer. Poles often initiated wildcat strikes, often in direct reaction to specific abuses by employers. (Unions, run by native-born white workers, were slow to recruit immigrants or ethnic and racial minorities, especially before World War I.) While workplace conflicts often involved arbitrary pay cuts, pay alone did not motivate all labor disputes. Bad working conditions, abusive treatment by foremen and contractors, and deductions for nonexistent services also stimulated the discontent of Polish laborers. Illinois Steel was a major employer of Poles and a source of ongoing labor disputes as employers cut back pay:

> Those who previously received one, two and three dollars per day are now doing more laborious work for a dollar, seventy-five and even fifty cents per day! But if this were only a regular daily pay! Unfortunately, it is not so. The company bet out contracts for the work, and the contractors brought the workers

to despair. When a month would pass there was nothing to ward off hunger with. How serious these conditions were is evidenced by the present strike. . . . And how was it possible for the worker to live with his wife and children under such conditions? How was it possible to avoid hunger? How was it possible to be patient? It is no wonder then that the strike broke out. After the meeting of the workers' committee, a delegation conferred with company officials, but a reply to their demands was refused. Only then did desperation grip the workers. The police were dispatched to break up the mobs of strikers gathering about the company plant. Police clubs swung freely among the strikers and many heads were broken. Those whom the police came in contact with and who were caught were immediately jailed and fined. Many innocent victims were taken to the criminal court. At the present time the company is replacing the strikers with Negroes, and wants to continue in operation with them.[28]

Another dispute at Illinois Steel in 1904 was typical of how such problems arose, especially when corrupt labor contractors added fuel to the fire:

It was said outright to the workers of the Illinois Steel Company in South Chicago that their pay will be cut. The workers marched upon the office in so great a number that the doors had to be barred to avoid trouble. After the police quieted the workers, an office employee said: "there is enough work for all those willing to work at the new scale." The workers were paying some agents, who claimed they were company agents, as much as 1 to 3 dollars. These agents promised workers that they would receive better jobs and more pay. The police had all they could do to restore peace and order after this new outbreak. The police were stationed in the repair shops, the supply rooms, and near the furnaces to guard the angered men from damaging these and at the same time protect the new [replacement] workers.[29]

Early Polish immigrants at times may have replaced workers of other ethnic groups who were on strike, although evidence for this is unclear. From a very early stage, Polish workers and community leaders were aware that acting as strikebreakers was not only bad practice if they wanted to receive better wages and conditions; it also brought upon them the scorn of other ethnic groups. In 1893, an editorial in the influential Chicago Catholic paper *Dziennik Chicagoski*, stated that Polish strikebreakers "gain nothing, but awaken against themselves the ever growing ill will of workers of all other nationalities. . . . We, the Poles, should for our own good and for the preservation of our honor as a people, leave the role of scabs, those drudges of capitalism, to the Negroes and the Chinese."[30] Although Illinois's large Polish communities were not particularly unified on many issues of the day, support for strikers against big employers was practically universal, from the small but vocal radical groups to the much larger centrist and Catholic groups.

Even small strikes were widely reported in the Polish press:

The employees of the Davidson Marble Company, among whom are more than a hundred Poles, have been on strike for the past week and a half. The strikers demand $2.25 for nine hours of work. Until a few days ago, the strike was entirely peaceful, but when the workers discovered that the factory was employing other men in their places, they picketed the street corners and prevented anyone from approaching the building. The new workmen, returning from the factory, were pursued and beaten. Three men were seriously injured, one of them

Polish workers employed at the Preston frame factory on 22nd Street, Chicago, circa 1900. Courtesy of Polish Museum of America Archives.

losing an eye in a fist fight. There was no more violence on the following day. The strike was instigated by the Irish, while the strikers are nearly all Poles.[31]

Strikes involving Polish workers frequently became violent. As despised outsiders, Poles and other new immigrants were widely viewed as a potentially dangerous element. Police and militia were poorly trained in crowd control, and employers often hired guards or armed strikebreakers to attack striking workers. Immigrant workers and their families, facing the loss of their income and security, fought back with fury. One of the first violent labor disputes involving Poles was the Lemont Massacre in May 1885, when Illinois state militia were called in to break up a strike at the Lemont stone quarry. The militia opened fire on the workers and attacked with bayonets, killing two Polish immigrants and wounding several others.[32] Lemont was the scene of another, even more violent confrontation a few years later. In June 1893, the heavily Polish labor force working on the Chicago Ship and Sanitary Canal went on strike after contractors reduced their pay. Workers had been forced to buy goods at a company store at inflated prices and were charged for the services of an apparently nonexistent doctor.[33] The company responded by bringing in a new workforce of blacks and whites, recruited in Georgia. On June 9, a large group of unarmed strikers approached the job site. They stopped at the site to count the number of "scabs" when a large group of black and white strikebreakers, armed with clubs and Winchester rifles and led by white foremen, attacked the workers without provocation. Shots rang out and the workers fled, pursued by the strikebreakers who paused only to shoot the wounded men lying in their path. Sheriffs' deputies arrived to support the strikebreakers and began arresting the striking workers for causing the disturbance. At least three and perhaps as many as nine men were killed and around twenty-four men wounded. The overwhelming majority were Poles. (Since strikers faced arrest, many of the wounded were treated at home, while the dead were often buried privately.) Among the dead was seventeen-year-old Polish immigrant Frank Kluga, who was not even involved in the strike but happened to be on his lunch break from his job at the nearby Santa Fe Railroad when he was gunned down at close range by strikebreakers.[34]

Poles also participated in the Pullman Strike of 1894, and in July of that year, several Polish immigrants were killed and injured when shots were fired into a crowd of bystanders at a labor rally.[35] Polish workers who struck against the Pullman Company or joined in sympathy strikes were hit especially hard when the strike failed. The economic depression that had begun the year before and the practice of many employers not to hire known strikers meant that many Polish immigrants remained jobless for months or even longer in the aftermath of the strike. The Chicago newspaper *Zgoda* printed an appeal from workers Jan Dluzak and Pawel Andrzyczka asking for help from the community for the strikers and their families:

> Dear Polish Brothers in Chicago! We have been without work for the past seven months due to the strike at the Pullman plant. . . . Many of the strikers of other nationalities have been back at work for sometime but we poor Poles are less fortunate, because we do not understand, speak or write the American language, and we haven't any bright prospect for the future, because it will be a long time before we go back to work, if then. We Poles are suffering the most and are the hardest pressed; many with their wives and children are on public charity, and are waiting from day to day for help from some unknown source. . . . The other nationalities remember their needy at all times, because they say "it is our duty to take care of our brothers." Why don't the Polish businessmen and workers of different organizations look into this matter of their poor brothers and help them, now in their hour of need. This is not merely a letter but a plea: please do not forsake us now.[36]

Among the most intensive labor struggles Polish workers engaged in was the Back of the Yards meatpacking strike in 1921 and 1922. By the early 1920s, Poles and other East-Central Europeans were the largest component of the workforce in the Back of the Yards neighborhood of south Chicago. Following an unsuccessful strike in 1904, wages in Chicago's packing industry remained stagnant even as the demand for the product and profits increased dramatically, especially as a result of World War I. After the United States entered the war, the government brokered a labor pact in the stockyards between the Amalgamated Meat Cutters Union and the packers, which increased wages and granted an eight-hour day in return for labor tranquility. As the U.S. economy entered a recession following the war, Chicago's four big packing companies—Armor, Morris, Swift, and Wilson—announced that they would no longer honor the wartime agreement and would cut wages by 45 percent by the end of 1921.[37] In November the union called a strike, and by December 5, 12,000 workers were on strike, over a quarter of the workforce. That number increased as crowds outside the packing plants swelled in size.

On December 7, large numbers of mounted and foot police poured into the Back of the Yards neighborhoods to suppress the strikers and keep the plants open. Furious battles erupted in the streets as the police faced not only strikers but the entire Polish community, including women and children of all ages. Police on foot and on horseback charged crowds, beating strikers with clubs and firing guns over their heads. Strikers fought police in the streets. Women threw bags of pepper into the eyes of police and police horses, rendering them temporarily helpless. Children hurled rocks and bottles at police from rooftops. The police fell back but tried again on December 8 and 9 as the violence escalated.

Outside observers were particularly stunned with the leading role of Polish women in the strike and riots. Women were the ones who directed the defense of their neighborhoods and led the men against the Chicago police with chants of "Beat the Cossacks! Beat the Cossacks!"—recalling a century of Polish resistance to Russian oppression. They fought the police not only as workers but also as wives, sisters, and mothers of workers whose ability to care for and feed their families was directly threatened by the wage cuts. *Dziennik Chicagoski* described the scene in its editions of December 8 and 9:

Women participated in the rioting this morning and they withstood the onslaught of the police longer than the men. . . . Amidst the crowds, women with ruffled hair and torn dresses could be seen scuffling with police as they tried to break up the gangs. . . . One of the women workers, Maria Buczyńska, pounced on Policemen Mueller and Jungblut. The crowd dragged them from their motorcycles and beat them. . . . A second important encounter took place at 49th and Racine Avenue. Here again, a woman, Miss Zofia Horoszka, threw herself at five policemen patrolling the area. One of the officers fell to the street as he was struck on the head with a club. Meanwhile Miss Horoszka escaped with her colleagues. When police tried to extricate her from one of the houses, they were showered with pepper; however, after a long battle, the police succeeded in making the arrest. . . . A woman was arrested at 49th and Racine Avenue after she flung a bottle at a mounted policemen, striking him with such force that he fell to the street.[38]

Despite the ferocity of the striking Polish workers and their families, the 1921 strike ultimately failed, and plants reopened under the lower wage regime. As *Dziennik Zjednoczenia* pointed out,

> The end of the strike does not yet mean return to former occupations, because the question that comes into consideration is whether the packers wish to accept the former employees back to work. The workers went out on strike because they were forced to it. The pay which they received for hard work in foul-smelling dark holes was not sufficient to feed a good sized family. It was not even sufficient for a single man to keep himself decently. . . . The workers have felt a terrible injustice caused by the owners of the packing houses, and have resolved to ask for their rights. They endeavored to present to the meat barons their unpleasant predicament, but all of their complaints received no response. Nothing else was left for the workers but to go out on strike. They went! Unfortunately, they did not assure themselves as to the certainty of coming out victorious. They were not told that other unions would not join their strike and that they were going out on strike on their own strength. Today, after two months of want, the Polish workers were told that they could call off the strike. We saw our fellow countrymen strikers yesterday as they waited at the employment bureau of Swift and Company; we saw how hundreds of them walked away from the window after being turned down, with no hope of receiving a job in the future. That is the tragedy of our ignorant Polish workingman. The Polish community ought to do something to make things easier for these poor souls.[39]

Although Poles in Illinois fought fiercely and courageously for their rights in the workplace, they did not succumb to the siren song of political radicalism. Support for workers was widespread across all segments of the community. While small groups of Polish socialists, Wobblies (i.e., International Workers of the World [IWW]), and even communists emerged in Chicago, they were dwarfed by the far larger Nationalist and Catholic groupings.

While the two larger factions disputed leadership of the community between them, both were firmly opposed to extremists on either the right or the left. A strong Catholic social movement, inspired by late nineteenth-century Polish positivism and Catholic teachings on the dignity of labor that emerged in the 1890s, played a major role in blunting any impulse toward extremism while staunchly defending workers against capitalist exploitation.[40] Another important factor is that in spite of the severe problems Poles faced in the industrial workplace, they were making steady material progress on the whole. They had come to America to better their situation, not to overturn the social order or start violent revolution. Labor exploitation was a roadblock they struggled against, but it failed to stop them from improving life for themselves and their families.[41]

The struggle of Polish workers for their rights in the workplace would continue throughout the 1920s and 1930s. Only in the late 1930s and 1940s, with a new wave of unionization in American

Polish bakers union, circa 1920s. The sign reads "Eat Bread Only with the Union Label" in both Polish and English. Courtesy of Polish Museum of America Archives.

heavy industry, would permanent progress be made. In Illinois as well as in other major industrial states, such as Pennsylvania, Michigan, and New York, Poles were a critical component of the union movement. Polish workers and Polish communities played a leading role in the effort to improve working conditions and provide better pay and fair treatment for workers across the country.

\* \* \*

The jobs available to Polish immigrants in Illinois were dangerous, low paying, and dirty. Poles were treated as replaceable cogs of industry and were often verbally and even physically abused by native-born Americans, especially when they protested low wages or dangerous working conditions. Yet, Poles took these jobs and took them voluntarily, knowing what they entailed. They did so because such jobs represented the best opportunity they had to make a better life for themselves and their families. Conditions in rural villages of East-Central Europe were often idealized by outside observers (including some middle-class leaders of the Polish community in the United States) who contrasted the supposedly idyllic green pastures of the Old Country with the smoky, gritty factories of America. Yet in reality the villages were places of tremendous hardship, poverty, and constant, degrading work that offered little opportunity for even the hardest laborers to better themselves. Farm work was not only hard but also, like the factories whence they journeyed to work, filled with accidents, disease, and early death for many. Observing the situation at a distance, it is tempting but inaccurate to see Poles as merely victims of industrialization, wrenched from green pastures of home to smoky, dirty factories. Poles came to Illinois well versed in hardship and the importance of lifelong toil. They chose to come and take the hardest jobs in order to create a better life for themselves and their families. There were many setbacks, tragedies, and failures along the way, but industrial Illinois offered real opportunities. And in spite of all the perils they faced, the Poles who came succeeded, and that success served as a magnet to draw their counterparts in Europe to the New World.

# 4

---

# WIARA: FAITH AND RELIGIOUS LIFE

Faith was central to the lives of Polish immigrants in Illinois. For the overwhelming majority of immigrants and their children, faith meant Roman Catholicism. Indeed, to be Polish in America meant being Catholic. Those Polish Americans who were not Catholic existed in a largely Catholic milieu, their identity formed by that milieu and in dialogue with and sometimes opposition to the Catholic majority. Of the Polish immigrants who settled in Illinois in the late nineteenth and early twentieth centuries, probably no more than 5 percent were non-Catholic. Although a sizeable number of Jews emigrated from the lands of the old Polish-Lithuanian Commonwealth to the United States and to Illinois, most developed a very different ethnic identity in America, usually preferring to identify themselves as Russian Jewish or simply Jewish American. Only a relatively small group of early Jewish immigrants—often political refugees—seem to have identified as Poles.[1] There were small numbers of Polish Protestants in Illinois, but in the early decades, aside from a single Baptist congregation in Chicago, most Polish Protestants seem to have joined congregations from other ethnic groups.[2]

Catholicism was the most important bond shared by gentile immigrants from rural Poland, initially far more meaningful than the nascent sense of Polish nationalism that spread gradually from the service gentry and urbanites to the peasantry. Faith was one of the few things binding together Poles from diverse regions of the old country. When Poles arrived in Illinois in significant numbers, their first impulse was to form a parish. As a result, parishes would become the main and foremost institution in the lives of Polish immigrants and their children. They would function primarily as religious centers, but they took on roles far more expansive than merely serving as place to worship once a week. Parishes were centers of community organization and social, cultural, political, and even economic activity. Thus parishes served as venues for the most significant and ambitious cooperative and organizational efforts as well as the battlefields for the community's bitterest conflicts. While Roman Catholic parishes predominated among Poles in Illinois, the same basic functions can be observed in the schismatic Polish National Catholic Church, whose parishes were often formed as a result of divisions within Roman Catholic parishes. Chicago was also home to a small Polish Baptist group.

### Founding Parishes

The first Polish immigrants often attended English-speaking Irish parishes or German parishes. As many of the early Polish arrivals in Illinois came from the German- or Prussian-controlled regions of Poland, most spoke at least some German, and quite a few were fluent in the language. As Polish immigration increased, so did pressure to form Polish parishes. In some cases, Poles parted quite amicably with their Irish or German counterparts, but in other cases the Poles felt they were being treated as second-class citizens. In 1882, the Polish missionary Father Leopold Moczygemba wrote from Lemont, stating, "The local parish has 300 Polish families and only 125 Germans, and the Poles are only tolerated; therefore, a Polish church must be built."[3] Polish parishes in Joliet, Kankakee, LaSalle, Peru, and DuBois also began when Poles left existing German parishes to form their own.

Polish immigrants began the process of forming a parish by creating a Polish church society, either in an existing Irish or German parish or on their own. Once the group had received the consent of the bishop, it would sign up sufficient members to prove that enough Poles existed in a particular locale to support their effort. They would then petition the bishop for their own parish. The Poles also had to raise money to build a church. If these conditions were met (or appeared likely to be met), a new Polish parish was born.

The first Polish church group in Illinois was the St. Stanislaus Kostka Society, founded in 1864 in Chicago. Due to a growing rivalry with a second Polish group—the Gmina Polska—the process of forming the first Polish parish in the state was delayed a few years as both sides lobbied the archdiocese with different plans. In 1869, the parish of St. Stanislaus Kostka was founded and a church built at Bradley and Noble Streets in Chicago (where the church stands today).[4]

The origin of Polish parishes was often fraught with rivalries, financial hardships, and difficulties in finding suitable Polish-speaking priests. The history of St. Valentine Parish in Peru noted, "The beginnings of this parish were hard. The perseverance and strong will of the founders overcame all obstacles. Members of the Society of St. Valentine took on the work, and in one fell swoop gathered two hundred dollars."[5] At its beginnings in 1901, the parish of St. Stanislaus in Kankakee was so poor that in order to build a church, the parishioners mortgaged their own homes.[6]

## Parish Life

Once approval for a parish was received, the building could begin. In smaller parishes and especially in rural areas, the first church building was often simply a wood-frame structure. Yet most Poles sought to put down brick-and-mortar foundations in their new homes and build the biggest and best they could afford, quickly replacing the first wooden churches with stone and brick. In larger urban parishes, churches were often towering neo-Gothic or neo-Romanesque structures. Nearly all the Polish immigrants to Illinois who built and paid for such churches had been born and

Sts. Peter and Paul Catholic Church and rectory, Spring Valley, Illinois, circa 1900. This was the first Polish parish in the diocese of Peoria, founded in 1891. Courtesy of Polish Museum of America Archives.

raised in thatched roof huts with dirt floors, often an attached shed for the family's livestock. They came to America to work in dirty and dangerous factories and lived in slum neighborhoods with few services. To build churches that would rival the storied cathedrals of Europe would be the greatest collective undertaking of their lives, representing an immense mobilization of resources for the new and impoverished immigrant communities. Yet on coming to America, they contracted with some of America's best architects, commissioned stained glass windows, and ordered the casting of huge bronze bells. The great Polish churches of Illinois were spaces to worship God and to gather for important community events, but they were so much more as well. They embodied and symbolized the collective hopes and aspirations of a new people in America. To nativists, Poles appeared to be troublesome foreigners; to socialists and radicals, they were part of the proletariat masses; to middle-class reformers, they were poor unfortunates in need of social uplift. But in their churches the Poles expressed who they truly took themselves to be.

Because of this, events like the dedication of a new Polish church took on great importance. In 1892, the parish of Our Lady of Perpetual Help was dedicated in Chicago, and Poles from across the city came to help the parishioners celebrate:

> The St. Mary of Perpetual Help Church was consecrated yesterday amidst solemn rites. Twenty-six Catholic societies led by an orchestra, took part in the ceremonies. Main, Laurel, 31st and 32nd streets were so crowded it was almost impossible to pass. The people of the neighborhood, mostly Poles, jammed the streets and sidewalks. The ceremonies began at three o'clock in the afternoon, when the societies from Town of Lake and 17th Street made their appearance, each led by a mounted marshal in colorful uniform and represented by a band. As these bands passed by, one by one, it seemed as if they were trying to outdo one another. . . . A sermon was given by Father Urban Raszkiewicz. [He] talked about the sacrifices in the Old and New Testaments. He emphasized the importance of observing Holy Mass on Sunday and compared the offerings made by the people to the church during biblical days with those of the present day. Contributions, attendance, and prayers play an important part in the Church of God. . . . Father Raszkiewicz urged all the Poles to unite and become a

harmonious whole. The fact that one came from a province and the other from another, should be forgotten. . . . The structure and interior decoration of the church are of unusual beauty. The edifice is patterned after the Roman and Byzantine styles of architecture. Although the portals are impressive, the spacious height of the interior of the church is even more so. The large tall pillars, the beautiful arches, the stained-glass windows, and the tall central dome are bewitching to the eye.[7]

Polish parishes in Illinois were supported by a working-class population with limited resources. Their very existence is a testimony to the importance Poles in Illinois have placed on them over the last 150 years. Contributing to the parish was an important part of belonging to the community, and even those of limited means sought to contribute something, even symbolically, during the hard years of the Depression. Chester Parks's single mother gave five dollars a year in 1924, but only two dollars a year by 1936. During the 1930s, Anna Procanin's family gave about ten dollars a year, increasing to fifteen dollars a year by the 1940s.[8] Because the amounts collected from parishioners were rarely enough to cover all expenses, most parishes hosted public fundraising events, such as benefit concerts and dances. At St. James Parish in Chicago, for example, "the main source of income came from different social activities, sponsored directly by the Parish and Church organizations, and particularly the Parish Carnivals—popularly known as 'The Saint James Parish Outdoor Fiestas.'"[9]

Parishes were the sites of the community's most important and memorable events and celebrations. Although early Polish communities were often riven with conflicts and rivalries, and Polish families were likewise divided by distance and generation, parish rituals emphasized symbolic unity. Processions featured the entire community, and programs of events were carefully designed to include representatives of as many constituencies as possible. In 1890, for example, the recently founded Society of St. Stephen at St. Stanislaus Kostka Parish in Chicago solemnly blessed the society's banner, which would henceforth be carried in all public events by members of the society. Proud members sent a report of the proceedings to the newspaper:

The members of the St. Stephen Society, at the parish of St. Stanislaus, celebrated the commemoration of a beautiful Polish banner, Easter Sunday. . . . At 9 o'clock, Easter morning, the procession started; the Society of St. Stanislaus came first because it is the oldest society of this parish, second came the Society of St. Casimir; third, the Society of St. Adalbert; fourth, the Society of St. Valentine; fifth, the Society of St. John Cantius; sixth, the Society of St. Stephen. These different societies paraded through the streets to the music supplied by the Society of St. Stanislaus, and returned to the church where a church mass was given, followed by a mass meeting in the church auditorium, where speeches by the Rev. Fathers and prominent leaders of Polish enterprises, were heard. The choir of St. Stanislaus sang songs, accompanied by a Polish orchestra. After the speeches, the societies marched through the streets with this new banner at the head of the parade, and many thousands of Polish people took part in the great ceremonies.[10]

Such celebrations blending religious and ethnic or nationalist themes have been a constant feature of Polish parish life from the late nineteenth century up to the present day. In 1936, for

example, St. Mary Magdalene Church in Chicago staged the parish's silver jubilee celebration in a way that would have been instantly familiar to members of the St. Stephen's Society nearly half a century earlier.[11]

For Poles in Illinois, the parish and its liturgical and paraliturgical practices provided an anchor of stability to people undergoing tremendous changes. Polish parishes were by no means replicas of the Old Country. Compared to their European counterparts, Polish American parishes were scenes of dramatic adaptation and change. Beginning in the 1870s in the wake of the First Vatican Council (1869–70), the Catholic Church had developed a response to the challenge of modernization and problems of urban, industrial life that emphasized greater lay involvement and new devotions, and addressed serious social problems through a range of new organizations. The Church

Polish American first communicant Florence Dankowski, in Chicago's Wicker Park Polonia, circa 1940. Courtesy of A. Gunkel.

in Poland was slow to adapt to these changes due to the intense pressure it faced from the Partitioning Powers, especially Germany and Russia. Free from such concerns in America and facing the problems of industrial life, Poles in the New World readily embraced many of the new initiatives that followed Vatican I. One example was Forty Hours' Devotion, a practice of forty hours of prayer before the Blessed Sacrament in which groups of parishioners and priests would take shifts praying continuously. Rarely conducted in Poland prior to World War II, it soon became a regular feature of Polish churches in Illinois.[12]

### Clergy

Although lay participation was at the heart of the Polish parish-community, clergy played a critical role, serving as the most important leaders of the new immigrant communities. Polish immigrants could have mixed views on clergy, sometimes treating them with great respect, other times viewing them with frustration. Many pastors and religious sisters who gave unstintingly of their time and talents to their struggling young communities were rightfully accorded pride of place in community memory and in historical and memorial books published for nearly every Polish parish in Illinois. However, at the same time, clergy could be the cause of equally great resentment and division.

Nothing better illustrates both potentials than the role of the Congregation of the Resurrection (known as the Resurrectionists) in Chicago's early Polonia and its leading figure until his death in 1897, Father Wincenty Barzyński. The son of a church organist, Barzyński was born in Russian-occupied Poland in 1838 and raised in a religious and patriotic home. After attending seminary, he served as chaplain to an insurgent unit in the January Uprising of 1863–64 against Russian rule. Forced to flee Poland, Barzyński ended up in Rome, where he joined the

St. Adalbert Parish (*left*) and Polish Youth Association home (*right*) on 17th Street, April 1901. Courtesy of Polish Museum of America Archives.

Congregation of the Resurrection. The Resurrectionists had been founded by exiled Polish priests following the failure of the earlier November Uprising in 1830–31. Rejecting armed revolution, the Resurrectionists sought to encourage spiritual, social, and cultural growth. Freedom from political oppression for Poles or any other group could come only when people built up their communities through prayer, hard work, and education. They felt a special mission toward the growing numbers of rural people migrating to urban centers in search of work, who were increasingly separated from networks of kin and community. In 1865, Barzyński was sent by the Congregation to serve Polish immigrants in the United States, and by 1869 he had found a home in Chicago.

Both Barzyński's admirers and detractors agreed that he was an organizational wizard with tremendous energy. He showed a particular talent for encouraging lay organizations and for building parishes, schools, and other church institutions. Assigned to the first Polish parish of St. Stanislaus Kostka, Barzyński became a leading force in the development of Polish Catholic institutions in Chicago. He created a parish bank that protected the small salaries of immigrant workers from saloonkeepers and provided a safe alternative to commercial banks (which most workers distrusted). The bank gave Barzyński financial clout, and he used it to loan money to build new Polish parishes and related institutions.

Soon acknowledged not only as the leader of Chicago's Polish Resurrectionists but also as the leading Polish clergyman in America, Barzyński sought to realize the Congregation's goals by creating a dense network of institutions—the parish-community—based in and around the parish church, which would meet all or most of the spiritual, social, cultural, and economic needs of Polish immigrants. The parish-community was to serve as a bulwark against rapid assimilation and against the perils of modern urban life, which included exploitation by capitalist "robber barons" and the seductive blandishments of radical and socialist agitators. At a time when American Catholic bishops struggled with polyglot dioceses and viewed newly arrived immigrant clergy with suspicion if not hostility, Barzyński was able to establish a special relationship with the Chicago archdiocese. So trusted would Barzyński become to the Catholic hierarchy in Chicago that it would closely consult him on nearly every major decision regarding Polish parishes in the diocese.

Historian Joseph Parot described Barzyński as the author of one of the most significant "brick and mortar" achievements of nineteenth-century American Catholicism: "Wherever a Polish colony settled, there Barzyński would build a church; and for each new church the Resurrectionists either supplied a pastor from their own congregation or made personal recommendations to the archdiocese on Polish-speaking diocesan priests." This led to the phenomenal growth of the parish-community system, "a system in which the Resurrectionists and/or Barzyński were either directly or indirectly involved on twenty-three separate occasions."[13] Parot goes on to note:

> For example, by the turn of the century in the West Town/ Logan Square area, the nucleus of which was formed by St. Stanislaus Kostka and Holy Trinity parishes, the community parish system encompassed six parochial grammar schools, two parish high schools . . . one college . . . several orphanages, two newspapers (the *Dziennik Chicagoski,* initiated by Barzyński himself and *Naród Polski*, the organ of the Polish Roman Catholic Union [PRCU]), the headquarters of the PRCU, hundreds of parish societies, several social welfare and cultural organizations and even one Polish-run hospital. . . .

Choir, musicians, and priests from St. John of God Parish, Chicago, circa 1920s–30s.
Courtesy of Polish Museum of America Archives.

All these institutions, needless to say, were administered on a predominantly Polish Catholic basis.[14]

By 1900, within these few square miles of urban terrain, St. Stanislaus had forty thousand parishioners, while a few blocks away Holy Trinity had twenty thousand parishioners, making them the largest Catholic parishes in the United States if not among the largest in the world.

Yet, Barzyński's achievements came at the cost of alienating significant groups in the Polish community. Nationalist leaders who wanted a stronger focus on liberating the Polish homeland fumed at the resources being plowed into his building projects and at his goal of having permanent Polish colonies in the New World. Barzyński's favoritism toward his Resurrectionist colleagues and their close allies alienated many other clergy, and the appointment of his own brother, also a priest, to a new parish in Chicago did not help. At a time when Poles were often discriminated against by Irish and German bishops, Barzyński's close ties to the Chicago archdiocese and his insistence on loyalty to the American hierarchy upset those who wanted better treatment of Polish immigrants in the Church and the appointment of more Polish-speaking clergy to positions of greater authority. Finally, the small but highly vocal radical and anticlerical elements among Polish immigrants hated the thought of any Catholic priest acting as the de facto leader of what was rapidly becoming the largest and most important Polish community in the United States.

Even after Barzyński's death, his legacy in Chicago continued, most notably in the relative degree of autonomy that Polish clergy enjoyed. Polish pastors in Chicago formed a kind of "league" within the city's archdiocese that decided how (or even if) to implement policies of the archbishop. Due to the specter of independentism and the enclosed nature of Polish parishes, archbishops in the 1920s gave the Polish pastors' league a fairly long leash in managing their affairs in return for loyalty, keeping independentism and trusteeism in check, and ensuring some semblance of administrative discipline in the often-fractious Polish parishes.[15]

While Barzyński's case was unusual in the scope of his impact on Polish history in Illinois, clergy had formed an important leadership class in the immigrant community for generations. Priests were often the most formally educated leaders among the earliest immigrants. Many served as intermediaries between different factions in the community, as well as between the parish-community and the larger society. They helped immigrants write letters, find jobs, and manage their money, and priests were often the ones to intervene with authorities if a parish member got in legal trouble. A history of Poles in East St. Louis recalled that "Father [Andrew] Janiszewski was the 'financial advisor' of the parishioners. Single men would turn over most of their paychecks to him to bank the money to insure that dubious saloons and gamblers would not take advantage of [these] vulnerable young men."[16] Pastors organized the community for efforts such as building a new church or school or collecting funds for Polish relief and other patriotic activities.

Capable, caring pastors had a formative impact on Polish parish-communities, and they were cherished in the collective memory of the places they served. Yet not all pastors were remembered with fondness, for the immigrant community had its share of priests who were less than capable stewards of their parishes, who alienated those they served with their management style, or who even acted abusively toward parishioners. Early clergy came almost exclusively from Europe, and some adjusted to America more readily than others, just like their fellow immigrants did. In some instances, European dioceses found that sending troublesome clergy to America was a good way to "clean house." By the second generation, a new crop of clergy—Polish-speaking but educated in America—came to the fore, providing sorely needed pastoral leadership.

While priests were the leaders of Polish parish-communities, women religious (i.e., nuns) played a vital and often forgotten role in the immigrant church, especially by the turn of the twentieth century. The creation of Polish parochial schools was a critical part of the Resurrectionists' vision of the parish-community, and here they were fully in accord with the stance of American bishops who had supported the development of Catholic schools since the middle of the nineteenth century. Early Polish schools in Illinois were often limited, and teaching duties were handled by the parish organist (who in European villages had usually doubled as the children's catechist) or by occasional itinerant laymen. This proved less than satisfactory, since the quality of teaching was often poor, pay was minimal, and there were never enough lay teachers to meet the demand. Orders of Catholic nuns proved to be the solution in Illinois and other states. For example, at Our

Lady of Częstochowa Parish in Cicero, parishioners founded a school in 1894 that was run by the church organist. Yet, as the parish historian noted, it was the arrival of teachers from the Sisters of St. Joseph in 1904 that "marked the formal establishment of a real 'grade' or 'grammar' school here at St. Mary's."[17]

There appear to have been at least eight separate orders of Polish Catholic religious sisters operating in Illinois.[18] Among the largest of the orders was the Congregation of the Sister of St. Felix of Cantalice, a Franciscan order known as the Felicians that was founded in Warsaw in the 1850s to serve the needs of the urban poor. Felicians operated Polish schools all across Illinois, but the Chicago province also served communities in Wisconsin, Minnesota, North Dakota, Nebraska, Louisiana, and Texas (and even operated a school at a Polish refugee camp in Mexico during World War II). Although Felicians mostly served Polish American communities, their service extended further. For example, Felicians staffed a school for the deaf that was operated by the Chicago archdiocese, and they also ran a hospital in Centralia.[19]

Annunciation Catholic School class, 1924. Courtesy of Polish Museum of America Archives.

Many of the early nuns to serve in Polonia came from Poland, but by the early twentieth century a growing number of immigrant women and their daughters entered convents in the United States. At a time when few Polish immigrants—men or women—had access to education beyond grade school and the lives of most women were circumscribed by family and work, entering religious life proved an attractive option for many intelligent and capable young women. Becoming a nun meant entering a life far removed from what their mothers and grandmothers had known—one that emphasized learning and service to the community and that was viewed with great respect and even reverence. The mobilization of Polish American nuns represented a tremendous influx of talent in service to God and to their struggling communities. Polish nuns did far more than simply teach school, however; they also created the entire Polish American school system from the ground up. They designed the curricula, wrote the textbooks, and managed both the financial and administrative sides of the schools. Beyond the school system, nuns were on the front line of social service in the state's young Polish communities. They founded and staffed hospitals. They created and managed a host of day cares, orphanages, nursing homes, and homes for unwed mothers. As we shall see, these roles were critical to the survival of the Polish community as it became increasingly subject to the stresses of immigrating to urban, industrial Illinois.

Guardian Angel Center, circa 1910. The center, operated in south Chicago by Polish nuns, served as a clinic, a day care for working mothers, and a women's shelter. Courtesy of Polish Museum of America Archives.

## Conflict

Although parishes were the seedbed for a plethora of community initiatives, they were also the scene of some of its bitterest conflicts. They brought together a wide range of people from different regional, social, and political backgrounds. Thus, control of parish resources and organizations and the prestige that accompanied it served as a bone of contention. As leaders of the parish, priests became the focus for either intense support or intense resentment. Strong-willed immigrant pastors clashed frequently with groups of equally strong-willed parishioners, usually over finances or issues of administrative prerogative. The pride of former peasants who took the place of old-world noblemen in building their own churches extended to controlling the parishes they had worked so hard to help build. After all, if the old gentry back in Europe hired the local pastor and paid his salary, shouldn't the new immigrant gentry in America receive the same privileges?

Such attitudes brought Poles into conflict with one another, but they also led to clashes with the existing American Catholic hierarchy, which was dominated by Irish American bishops along with quite a few German American prelates. Irish Catholics, facing intense nativist prejudice, were particularly sensitive to charges made by many Protestants that the American Catholic Church was a hotbed of foreigners who refused to speak English or to assimilate into the mainstream of society. German immigrants had first challenged Irish bishops in the late 1700s and early 1800s over the issue of whether lay trustees could exercise legal ownership and administrative authority over parish churches. Over time, however, more German Americans had joined the ranks of American bishops, reducing (but not completely eliminating) cultural conflicts between Irish and German Catholics. In addition, the practice of designating "national parishes" set aside for the use of a specific ethnic group became widespread, though some bishops resisted forming such parishes. By 1884, the Third Plenary Council of Baltimore, with the support of Rome, firmly placed legal ownership of parish property in the hands of bishops. This set the stage for potential conflict with newly arriving Polish Catholics.

For many early bishops, the Poles, along with their language, culture, and history, seemed as incomprehensibly foreign as they did for many other Americans. As Polish immigration increased and more and more Polish national parishes were proposed, the bishops' sought to promote "Americanization" and get the newcomers to conform to established practice. Most Poles saw this as a serious threat to the integrity of their new communities.[20] Polish immigrants, both lay and clergy, often found relations with American bishops frustrating. While many bishops viewed the Poles as stubborn, fractious, and demanding, many Poles felt the bishops were hostile to their culture and language. A few prelates did try to learn Polish and to relate more closely to Polish Catholics. Bishop Henry Althoff of Belleville was one. A man with a gift for languages, Althoff picked up Polish while serving immigrants in Nashville (he also spoke German and French and could converse in Lithuanian, Croatian, and Italian).[21] But Althoff was an exception. Most bishops preferred to work through one or a few trusted Polish-speaking priests who would serve as their intermediaries with the Polish newcomers.

One of the most intense sources of conflict was the appointment of pastors. Polish immigrants greatly outnumbered available priests, and few sons of immigrants had the connections or the educational background to enter American seminaries prior to 1900. Priests from Europe filled the void, but their numbers were always limited, and the problem was exacerbated by the practice of a few European bishops who sometimes saw America as a convenient place to get rid of their most troublesome or least able priests. On the American side, some bishops were slow to allow Polish priests into their diocese or even resisted them altogether. According to one early Polonia historian, Bishop James Ryan of Alton (now Springfield) "does not want any Polish priests."[22]

Americanizing bishops (those who sought to Americanize Poles) had a polarizing effect on Polish immigrants and Polish clergy. Loyalists wanted to maintain strict obedience to the bishops while quietly proving their worthiness for future positions of church leadership. Nationalists felt that Americanizing bishops were violating their duties as faithful pastors in failing to respond to the cultural and linguistic needs of the Poles. One Polish priest speaking at a January Insurrection celebration railed, "These Americanizers had better forget about the Polish children, because they shall never be able to work their wishes on the Poles."[23] Numerous letters and petitions of protest from Polish Catholics in Illinois were sent to the apostolic delegate and other church officials, opposing decrees and actions of bishops who were viewed as anti-Polish or who pushed Americanization too strongly.[24] A conflict over the ownership of Holy Trinity Parish had to be resolved by the intervention of the Church's apostolic delegate to the United States, who brokered a solution that left the parish without a pastor for a period and neither party entirely satisfied.[25]

These differences culminated in open conflict in Chicago in the 1890s at the parish of St. Hedwig. The parish's pastor, Father Joseph Barzyński, was the younger brother of Father Wincenty Barzyński. In 1894, the elder Barzyński appointed Father Antoni Kozłowski as an assistant to Father Joseph to help manage the fast-growing parish. In contrast to Joseph Barzyński's stolid and uninspiring nature, Kozłowski was young and charismatic, and he immediately attracted a large following of younger parishioners, especially young women. The younger assistant and the older pastor disliked each other from beginning, and the power struggle between them sent the parish into turmoil. For the Resurrectionist leaders of Chicago's Polish clergy, Kozłowski's ties to dissident theologians in Rome who had opposed Vatican I and were instrumental in the fostering the Old Catholic schism in Europe were especially troubling.[26] Wincenty Barzyński would later admit that he had overridden his own brother's objection to Kozłowski's appointment and made a terrible error of judgment:

> As I look upon the crafty execution of the affair in your parish, for which every Catholic and Christian heart suffers great pain, for which every honorable Pole is ashamed, I see that the foes of Poland are joyous and that the enemies of the church have cause to sneer. Therefore, I crumble with anxiety before God and consciously feel that I am obligated to make a sincere effort to correct the wrong. . . . Some say that my brother is at times rude in his expressions and is easily roused to anger. But, on the other hand, no one can accuse him of ever being a flatterer, hypocrite, cheat or conspirator.[27]

While Wincenty Barzyński tried to the stem the growing discontent, the failure of the St. Stanislaus parish bank and his reluctance to compromise with nationalists who were yet loyal to the Church fueled a movement of radical independentists who sought direct control over parishes, if not an outright break with the Catholic Church. In Cleveland and Buffalo, dissident priests and parishioners had already formed "independent" parishes or tried to take over existing Roman Catholic parishes. In Chicago, Reverend Kozłowski was dismissed from his post at St. Hedwig by the archbishop after he was caught circulating a petition to remove Father Joseph Barzyński (his own superior) from the parish. Kozłowski and his supporters refused to budge, however, and challenged both the pastor and the archbishop. As the U.S. apostolic delegate sought to investigate the claims and counterclaims, tensions rose at St. Hedwig. When a group of men threatened Father Barzyński and prevented him from saying Mass, a virtual civil war was in the making. In February, a mob of hundreds of Kozłowski supporters forced Barzyński to flee the rectory for his own safety. The mob eventually broke through a police cordon and into the rectory, looking for Resurrectionist priests to lynch. Police who tried to halt the looting of the building were assaulted with clubs. Soon hundreds of police descended on the parish, fighting an all-out battle with the independentists. Police finally cleared the scene at gunpoint after hundreds of arrests and injuries. Attempts to reach a solution failed when independentists rejected the bishop's compromise candidate for a new pastor.[28] As a result, Kozłowski and his supporters left the church and formed their own parish under the auspices of the Old Catholic Church, a minor schismatic movement based in Holland.

In 1897, independent Polish parishes in the United States formed the Polish National Catholic Church (PNCC) under Reverend (later bishop) Franciszek Hodur of Scranton, Pennsylvania. Although it accepted most Roman Catholic theology, the PNCC rejected the role of the papacy, allowed lay control over parishes, and emphasized the use of Polish (rather than Latin) as the language of the liturgy.[29] As one PNCC newspaper in Chicago noted, "Members of the Polish National Church are the sole legal owners of the church buildings and all other church estates. All parishioners, through specially appointed committees, manage the parish wealth." Although never a true Protestant church, the PNCC nevertheless viewed faith as a relative matter of personal choice: "A church ought to be an association, of which everyone can be a member on his own accord. If someone does not feel the need of religion, nobody must judge him for it."[30] Parishes and individuals usually joined the PNCC in the wake of disputes between pastors and groups of parishioners in an existing parish. While independentism gained a toehold in many Polish communities, its appeal was limited. In Chicago, the most significant PNCC institution was All Saints Church, which was founded in 1895 by Reverend Kozłowski and his supporters. It later became the seat of the Western Diocese of the PNCC.[31]

The appeal of the PNCC remained particularly limited in Illinois not only due to the effective development of the Resurrectionists' parish-community system and the institutions it created but also by the fact that most of those who wanted a greater role for Poles within the American Catholic Church and many of the most effective voices in support of that role stayed with the Church and worked for their goals from within. The death of Father Wincenty Barzyński in 1899 also removed a flashpoint from the conflict. Although an effective leader and builder, Barzyński had a polarizing effect on many in the immigrant communities. While the PNCC as a whole remained small, its impact on Illinois was further limited by the fact that Polish clergy in Chicago were far better organized, more effective, and more trusted by

All Saints Polish National Catholic Church on Chicago's Lubeck Street, 1908. This was the first and best known of the Polish churches in Illinois that broke away from the Catholic Church. Chicago Sun-Times/Chicago Daily News collection, Chicago History Museum, DN-0006537 (cropped), copyright © Sun-Times Media, LLC, all rights reserved.

non-Polish bishops than in many other dioceses—all part of
Barzyński's legacy. The PNCC would ultimately have a total of
eight parishes and one mission in Illinois, many of which were
formed by local conflicts within particular Catholic parishes that
resulted in a disaffected group leaving and forming a national
parish. Most remained extremely small in size and did not last
long.[32] Although a precise number of PNCC adherents in Illinois
cannot be established with any certainty, one highly sympathetic
author in 1944 claimed the church had twelve thousand members
in Chicago.[33] This would have constituted about 2.4 percent of
Poles in the Windy City.

To be sure, Illinois's large Polonia contained those who openly
despised the Catholicism of their neighbors. In 1937, for example,
Maryanna Bort wrote to Toledo's *Ameryka-Echo* from Chicago
to say, "I cannot get into my head how a person can be so stupid
as to not understand that Roman priests are our most dangerous
enemies. All of them work only for the rich."[34] Chicago's Polish
socialists even sponsored a short-lived weekly called *Bicz Boży*
(Scourge of God) devoted to attacking Catholics and especially
Catholic clergy. A typical piece began, "Not long ago there was
a report made that one of our Polish students, who was taking a
higher course in one of the parochial schools, succeeded in signing
his name without any assistance. . . . A very careful investigation
was made in order to determine if there are any more such pearls
among our parochial students. The investigation failed to find another one. Evidently it was only an accident."[35] Such attacks closely
paralleled the rhetoric of late nineteenth- and early twentieth-
century American nativism, as well as anti-Catholic groups like
the American Protective Association. Despite the fact that many
Poles felt American bishops never treated them with the respect
they deserved, the centrality of faith to the everyday lives of most
Polish Americans and the ownership they felt in their own parish
organizations caused anti-Catholic rhetoric to backfire.

Although many American bishops continued to view Poles
with disdain for decades, the growth rate and importance of Poles
within the American Church could not be so easily ignored, especially by representatives of the Vatican sent to America to report
on the condition of immigrant parishes. In 1908, Father Paul
Rhode, a Polish priest serving the parish of St. Michael in South
Chicago, was ordained as the first Polish American bishop, serving as an auxiliary bishop in Chicago until 1915 when he became

bishop of Green Bay, Wisconsin. The announcement of Rhode's ordination caused intense joy in Chicago's Polish enclaves and communities across the country. *Dziennik Chicagoski* opined, "We wholeheartedly call this the greatest and happiest moment of our lives. . . . The thing that is most important is that after all these years that the Polish people have worked hard and undertaken every step to build and uphold the Roman-Catholic religion, they have at last received their reward by having a Polish bishop at the Chicago archdiocese."[36]

Bishop Rhode's ordination signaled the beginning of the end to one of the most divisive periods in the early Polish community in Chicago and beyond. Although conflicts over parish control and the place of Polish language and traditions in parish life never entirely disappeared (even into the twenty-first century), and there was little contact between most Roman Catholic and PNCC Christians until well after World War II, the most intense period of discord came to close. In its place, new issues arose for the growing Polish American population of Illinois, including their role in supporting Polish independence and the seriousness of social problems plaguing Poles in urban slums. To face these issues, a new and greater effort would be needed.

# 5

## POLONIA: POLISH COMMUNITY LIFE IN ILLINOIS

Community life for most Polish immigrants in Illinois began in their parish churches, but it did not end there. A rich array of organizations and activities has characterized the state's Polonia since its beginning. The story of this organizational life is only partly remembered by many Polish Americans today, and it is little known to the wider population. Polish communities in the late nineteenth and twentieth centuries had a high degree of self-sufficiency but also tended to be inward looking. Early native-born commentators often referred to Poles as "clannish" or insular.

Polish immigrants and their children were "joiners," and they created and enrolled in scores of organizations and institutions devoted to nearly every imaginable facet of public life. For example, the medium-sized parish of Our Lady of Częstochowa in Cicero had eight hundred families and supported a huge roster of organizations by its twenty-fifth anniversary in 1920: seven separate societies of the Polish National Alliance, five of the Polish Roman Catholic Union, four of the Polish Falcons, two affiliated with the Catholic Foresters, and two from the Polish Women's Alliance in addition to several independent societies for men and women, including "The Association of Free Polish Women in the Land of [George] Washington."[1] The dense network of organizations and associations substituted in a small way for the separation from their home villages and families.

It would be hard to produce a complete chronicle of the activities and groups that made up the Polish communities of Illinois. There were informal networks of kin, friends from the same villages in Poland, workers who toiled in the same sections of a factory, neighbors from the same block, bridge clubs, and drinking buddies. Parishes alone contained a wide array of groups—altar and rosary societies, sodalities for young men and women, and usher's clubs to name a few. All of these networks (both inside and outside the parishes) overlapped and reinforced each other, creating a matrix of belonging that gave structure and meaning to the lives of Poles in Illinois.

## Schools

After the building of a parish church, the highest priority of Polish immigrants was to build a school. In some cases, parishioners used the same building. In Evanston, the founders of Ascension Parish created a combined church-school building to save time and resources.[2] By World War II, there were forty-six Polish parochial elementary schools in Chicago and another thirty-one in the rest of the state, in addition to eighteen Polish high schools throughout Illinois.[3] During the peak of the "Polish baby boom" of the 1920s and 1930s, the larger urban schools had annual enrollments of between two and three thousand children.

Polish schools featured a bilingual curriculum, often with half the day in English and the other half in Polish. Subjects like American history were taught in English while literature and religion were often in Polish. Angela Mischke, who attended

Gathering of the St. Stanislaus Society at St. Stephen Parish, Chicago, on the nine hundredth anniversary of the birth of the saint, May 1936. Courtesy of Polish Museum of America Archives.

Holy Trinity, recalled that the school day began with Mass and prayers, then calisthenics:

> On alternate days, this was followed by catechism and Bible history both in Polish. Then came arithmetic in English. After recess we had Polish reading, writing, grammar and history. Afternoons were devoted to English studies: reading, spelling, grammar, American history and in higher grades literature and civics. Once a week the girls had lessons in needlework. The boys attended gym classes. . . . Beginning in 7th grade girls were taught shorthand, typing and correspondence, i.e., how to write a business letter. In those days most of the girls after finishing 8th grade and reaching the age of 14 would seek employment. Father Kazimierz Sztuczko, pastor of the parish, initiated a program to encourage them to continue the course in the evening and try for better jobs. Many did—I did.[4]

Most children went to school through at least the sixth grade before going to work, though staying through the eighth grade became more common in the years leading up to World War II. Although church and community leaders constantly stressed the need for education, the economic needs of the family were paramount. Classes were large and in the urban neighborhoods, many of the students came from tough backgrounds and could be disruptive. Discipline was, by modern standards, harsh, but there was little alternative. Chester Parks's widowed mother struggled to keep him and his brother out of gangs and in school. He recalled that "tuition at [Holy] Trinity in the 1930s was 75 cents per month per student. . . . There were 46 boys in my class, and only the rector and another priest were in the class picture. . . . The poor nuns seldom received any credit for the near impossible task of teaching such a brood of misfits, delinquents, and malcontents." Despite this, Parks eventually attended Holy Trinity High School, achieving a level of education that few of his grammar school classmates did.[5]

In the late nineteenth century, high school graduates were still relatively rare in American working-class communities where people had almost no access to education beyond high school. The efforts by Polish immigrants to establish high schools and even colleges demonstrate a strong aspiration to take advantage of the greater freedom and opportunity afforded by life in America and provide a better future for the next generation. In 1890, St.

Stanislaus College was founded by the Chicago Resurrectionists. It was based on a European *gimnazjum* model of education, which roughly equated to a college preparatory high school for boys ranging from age thirteen to eighteen. *Dziennik Chicagoski* noted, "Examinations were held in the first class of St. Stanislaus College, opened this year, before assembled guests, who were anxious to learn what subjects were being taught at the college. . . . The first class numbered 12 students. When they have become men and occupied responsible positions, it will be a pleasant recollection that they were the first students of the Polish St. Stanislaus College of Chicago."[6] Students took exams in Polish, English, German and Latin, and by 1909 enrollment had grown to 201 students and 15 teachers. Prior to World War I, St. Stanislaus converted to an American-style high school curriculum. In the early 1930s, the school took the name Weber High School and continued in operation as a Catholic high school until 1999.[7]

By the time of World War II, there were eight Polish Catholic girls' high schools and five for boys, plus six that were coed (two more were opened after the war). Every one of these institutions was funded entirely by the Polish community with money raised directly from parish members as well as fundraisers ranging from theater productions to dinners and concerts. Although many of the city's Catholic leaders questioned why the Poles needed their own high schools, the Polish community and its clergy were undeterred. When Holy Trinity High School for boys dedicated its new building in 1928, virtually all of the donors to the new facility had Polish names. The school served the Polish community but drew a few students from other ethnic groups as well.[8]

Although parochial elementary schools and religious high schools and colleges provided the bulk of Polish education in Illinois, other educational endeavors were also common, in particular adult school programs. These programs addressed the educational gap experienced by immigrants who had had little opportunity to go to school in Europe. The Chicago Public Schools, settlement houses, and many parishes offered adult courses.[9] English-language classes were the most popular, but most schools also offered courses in math, history, and bookkeeping, as well as sewing and cooking classes for women.[10] In 1908, the PNA founded a series of six schools for adults at Chicago community centers that by the 1930s had annual enrollments of over one thousand. A similar but smaller effort was begun by the Polish section of the Socialist Party, which was given the name Polski Uniwersytet Ludowy or Polish People's University. A second Polish People's University founded by Polish civic leaders started in 1926 and had three thousand attendees by the early 1930s.[11]

### Libraries, Periodicals, and Reading

In addition to formal schooling, there was a tremendous demand for reading material among Polish immigrants. Many Poles arrived illiterate, and some stayed that way throughout their lives. Others learned to master basic reading, and even those who did not often had other immigrants read to them whether on the job or at home. Recent research has shown that Polish communities in Illinois and elsewhere sustained a huge number of newspapers and book publishers.[12] The publishing catalogues of some Polish immigrant publishers contained as many as ten thousand titles by the time of World War II. Books published included devotional and prayer books, self-help titles, political tracts, Polish classics, translations of popular American and European authors, and both fiction and nonfiction works by immigrant authors themselves. Poles also imported books published in Europe, though it was usually less expensive to publish the same titles in the United States. Polish American publishers specialized in cheap paperback editions that were well within the price range of the average worker. Many novels were serialized in newspapers and then published as books.

Helena Chrzanowska, who worked for the Polish publishers Michał Kruszka and Jan Smulski in Chicago much of her life, recalled, "The records in my old ledgers show that a grand total of between 375 and 400 thousand Polish volumes came off our presses annually during the years 1903 to 1933. . . . Our neighbors and competitors, the Polish Publishing Company . . . was publishing about the same number of books."

Middle-class Polish woman posing with a book, Chicago, circa 1890s. Polish immigrants supported a wide array of publishing operations in Illinois. Courtesy of Polish Museum of America Archives.

Two Polish-run book binderies were kept in constant operation to meet the demand. "Besides the many text books printed to equip the Polish schools throughout the States," Chrzanowska recalled, "we published Polish classics, fiction, poetry, song books, dream books and theatrical books, cook books, novenas, Stations of the Cross and such a huge amount of miscellany that we regularly employed salesmen to pack it in their valises and canvass the communities for sales."[13]

Poles in Illinois also read books from publishers in other states, most notably the Paryski publishing house in Toledo, Ohio, arguably the most successful immigrant publisher of the early twentieth century. Nevertheless, Paryski's anti-Catholic views and its willingness to publish what some considered tabloid-type work met with the strong disapproval of Illinois's Polish Catholic leaders. Chicago itself developed a robust Polish press and publishing industry. The city was home to hundreds of Polish periodicals, ranging from well-established daily and weekly papers to organizational newspapers and yearbooks of fraternal societies, papers of political parties, satirical magazines, and periodicals for children and young people.

The first Polish publisher in Illinois was Władysław Dyniewicz, who settled in Chicago in the 1870s and started the first weekly Polish newspaper, *Gazeta Polska* (Polish Gazette). Like many immigrant publishers, he branched out beyond newspapers into commercial and book publishing. His house produced books and pamphlets for the city's growing Polish parishes, songbooks, schoolbooks, and a wide variety of fiction and nonfiction. A partial listing of his book-publishing endeavors shows the wide range of work that appealed to a Polish immigrant readership. This included translations of well-known writers such James Fenimore Cooper, Daniel Defoe, Leo Tolstoy, and children's author Franz Hoffmann. Polish romantic and positivist authors, as well as those writing history, comedy and satire, and poetry, were also represented.[14]

Because even the inexpensive books were not always affordable on a worker's salary, and because Polish immigrants with limited English were not especially welcomed at most public libraries, many Polish organizations opened their own libraries and reading rooms.[15] Parishes often had small libraries of religious works, while socialists and other radicals created reading rooms for their literature. By World War I, both the Polish National Alliance

(PNA) and Polish Roman Catholic Union of America (PRCUA) had opened libraries, the latter being the genesis of the book collection of the Polish Museum of America.

Angela Mischke and her younger brother Karol read serialized novels in Polish newspapers, cutting out each installment of favorite books and pasting them in a scrapbook each week.

Father never discouraged our love of books. In fact shortly after our arrival he made a point of obtaining a card to the Polish National Alliance library. The library had "A" section books for children, section "B" educational, and "C" books for adults. I have since forgotten the name of the kindly librarian who came to know us well. I recall his kindly face and his manner of handling the children. When selecting books, we'd often request a book from the "C" section. Invariably they were out. The old gent then substituted our choice and thus guided us into reading books proper for our age. How wonderful was the world of books. And how beautifully the Polish authors wrote. We often read books of other authors in translation, such as Conan Doyle's "Sherlock Holmes" and Charles [Karl] May's great stories of adventures in far off lands.[16]

Poles in Illinois published and read an astonishing number of newspapers and other periodicals. They ranged from large daily newspapers to weeklies to monthly magazines.[17] Some had a life span of only a few issues, other have remained in publication for over a century. They covered every stripe of political interest. Some were dedicated to youth or the elderly, others to subjects like sports or satire. Because Chicago was home to so many Polish organizations, their publications were not only read in Illinois but throughout the United States. During the 1890s and 1900s, there were hundreds of Polish-language periodicals circulating in Chicago. During and after World War I, the number of Polish publications fell markedly, but overall circulation increased as the periodical market consolidated. The hard years of the Depression caused the demise of a number of papers, but Chicago continued to support two Polish-language dailies into the 1970s.

A typical Chicago Polish-language daily paper in the 1920s averaged between twelve and twenty-four pages. The first few pages were usually devoted to U.S. and world news. Stories about Poland featured prominently. Dailies like *Dziennik Związkowy* (published by the PNA) and *Dziennik Zjednoczenia* (published by the rival PRCUA) could have "city editions" for local readers featuring news from Chicago. Many papers featured round-ups of stories from other newspapers in other cities and countries, including other Polish American newspapers. Prominent organizations—usually ones whose stance on important issues matched those of the editors—were given space to report on their activities. Newspapers run by fraternal societies also collected reports on activities of their local branches across the country, usually written by correspondents in those communities. By the 1920s, most dailies had a regular page devoted to women's issues, nearly always written by female correspondents. Stories of famous or prominent Polish women were a common theme along with practical advice for immigrant women managing households, such as home remedies or time-saving tips. Sports pages became another important and regular feature in many newspapers, and by the mid-1920s most of the Polish daily papers had their own cartoon strips with titles like "Figle Antka" (Trickster Tony) or "Klopoty Pani Safandulskiej" (Mrs. Galoot's Troubles). Finally, newspapers frequently published serialized novels in weekly installments. These ranged from classics of Polish- and English-language literature to didactic works on religion, politics, or science. As more and more books became available to immigrants in the 1920s, this practice gradually declined as newspaper preferred to sell their readers books and reserve space in the paper for shorter articles and advertising.

## Fraternal Societies

After parishes and their schools, the most important Polish organizations in the state were fraternal insurance associations and their many local societies. Fraternal insurance companies began in the nineteenth century as a way to provide low-cost death-benefit insurance to workers. For most working people, regular life insurance was impossible to obtain, especially for men working in industries with high accident and death rates, such as meat-packing, steel, and coal. Such groups became very popular with immigrants in the mid-nineteenth century, including Irish and Germans. As Poles arrived in larger numbers, they too formed fraternal societies. Although these began merely as insurance societies, they proved to be ideal organizations for immigrants to get involved in cultural, social, and political activity. In a day and age when new immigrants had little chance to participate directly in American politics, fraternal societies allowed immigrants to develop leadership skills and practice democracy. Nearly all fraternal societies had written constitutions and bylaws. When leaders were elected, proper voting was carefully scrutinized by all members to ensure fairness.

Due to the sheer size of the Polish settlement in Chicago, the city became an important center and headquarters for three of the largest Polish fraternal groups in America, each of which had (and still has) constituent societies spread across Chicago, Illinois, and throughout the United States. The first of these was the Polish Roman Catholic Union of America (PRCUA), founded in 1873 in close association with the Chicago Resurrectionists as part of the congregation's efforts to create close-knit local parish-communities with a range of Catholic organizations that would meet the needs of all parishioners. From its origin, the PRCUA emphasized the centrality of Catholicism to Polish identity. Members had to be Catholics in good standing and of Polish or Ruthenian decent. The PRCUA emphasized Polish Catholic positivism and efforts to build viable communities in the United States.[18]

A second important group, the Polish National Alliance (PNA) was founded in 1880. Where the PRCUA emphasized the religious character of Polishness, the PNA was created as a secular, nationalist organization. Members had to be Polish but did not have to be Catholic (though nearly all were). Inspired by the example of Polish Romanticism, the PNA saw itself as the American part of a worldwide effort to gain freedom for the oppressed homeland. PNA leaders saw Poles in America as the "Fourth Partition" of Poland. Rather than develop parish-communities, PNA's early leaders wanted Polish immigrants to assimilate into American society while maintaining their Polishness and use their positions in America to aid the Polish cause.[19]

A third significant Polish fraternal was created in 1898. Until 1897, when the PRCUA began to allow wives of members to join, Polish fraternals excluded women. Given that women were critical to the development of Polish cultural and family life in America and many were working in mills and factories, there was an obvious need for a fraternal that not only provided insurance for women but also promoted the role of women in the young immigrant communities. The Polish Women's Alliance was founded in Chicago to respond to those needs. Its founders were educated middle-class immigrants who blended Polish nationalism with a concern to community building and social reform in Polonia.[20]

A fourth fraternal, the Polish Alma Mater, was founded in 1897 as a society for young people, though it never achieved the size or reach of its larger counterparts, which also had their own youth sections by the 1920s.[21] In addition to the Chicago-based fraternals, Poles in Illinois also joined societies from organizations such as the Polish Falcons, a fraternal group based in Pittsburgh. The Falcons sought membership among younger immigrants and emphasized physical fitness through gymnastics and other sports, modeling themselves after similar societies in Germany, Bohemia, and Poland. Members of the Polish National Catholic Church (PNCC) joined the Polish National Union—Spójna—based in Scranton, Pennsylvania.

Membership requirements varied from group to group but usually shared common themes. Fraternal membership was not merely about joining an organization. The societies sought to enforce norms of good conduct and good citizenship. Most groups insisted that their members refrain from chewing tobacco or smoking at meetings, as well as from drunkenness and immoral or illegal behavior. Members had to be law-abiding Americans and also good Poles. This included working for the betterment of fellow members as well as the community, the parish, and in many cases the cause of Polish independence. The Fraternal Aid Society of St. Michael the Archangel in Radom, established in 1874, was open to Roman Catholic men of good character, between the ages of twenty-one and fifty who were free of any debilitating illness

Members of Polish Falcons' Nest 44, Chicago, circa 1910s. The Falcons were a young people's athletic society that emphasized patriotism. Courtesy of Polish Museum of America Archives.

at the time of joining.[22] The Fraternal Aid Society of the Polish Artillery under the Patronage of St. Stanislaus Bishop and Martyr was founded in 1905 "to assist [members] in cases of sickness and death, to do good works for our neighbors and . . . for the love of our Polish fatherland."[23] Members were expected to pay regular dues that would be pooled and used to pay for members' funerals and to take care of their families if they died or were too sick or injured to work. Societies often took their names from Catholic saints—and Polish ones most often—as well as heroes of Polish and American history or important literary figures. Some of the men's societies adopted a paramilitary flavor and dressed in military garb. Women's societies often took their names from important women in Polish history, such the legendary Queen Wanda or Emilia Plater, a hero of the November Insurrection of 1830/31.

Relations between Illinois's major Polish fraternal societies were often rocky in the period between the founding of the PNA in 1880 and World War I when the common desire to help Poland that emerged during World War I helped tamp down internal strife. The PRCUA and the PNA in particular represented two opposing camps within Polonia and two differing visions on the place of the Polish community in America and approaches to gaining Polish independence. The PRCUA emphasized building up the community-parish in America to preserve the faith and identity of the immigrants. This included a strong emphasis not only on education and social reform but also on relative isolation from the American mainstream. Polish independence was important, but it would only be achieved when Poles better developed their own moral, cultural, and economic resources. To its foes in the PNA, the PRCUA was too close to the Chicago Resurrectionists (and the clergy in general), too focused on Catholicism to unite all Poles, and not sufficiently concerned with Polish independence. The PNA emphasized Polish independence and saw American Polonia as a transient result of Poland's partitions. If Poland gained its freedom, the need for emigration would fade away. To its critics in the PRCUA, the PNA slighted the crucial role of Catholicism in Polish history and identity and failed to appreciate the needs of the Polish communities in America. The PRCUA saw itself leading a broad coalition of like-minded groups, while the PNA believed it needed to absorb other Polish groups in America to create a single unified front for the sake of Poland.

The rivalry played out in the pages of competing newspapers sponsored by the two groups and their allies. Furious and abusive rhetoric flew back and forth in the pages of the press, resulting in frequent libel suits, and societies of the rival organizations sought to outdo each other in staging commemorations of important Polish holidays. While the PRCUA was founded earlier, PNA grew bigger and faster as it allowed for the creation of more societies and in more parts of the country. This in turn provided more opportunity for local leadership. Until about 1900, the PRCUA had fewer but somewhat larger societies, with its core membership focused heavily on Chicago and environs, while the PNA was had more societies distributed more broadly. Although the rivalry among the leaders was bitter, most pastors and other leaders at the local level managed to keep conflicts between the rival societies to a minimum, and by World War I most large Polish parishes in the state hosted societies from both groups as well as their smaller counterparts. The intensity of the rivalry also forced both groups to sharpen their focus, improve their outreach to members, and address both the needs of the Polish community in America and aspirations for Poland's independence. The PNA developed a more comprehensive approach to the needs of Poles in America while the PRCUA began to support more vigorously the cause of Polish independence.[24]

## Self-Help

Poles in Chicago faced a wide array of social ills—substance abuse, violence, gangs, family breakdown, and poverty. Across America, Progressive-era social reformers sought to address such problems in a variety of ways, but efforts directed at new immigrants often demanded cultural and religious assimilation and at times treated immigrants as second-class citizens whose backgrounds themselves were the cause of social problems. Less well known is the fact that in many immigrant communities—and among Poles in particular—a social reform movement arose that drew on the approaches of mainstream reformers while trying to help immigrants in their own languages and in a way that was culturally more sympathetic.

Chicago's poor had only limited access to healthcare at the end of the nineteenth century, and this was especially true of Polish immigrants who also faced a language barrier if they needed the services of a doctor or hospital. In June 1889, Blessed Mother

Frances Siedlicka, founder of the Sisters of the Congregation of the Holy Family of Nazareth, visited Illinois and "was accosted by the crying need and clamoring requests of the Polish immigrants for a hospital where they would understand and be understood in their illness."[25] Siedlicka directed her sisters in Illinois to begin planning to create a charity hospital to serve the Polish community. To found such an institution in a poor, working-class location during the depths of a severe economic recession in the early 1890s must have seemed like a pipe dream. Yet by 1894, the sisters had raised enough money to open St. Mary of Nazareth Hospital, which admitted its first patients in May. Since people tended to go to the hospital only if they were too sick to work and had exhausted other resources, few patients could pay. At the end of the first year, the hospital's income was $126, and several times the hospital almost had to close its doors. The Nazarene sisters canvassed Polish neighborhoods on foot and by buggy to raise operating funds, which often manifested in the form of loose change, and Polish societies held a nearly continuous menu of benefit plays, concerts, and other events to raise money. The hospital later opened a nursing school, and by World War II it had trained 750 nurses (3,000 by 1986). The majority of the hospital's patients were Poles, though it served people of all groups, especially Catholic Italians, Slovaks, and Ukrainians from the surrounding Chicago neighborhoods.[26] The hospital remains open today under the name Presence Saints Mary and Elizabeth Hospital, continuing its mission as a Catholic hospital and serving the entire community.

The Sisters of the Resurrection was founded by Polish mother and daughter Celine and Hedwig Borzecka in 1891. In 1900 they purchased land on the far Northwest Side of Chicago, building Resurrection Academy for educating girls and women (currently Resurrection College Prep High School) and Resurrection Hospital, now part of Resurrection Health Care, the largest Catholic health system in Chicago, cosponsored by the Sisters of the Holy Family of Nazareth.

To help young women in crisis pregnancies and mothers who had to work, Father Ludwik Grudziński established Guardian Angels Nursery and Home for Working Girls at St. John's Parish near the Union Stockyards. By the 1920s, the facility had become a full-fledged community clinic that included a playground, dispensary, operating room, X-ray room, and pharmacy. It had three doctors on staff, plus nursing sisters. Although the clinic catered mostly to the needs of the huge Polish community, it was open to all. One of the staff doctors, Dr. W. J. Schnieder, wrote, "As chief of staff of the dispensary I am warranted in saying that no meritorious case was ever turned down because of color, nationality or religion. At the request of Rev. Louis W. Grudziński we aided all patients that needed medical attention and had no means of paying for it. Among those we had people of numerous national and racial groups living in the community."[27]

A similar motivation was behind the creation of St. Joseph's Home for the Aged, which opened in 1894 under the care of the Franciscan Sisters of the Blessed Kunegunda. The home took care of some two hundred elderly immigrants, only a few of whom had any means of support. The home was funded entirely through donations from the community and with the help of doctors and nurses who donated their time.[28] Similar efforts were made on behalf of children. Poles in Illinois supported two orphanages. St. Vincent's Orphanage, opened in 1899, operated until 1910 when it was refounded as St. Hedwig's Orphanage and moved to Niles. By the 1920s and 1930s, the orphanage also operated two schools, the Polish Manual Training Center for Boys and St. Hedwig Industrial School for Girls.[29]

By the first decade of the twentieth century, social reform had become an important theme among Poles in the state. In spite of the community's poverty and its marginalized status, community reformers never took refuge in self-pity but tried to address the scourges of alcoholism, crime, and juvenile delinquency with the limited resources at their disposal. While the American temperance movement with its anti-immigrant and anti-Catholic overtones was rejected by most Poles, a Polish American temperance movement fostered by social reformers and clergy had some success. With Chicago as its epicenter, the movement founded a newspaper in 1911, *Abstynent*, and placed articles in numerous Polish newspapers, especially those based in the Windy City.[30]

In 1912, a group of educated middle-class Poles founded the Chicago Society as a branch of the PNA. The group's goal was to foster social reform. One of its signal achievements was the creation of the Polish Welfare Association (now known as the Polish American Association) in 1921. Initially under the patronage of the Archdiocese of Chicago and later becoming independent, the group was founded to combat juvenile delinquency, which was becoming an epidemic in the Polish community. With volunteers and Polish-speaking social workers, the Polish Welfare Association worked with parishes, the court systems, and juvenile detention facilities to turn young people around and provide alternatives to crime and substance abuse. The association later branched out to other areas of concern, such helping the unemployed find work, assisting newly arrived immigrants from Poland, aiding those in the clutches of substance abuse, and working with victims of domestic violence.[31]

The founders of these groups were often all or mostly women. The great majority of Polish-speaking social workers during the first decades were women who were supported by a large cadre of educated middle-class women, many of whom were already active in Polish fraternals, parish societies, and cultural groups. The motive for founding such groups was to protect not only vulnerable individuals but also the community as a whole. When the Polish Society for the Protection of Women began in 1917, one of its founders, Helena Setmajer noted,

> Were we only to stop and consider the predicament of our Polish women and girls, we would all no doubt unanimously agree that it is our duty as Poles to give help and advice to those who need them. If we would take the trouble to examine the court records, we would find innumerable cases which, by being dragged through the courts, bring shame and dishonor not only to the family in question but to our entire nationality as well. We Polish women who sympathize with and understand the terrible lot of the victims of our social indifference, are called upon in the first place to make a united effort to remedy the evil.[32]

She listed the society's goals as:

1. To give advice and protection to women and girls of Slavic ancestry, especially to Polish women.
2. To defend the reputation and honor of these women and girls, when the need arises (in a legal sense).
3. To make free employment service available to them and to contact employers.
4. To gain admittance to hotels and restaurants, where a large majority of these girls work, for the purpose of extending moral control and protection over them, such control and protection to be in the form of appropriate

lectures and evening school classes in English reading and writing.

5. To organize clubs for these women where they can spend a few hours each week in proper relaxation and listen to morally strengthening lectures, and where they can learn handicraft, either for their own use or for use of charitable institutions.[33]

The combination of moral uplift and practical assistance was a hallmark of Progressive-era reformers, and throughout this period Illinois's Polish community created a wide range of organizations and institutions that were fully in tune with the spirit of the age yet distinctly Polish and tailored to an immigrant community.

## Regional Clubs

The number of social clubs in Illinois Polonia is impossible to calculate, as many were small groups of relatives, friends, and associates who gathered for activities such as card games, eating and drinking, or to reminisce about life in the old country. Yet, in Chicago a unique groups of social organizations developed among immigrants from the highlands and the foothills of Małopolska in southern Poland and later other regions. Polish highlanders, or *Górale*, shared a common dialect and distinct patterns of folk culture. They immigrated in large numbers to South Chicago beginning in the 1890s through a process of chain migration from specific villages and towns. There they were joined by neighbors from villages in the foothills and valleys of the same region. So many came that Chicago was said to have more *górale* than the Podhale region from which they originated.[34] Regular return migration kept alive strong ties to their ancestral communities, and *górale* created a series of organizations based on their common origins in those places. Two different umbrella organizations evolved to embrace these immigrants. The first was the Polish Highlanders' Alliance of North America, founded in 1929, which drew members from the Tatra Mountains and the Podhale mountain district. The group mirrored similar local associations that existed in southern Poland. According to one early member, the impetus for the formation of highlander clubs was the sense of isolation from family and friends felt by many early immigrants. The first society of highlanders formed in 1928 at St. Adalbert Parish in Chicago, consisting of people exclusively from the Nowy Targ district of Poland. In addition to providing a place to socialize with fellow immigrants from the same area, the groups provided assistance for their home villages and emphasized the preservation of *górale* subculture, including its music, dance, crafts, dress, and dialect.[35]

A similar organization, grouped together under the umbrella of the Alliance of Małopolska Clubs, known as the Alliance of Polish Clubs (founded in 1928), initially included people from towns and villages in the foothills and valleys of southern Poland. Like their highland counterparts, these clubs provided help and support for compatriots coming to America and a friendly place to catch up with news and gossip. The clubs also raised funds for their home villages. Throughout the Małopolska region of Poland, travelers often come across impressive churches in small villages built with support from compatriots in Illinois.[36] For example, former residents of Łęki Górne near Dębica in south central Poland founded Club Łęczan in 1923. The club's jubilee books proudly show funds raised to buy a new bell for their hometown church along with other charitable causes. In 2012, the club celebrated its ninetieth anniversary.[37] Although many of the earliest regional clubs hail from southern Poland, they were joined in the years following World War II by similar associations made up emigrants from other towns and cities with a significant population in Chicago.

## Sports and Youth

For most immigrants from peasant villages of Europe, the modern concept of organized sports was a new idea, and this was no exception for Poles. Yet, like most immigrants, they embraced American sports with a passion. While poverty, discrimination, and language barriers kept Poles out of mainstream society, sports provided a level playing field with common rules where participants could be judged by ability rather than ethnicity, race, or class. Sports also provided the young Polish community with ready-made and recognizable heroes such as Stanisław "Zbyszko" Cyganiewicz, an athlete with a powerful physique who became one of the pioneers of professional wrestling in the United States, or Johnny Lujack, a Notre Dame University Heisman Trophy winner who went on to star for the Chicago Bears.[38] Poles in southern Illinois who rooted for St. Louis teams thrilled to the exploits of baseball great Stan Musial. Accounts from early Polish newspapers show that long before many Poles became citizens, they were local sports fans. Baseball developed a huge following among Polish immigrants, and in the summer streets and vacant lots in Polish neighborhoods turned into makeshift diamonds. Chicago's Polish street gangs often doubled as baseball teams when they weren't getting in trouble.

By the 1920s and 1930s, nearly every major Polish American organization in the state was sponsoring its own sports teams, as were all the state's Polish Catholic high schools. For example, by the mid-1930s the PRCUA sponsored seventy-three basketball teams, fifty-two softball teams, thirty-seven baseball teams, and six bowling teams as well as some volleyball teams. The PNA sponsored even more sports clubs. Because it was such a major center for Polish life in the United States, Chicago also hosted yearly tournaments where Polish sports teams from around the country came to compete.[39]

In addition to sports, Polish organizations sponsored scouting organizations for both boys and girls. The first scout troops began during World War I and were linked to support for Polish independence but continued to grow after the war due to the need for programs for the community's huge cohort of young people. The PNA created an independent scouting organization modeled after the Hacerstwo (Scouts) movement in Poland. The organization claimed fifty thousand members nationwide in the 1930s, but the Depression and World War II put an end to it until a new wave of Polish immigrants arrived after the war. The PRCUA boy scouts were affiliated with the Boy Scouts of America, and by 1936 there were thirty-six troops in the greater Chicago area alone. The PRCUA formed a separate scouting organization for girls—Córy Zjednoczenia (Daughters of the Union) as well as Cub Scouts, Junior Daughters, Senior Daughters, and a troop of Sea Scouts

Baseball team from St. Adalbert Parish, Hegewisch, Illinois, 1931.
Courtesy of Polish Museum of America Archives.

who practiced nautical skills on Lake Michigan.[40] Both PNA and PRCUA scout groups had their own publications, and most major Polish organizations also created summer camps. These camps were open to scouts but also to other Polish young people, many of whom received support to attend since their families lacked the means, especially during the hard years of the 1930s. The camps were located in rural areas of Illinois and featured a wide variety of outdoor activities designed to get young people away from the troubles of city life, to teach crafts and build teamwork, but also to have fun with their peers from around the city and the state.

### Business and Professionals

Poles in Illinois were overwhelmingly industrial workers, but the size and complexity of the Polish community allowed for the development of Polish-run businesses and a small professional class as well. A proportion of trade in Polish neighborhoods was run by Jewish merchants, mainly those with origins in Poland and Eastern Europe, reproducing a pattern of ethnic relations that was familiar yet often fraught with mutual tension. Polish Jews arriving in America likely had more commercial experience than their gentile neighbors, and they were often able to take advantage of established networks of Jewish merchants who helped their compatriots (often relatives or people from the same hometown) get started in business. Jewish merchants often spoke the languages of their gentile neighbors and were more likely to extend credit to them than were most American stores. During periods of strife, there were sometimes calls to boycott Jewish stores in Polish neighborhoods. This was most notable during the long, hot summer of 1919, when tensions over the role of Jews in newly independent Poland riled both communities, leading to a battle in the pages of Polish and Jewish newspapers in Chicago that featured heated accusations of treachery, anti-Semitism, and charges of un-American activity.[41] Polish newspapers called for boycotts of Jewish businesses, while Jewish newspapers portrayed Chicago's Poles as a menace to Jewish life and property. The rhetoric was not acted upon, however, as Poles continued to shop in Jewish stores and Jews continued to open their stores to Polish customers.

While Poles were slower to open businesses than their Italian or Jewish counterparts, Chicago developed a sizeable Polish business community by 1900 (see figure 5.1). The most common sort of business to enter was saloonkeeping. Startup costs were moderate, and with the proper connections, a liquor license could be had for five hundred dollars. The demand was high, since saloons served as clubs for the city's large population of unattached, male factory workers. In addition to alcohol, saloons provided cheap food and camaraderie. Some saloons even kept a supply of newspapers and reading material. They were places for political organizing, and they even served as voting stations at times. Saloonkeepers were viewed with ambivalence in Polonia. They were sometimes denounced for exploiting workers, especially given Polonia's serious problems with drunkenness. Other saloonkeepers were viewed in a more favorable light, and some parleyed their businesses into larger enterprises or political careers. Aside from saloons, Poles also opened many restaurants, bakeries, and small grocery, butcher, and tobacco shops. Since women and children were generally not allowed in saloons, ice cream and soft drink parlors provided places where families could go on special occasions to indulge their sweet tooth.

Professionals, such as doctors, lawyers, and dentists, were a consistent and well-established presence in Chicago's Polish business community. Many of them doubled as leaders of important community organizations and fraternal associations. Another important group of businesses included community banks and savings and loan associations. The latter were popular among immigrants for obtaining mortgages. By 1930, one Chicago directory listed 17 Polish community banks and 120 savings and loan associations.[42] A wide array of other businesses rounded out the "Polish downtowns" of the city: printers, book and music stores, photographers, and even a shop that sold banners, badges, and other organizational knickknacks to the growing number of

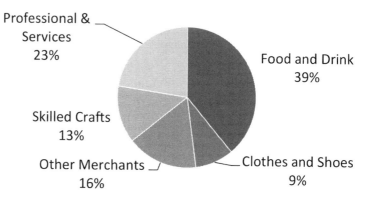

Pie chart of the Polish business community in Chicago, 1903. Created by the authors from *Polish Directory for the City of Chicago* (1903; reprint, Chicago: Polish Genealogical Society, 1981).

Professional & Services 23%

Food and Drink 39%

Skilled Crafts 13%

Other Merchants 16%

Clothes and Shoes 9%

Polish fraternal and parish societies.[43] A number of Polish manu-facturers also sprang up. In addition to the printers and publishers noted above, there were Polish dairies, packinghouses making sausage and other meat products, and a Polish brewer—the White Eagle Brewing Company in South Chicago.[44]

Nearly every Polish community in the state had some Polish businesses. East St. Louis developed a robust Polish business com-munity by the 1930s, which aside from the ubiquitous saloons and grocery stores included furniture stores, funeral parlors, barbers, insurance agents, hardware stores, and gas stations.[45]

The matrix of groups—formal and informal—that gave struc-ture to Illinois Polonia intensified throughout the first half of the twentieth century and existed as long as coherent parish-com-munities existed. Although much of this organizational richness faded with the economic and demographic changes of the 1960s and 1970s, it never entirely disappeared as new generations of Polish immigrants arrived and created their own organizations, sometimes joining existing Polish groups but often developing their own groups as well.

# 6

## CZYKAGO: CAPITAL OF POLONIA

Polish Americans in Illinois and beyond—as well as many other Illinois residents—have long proclaimed that Chicago is the "second largest Polish city" in the world.[1] The fact that the claim probably is not true today and may not have been true in the past is immaterial. At several points in the city's history, Poles were the largest immigrant or foreign-born group in the city. Poles were the largest group of newcomers to the city during the period of its greatest growth. These were more than just new inhabitants or workers in Chicago's industries. Poles founded and built many of the neighborhoods on both the North and South Sides of the city, as well as in the adjacent urban areas of Cook County.[2] Even after large-scale Polish immigration was cut off by Congress in 1924 due to rising nativist sentiment, the Polish population continued to grow due to a "baby boom" among immigrants as well as migration to Chicago from other Polish communities around the state and the nation.

The Poles who immigrated to Illinois and other parts of the United States in the decades prior to 1924 were overwhelmingly young men and women of childbearing age. Some were married in Europe before arriving, but many found spouses in the New World. The unprecedented size and youth of this wave of immigrants instigated this baby boom in the years that followed as immigrants got married had families of their own. In many Polish communities during the first decades of the twentieth century, half or more of the population was age sixteen or younger. Of all children of Polish immigrants still alive in 1960, one-third were born in the period 1916–25, and another quarter were born between 1906 and 1915.[3] Although the baby boom affected all Polish communities to one degree or another, it had a disproportionate impact on Chicago due to the concentration of young Poles and the fact that Chicago continued to attract Polish immigrants to a degree matched in only a few other communities in the United States. Poles not only made up a significant portion of Chicagoans, but, in the first half of the twentieth century, they also comprised a disproportionate segment of the city's young people. Those young Poles would help give Chicago its unique identity as the city of broad shoulders (table 6.1).

## Politics

Despite the large number of Poles in Chicago, their presence among the ranks of the city's political movers and shakers never matched the size of their community. The self-contained nature of many Polish parish-communities kept the focus on internal affairs and intragroup politics. The sheer size of Chicago Polonia and the diversity of its origins kept it from truly uniting to win offices at the state or local level. In Chicago's often fractious ethnic politics, Poles were a large enough group to discourage coalitions

Table 6.1. Poles in Chicago, by Nativity and Mother Tongue, 1890–1940

| Nativity | 1890 | 1900 | 1910 | 1920 | 1930 | 1940 |
|---|---|---|---|---|---|---|
| Foreign-born Poles | 24,086 | 59,713 | 125,604 | 137,611 | 149,622 | 137,837 |
| U.S.-born Polish Americans | | 112,433 | | | 251,694 | |
| Total Poles, by nativity | | 172,146 | | | 401,316 | |
| Language | | | | | | |
| Foreign-born Polish speakers | | | 126,059 | 139,360 | 130,439 | |
| U.S.-born Polish speakers | | | 104,073 | 178,978 | | |
| Total, by mother tongue | | | 230,132 | 318,338 | | |
| All Poles as a percentage of Chicago's population | | 10.1 | 10.5 | 11.8 | 11.8 | |

*Source*: John Radzilowski, "Conflict between Poles and Jews in Chicago, 1900–1930," *Polin: Studies in Polish Jewry* 19 (2007): 117–33.

with other ethnic groups who feared they would be dominated by the Poles, and yet the Poles were never numerous enough to elect their own candidates without support from other communities. Although there were some very successful Polish politicians, such as members of the Rostenkowski family, there has never been a Chicago mayor of Polish descent.[4]

Up through the 1950s, Poles in Chicago generally supported the Democratic Party machines that ran the city. Although there were always groups of Polish Republicans, including some of the prominent leaders of the PNA, the Democrats dominated the Polish vote. At the ward level, Poles were rewarded with some level of control and perks for loyalty. During the 1880s through the 1920s, Republican efforts to restrict parochial schools, support

Daniel Rostenkowski (1928–2010) in front of the Czerwone Jabłuszko (Red Apple) grocery, Chicago, 1990. Rostenkowski served in the U.S. Congress from 1959 to 1990 and also as a Democratic committeeman of Chicago's 32nd Ward, positions he even held simultaneously. Members of his family have been prominent in Chicago Polonia since the 1890s.
Courtesy of Polish Museum of America Archives.

temperance, and equivocation on anti-Catholic groups like the American Protective Association (APA) drew the ire of many community leaders, including the clergy.[5] In 1894, an editorial in the Resurrectionist-run *Dziennik Chicagoski* explained the case for the Democrats to their immigrant readers using the familiar question-and-answer format of the *Baltimore Catechism:*

> For whom should the Poles vote?
> The Democrats.
> Why should we vote for the Democratic party?
> Because in reality it is the people's party and it stands for freedom. . . .
> Who are restraining the millionaires and exploiters?
> The Democrats.
> Who condemns Pullman so severely?
> The Democrats.
> Who condemns the wicked APA?
> The Democrats. . . .
> Are there any Polish candidates on the Republican ticket?
> No, there are none.[6]

The Democratic Party's position on the Yalta Accords that gave Poland to Soviet domination after World War II helped to erode some support for the Democrats and the post–World War II wave of Polish immigrants was far more likely to vote Republican. Nevertheless, Poles remained in the Democratic fold into the 1980s despite the deepening divisions in the party following the Vietnam War.

Some Poles were active in the Socialist Party and other radical groups in Illinois, mainly in Chicago. (It is unclear whether these groups had much following outside of the greater Chicago area.) The first Polish socialist newspaper was founded in 1886, and there were small anarchist and socialist parties active by the 1890s, some of which were involved in the Polish-speaking local branches of the tinsmiths and carpenters unions.[7] Radical groups like the socialists drew on a small secular contingent of immigrants, as well as on individuals who were strongly anticlerical or who belonged to the Polish National Catholic Church. Like their mainstream counterparts, though, socialists were often divided over their approach to affairs of the Polish homeland.

The Alliance of Polish Socialists formed in 1900 in Chicago, and its newspaper *Robotnik* (the Worker) emphasized international socialism and punctuated its pages with calls for mass violence. One edition, for example, carried a poem by a Polish carpenter titled "Don't Spare the Bullets or the Bombs." A second socialist paper, *Dziennik Ludowy* (the People's Daily), founded in 1907 by the Polish section of the Socialist Party, placed more emphasis on Polish independence. The size of the Polish socialist contingent in Chicago and elsewhere was not large enough to support two rival papers, and *Robotnik* went into a decline in 1908 from which it never recovered.[8] Chicago was also home to a Polish enclave of the even more radical International Workers of the World (IWW), also known as the Wobblies, which published a newspaper occasionally between 1908 and 1917.[9]

At their height just before World War I, there were probably no more than thirty-one hundred Polish Socialist Party members (in two rival groups) in the entire United States and perhaps around four to five hundred in Chicago.[10] This does not count Poles who may have sympathized with the socialists or voted for socialist candidates as a protest vote. In 1924, for example, an estimated 14 percent of Chicago Poles voted for Progressive Party presidential candidate Robert La Follette. Socialist candidates for local office fared even worse. In the 1919 mayoral race, less than 2 percent of Poles voted Socialist, while 16 percent voted for the more moderate Labor Party and 54 percent for the Democratic Party candidate.[11] As historian Edward Kantowicz noted, "Most Polish voters rejected the socialist alternative."[12] Although the opposition of clerical and secular nationalist leaders and the division and infighting among Polish leftists played a role in the radicals' poor showing, the main reason for their limited influence was the steady economic and cultural progress made by the immigrants themselves. They were slowly though often painfully making a better life for themselves and their children seem possible without any appeal to revolutionary violence. As historian Adam Walaszek noted,

> Both the socialists and the IWW encountered considerable difficulties. They tried above all to convince workers that in accordance with Marxist social and economic thought, capitalists had robbed the workers. . . . Moreover, in the Polish-American newspapers and through Polish ethnic organizations in churches and schools, a different type of argumentation was driven home to them. Quite often Polish immigrants found it easier to accept these other voices, as they spoke of convictions and values

familiar from the Old Country. According to these arguments, the best way to success led through one's own effort, frugality, hard work and competition. Some trade unions, realizing the way to use these precepts effectively, quoted these elements of the work ethic in their campaigns.... They managed to attract thousands of "new" immigrants, while the IWW employed too many concepts and questioned too many convictions and values. Why should people who had only recently arrived in the United States let themselves be carried away by slogans which undermined the very goals for which they had left their native villages? After all, step by step, they were approaching this goal. Why should they wish for radical change?[13]

## Aid for Poland

Despite the divisions among Poles in Illinois and Chicago, there was nearly universal support for the cause of Poland and its freedom and independence. Because it was the headquarters of so many leading Polish American organizations, Chicago became the hub of activity to support Poland politically, financially, and morally. Initially, groups like the PNA, which put the highest priority on aiding the cause of Polish independence, maintained ties to Polish exile groups in Switzerland, which included providing some financial assistance. By the beginning of the twentieth century, however, Polish Americans worked directly on Poland's behalf. In 1899, a coalition of Polish American groups sent an appeal to the International Peace Conference at The Hague asking the delegates to address the cause of Poland.[14] The 1905 Revolution in Russia and the School Strikes in Prussia in 1906–7 galvanized Polish organizations, especially the PRCUA, PNA, and PWA, to begin raising funds for Polish relief, to assist Poles displaced by violence or natural disaster, and to bring Polish issues to the attention of American officials at the state and national levels. Mistreatment of Poles in Germany led Polish-owned businesses across the city to stop selling German-made products.[15] In 1912, a broad coalition of Polish groups joined together to form the Komitet Obrony Narodowej (KON or National Defense Committee), which soon made its headquarters in Chicago. By 1914, however, divisions over which Polish factions to support in Europe and the role of socialists in the KON caused most of the major Polish fraternal groups to leave the committee. With the support of pianist and statesman Ignacy Jan Paderewski and under the leadership of Bishop Paul Rhode, the PRCUA and other Catholic groups formed the Polska Rada Narodowa (PRN or Polish National Council).[16]

From the start of the First World War, Poland became a battleground for Russian, Austrian, and German armies, creating a humanitarian crisis. In October 1914, the PRN joined with the PNA, PWA, and the Falcons to form the Chicago-based Polish National Relief Committee. The KON was reduced to a small group, consisting mainly of Polish socialists and the PNCC. The KON's support for a new Poland aligned with Austria-Hungary became a major problem as the United States entered the war in 1917. The PRN joined with the Polish National Relief Committee to create the National Department in 1916, which served as the political arm of a largely united American Polonia. The National Department and the groups it incorporated favored the Entente Powers and had a strong distrust of Germany, which only grew after 1917. By the end of 1914, Poles in Chicago were raising significant sums of money for Polish relief.[17]

When the United States entered the war in April 1917, Chicago's Poles responded with vigor, seeing the war as a chance to show their loyalty to their adopted country and to work for the cause of a free Poland. The editors of *Naród Polski* wrote,

Leaders of the Polish National Alliance, 1894. Courtesy of Polish Museum of America Archives.

War! War!

War in defense of human rights, in the name of liberty, in the name of the people.

War!

And the Star Spangled Banner is our banner. . . . The time now has come for the greatest trial. And what is happening? In the home of the Polish Roman-Catholic Union, atop which wave Polish and American flags, a recruiting station opened up, at the end of the past week. . . . Addressing all Poles in Chicago, and especially the young men who desire to follow in the footsteps of Kosciuszko and Pulaski and offer their services on the altar of their adopted country, which has given them shelter, freedom and a chance to earn a living . . . it is only proper to appeal to them, it is desirous that they join the army through this Polish recruiting station, by which they will render a service to their nationality.[18]

Poles joined the American army in large numbers, which caused favorable comment even in the pages of Chicago's English-language newspapers. In addition, a separate Polish army began recruiting Poles in Chicago and across the country who were unable to join the U.S. forces due to language or citizenship barriers. This force, known as the Blue or Haller Army, would train in Canada and fight with the French army on the Western Front, and later as part of the army of a newly reconstituted Poland. "The Chicago recruiting headquarters of the Polish Army have been opened in the Polish Women's Alliance Building," wrote *Dziennik Związkowy*. "The long-awaited action, then, has finally begun, and now it is up to us and to the Polish youth to see that the Polish Army numbers thousands upon thousands of men, so that we can show the world that a Pole knows who his enemies are and that he knows when the time for action has come."[19] According to one estimate, 3 percent of the entire Polish population of Chicago entered military service during the first year of America's involvement in the war. In addition, twenty-five thousand Chicago Poles volunteered for the Polish Blue Army. The first Chicago soldier to die in combat during the war was Peter Wojtalewicz, who had grown up in St. Adalbert Parish.[20]

America's entry into the war threw the lobbying and relief effort of Chicago Poles into overdrive. Poles not only raised money for Polish relief but also for the formation of a Polish Army to fight alongside the Entente Powers. Poles were also called on to raise money for the American war effort though a series of war bond drives. The newspaper *Polonia* told Chicago Poles to buy government bonds and less expensive thrift stamps: "Every time you . . . buy a little 25c stamp you . . . are doing something for the country. Appealing to the people; to women who manage our households, to the children, to laborers, and to workers in general, the government is more generous than to large investors, who loaned billions of dollars and will lend more. . . . Before you buy something, think if you could not get along without this particular article. If so, use that money for buying Thrift Stamps. . . . Do not delay!"[21] Newspapers and community leaders urged Poles to outspend other ethnic groups in Chicago in buying government bonds, especially the Germans.[22] Nationally, working-class Polish communities bought an estimated $68 million in government bonds.[23]

As the war in Europe drew to a close, Germany faced total defeat, and the Russian and Austro-Hungarian Empires collapsed in the chaos of revolution and civil war. In 1918, after 123 years of foreign subjugation, Poland regained her independence. Poles in America rejoiced, but the new Poland soon faced serious threats. After years of war and occupation, the economy was in ruins, and poverty and disease ran rampant. Russia's new Bolshevik rulers cast ambitious eyes westward toward Poland as the pathway to reach the industrialized workers of Europe. As Poland struggled to knit itself together and stand up to foreign invasion, Polish communities in America were called on to help once again, and yet again, Chicago became the center for organizing assistance to the homeland. Poles were urged to buy Polish government bonds and to contribute for food, clothes, and medicine to prevent deaths from hunger and disease. Other contributions were taken up to support the Polish armed forces as they struggled against a massive Bolshevik invasion in 1920. Polish organizations in Chicago collected money from Poles all over the United States and all over Illinois and forwarded it to Europe. Polish parishes and community groups also collected funds. Parishes held special benefits and fundraisers while schoolchildren collected nickels and pennies. For many parishes, their contributions to the Polish cause remained a source of pride for years. St. Adalbert Parish in East St. Louis collected $19,590.95 for Polish relief in the years 1917–21.[24] In a single collection in October 1918, the parish of St. Stephen in Chicago donated $2,524.44, while the parishioners of St. John Cantius gave $1,434.95 in cash, $2,700 in Liberty bonds, $100 in checks, and $127.46 in postage stamps (for a total of $4,362.41).[25]

In August 1920, outnumbered Polish troops—including volunteers from Illinois—won a stunning victory over the invading Red Army near Warsaw. The victory secured Poland's independence for the next twenty-one years. The establishment of an independent homeland inspired some Chicago Poles to return to Poland to help the country rebuild or to open businesses. Those who did found a country in ruins, and the expertise and skills they had learned in America were either not needed or actually resented by Poles who saw the returning migrants as interlopers taking advantage of the country's poverty. Many returned to America. While helping to win Poland's freedom had been a defining cause of so many Polish Americans, by the 1920s most realized that America, not Poland, was their home. Ties to Poland remained strong, and helping relatives in Europe and the communities where they were born was still important. Yet the establishment of a free Poland signaled to Poles in Illinois and around the country that they were now and always would be an American ethnic community.

### Problems of Urban Life

As the Poles of Chicago struggled for Poland's freedom, they faced the threat of increasing social problems at home, which stemmed from the age and size of the city's Polish community. Immigrants were highly mobile, leading to severe strains on marriage and family life. Young immigrants without strong family bonds in America and American-born youth growing up in poverty with limited access to education and outside activities fell prey to numerous social ills. Parents worked long hours and struggled to learn basic English, but young people adapted far faster to the norms of urban

Boys in scout uniforms holding American and Polish flags during a parade or demonstration, circa 1917. Courtesy of Polish Museum of America Archives.

life in Chicago. Parents often had a hard time controlling their children as those children learned to operate in American society more effectively. The organizations and culture developed by the city's Polish immigrants did not immediately appeal to their second-generation children. At the same time, those children were often excluded from mainstream American culture and society by prejudice and discrimination, but they also found themselves in competition with young immigrants and migrants from other ethnic and racial groups that were also flocking to the city. As their parents struggled to make a home in Chicago, their children struggled to find their place in between their parents' Polish roots and the realities of urban life in early twentieth-century America.

Alcoholism was a plague on early Polish communities. With money in their pockets, weakened family ties, few activities outside of work, and plenty of available saloons, immigrants took to drinking. Polish newspapers, and especially the Catholic press, constantly sought to highlight and warn readers of the problems of alcoholism: "Polish people in this country abuse themselves beyond limit," raged *Naród Polski*, "men are drunkards, women are drunkards, and innocent children looking at this get used to bad habits."[26] Drunkenness, the paper noted in 1912, brought on other problems: "The people dance and drink, and drink and dance, and when they get weary of dancing and drinking, when their heads begin to swim, then presto! One after another: battle, disgrace, jail."[27] Nor was this problem lost on the Polish community's detractors. One exaggerated English account stated, "on Saturdays, 100,000 of them get dressed in the best to congregate in Little Poland and get roaring drunk."[28]

Another significant problem was crime, juvenile delinquency, and street gangs. Between 1900 and 1925, arrests of Poles increased by two and half times, and Poles were being arrested in numbers disproportionate to the overall population. Youth crime was a major part of this increase. By 1925, one-quarter of all boys and almost one in five girls in the Cook County juvenile system were Polish. A University of Chicago study from the 1920s found that Poles had the highest number of street gangs of any group in the city—almost 150 gangs, compared to 75 Irish, 63 African American, and 48 Italian gangs.[29]

Polish gangs engaged in a wide variety of criminal activity, including vandalism, petty theft, and jackrolling (luring and robbing gay men searching for sex partners or robbing drunks too inebriated to defend themselves). At a time when neighborhoods were sharply divided by race and ethnicity, Polish gangs fought each other and rival ethnic gangs over control of streets, alleys, and parks. These battles could be very violent, involving knives and other hand weapons and occasionally firearms, resulting in frequent injuries and deaths. One report noted that "the residents of a Polish colony . . . led by such gangs as the 'Hillers,' who dug themselves in along canals, would wage pitched battles with the Greeks and Italians from the southwest. A boy was shot through the heart in one of these fights."[30]

Although organized crime in Chicago was most famously dominated by the likes of Al Capone, there were also Poles in organized crime during "roaring twenties." Joe Saltis, known as "Polack Joe," was of Slovak origin, but he seems to have sometimes identified as a Pole and had a large number of Polish gangsters on his payroll. Saltis ran one of the most lucrative bootlegging operations of Prohibition era and dominated much of South Chicago. Hymie Weiss was another infamous Polish gangster. Born Earl Wojciechowski, he changed his name to the tougher- (and Jewish-)sounding Weiss when he embarked on a short but extremely violent life of crime.[31]

Although some in the Polish community blamed authorities for disproportionately targeting Polish youth, most leaders were forthright about the need for Poles to attack the problems of crime, delinquency, and substance abuse without excuses. In 1911, when a group of young Poles was sentenced to death for a murder, *Naród Polski* wrote, "In a few days four bandits will be hanged; young Polish men just beginning life. . . . They killed an innocent man without mercy. How did they become such cold-blooded murderers? Who injured and hardened such hearts? Who is to blame?"[32] A wide range of social reform efforts, including several organizations devoted entirely to these problems, emerged in the 1920s and 1930s (see chapter 5). Often it was within families that the struggle to address these problems was won or lost. Reverend Paul Fox, a Polish Protestant minister working at Laird Community Settlement House in Chicago, noted, "The average Polish family, has been far from succumbing to the unfortunate situation. It has struggled against the current vigorously, courageously, and in many instances, heroically."[33] While problems in the Polish community did not disappear overnight—they continued to plague Poles to some extent through the 1950s—the uncompromising moral stance of community leaders, the work of social reformers, the experience of the Depression and World War II, and the "aging out" of the second generation of Polonia gradually reduced these problems to the point where they were largely forgotten by the descendants of those who experienced them.

In addition to the very real problems of adjustment to urban Chicago, Poles and other recent immigrant groups were often disparaged by nativist groups in Illinois and beyond who saw them as unwilling and unable to assimilate and become "real" Americans. Large urban concentrations of immigrants—like the Poles of Chicago—which experienced more than their share of urban social problems, were a particular target. This wave of nativism reached its height during the 1920s when Catholic immigrants like Poles were targeted by groups such as the Ku Klux Klan who saw them as criminals and a danger to America. When a Polish woman was brought before a pro-Klan judge on bootlegging charges, he commented that "some of these foreigners come here to make money and find moonshining the easiest way of doing it. I say that we need the Ku Klux to put a stop to some of these practices."[34] The Poles actively fought against groups like the KKK and opposed nativist legislation designed to deprive immigrants of rights enjoyed by other Americans. In 1927, the editors of Chicago's *Dziennik Zjednoczenia* noted,

> In the years which followed the world war a chauvinistic movement was created by a group of American people of Anglo-Saxon descent, who wished to exercise this belated spirit of patriotism. Although it was much too late for this group to fight and participate in the hardships of war . . . this group began an intensive hunt for a non-existent foe of the Star Spangled Banner, under the guise of true Americanism. In this manner they spread a spirit of intolerance which is contrary to the principles of a free nation, as set forth by the founders of this glorious United States. The surprising attack of chauvinism was so sudden that the greater part of the loyal and law abiding people at whom this attack was directed were caught unawares. Agitation and unfair propaganda, directed at all foreign groups brought the results desired, by this chauvinistic group, to a point where the clever ruse bad swayed the opinion of the patriots and citizens on the side of chauvinism.

The paper called on the community's veterans to unite and get organized as the best answer to nativism: "We know that several hundred thousand soldiers of Polish descent served the country bravely. . . . Records of the War Department indicate that the Polish people had the largest percentage of enlistment, in proportion to the population. Let us then ask, is this display of loyalty not a proof of good citizenship? We say yes, it exceeds the loyalty of those 100% Americans who stood on the side lines and let the parade go by."[35]

Poles were seen as second-class citizens by many of Chicago's elite. Poverty, lack of access to education, and common ethnic stereotypes served to place Poles just above African Americans in the city's racial and ethnic hierarchy. As one Polish Chicagoan noted, "If you got a job, no matter what your qualifications were, if you had '-ski' at the end of your name, they'd say 'here's the mop and here's the pail.'"[36] Anti-Polish attitudes would persist in Chicago for decades, only fading gradually by the 1980s and 1990s.

### Polish Museum

Chicago's concentration of Poles allowed Polonia to create and sustain singular institutions that other Polish centers in the United States could not. The Polish Museum of America is the best example of this. Its origins date back to the creation of the library of the PRCUA before World War I. As years went by, the PRCUA library also began to acquire archives and historical artifacts under

Polish court session, August 1915. Chicago operated a Polish-language court in the early part of the twentieth century to handle the large volume of cases with defendants who spoke little or no English. Courtesy of Polish Museum of America Archives.

the direction of Mieczysław Haiman, a scholar, writer, and one of the first historians to study the history of the Polish community in the United States. In 1936, the PRCUA donated space to open the Polish Museum of America (PMA), the first museum dedicated to the history and culture of an American ethnic community.

The museum soon acquired a number of important collections. Among the most important of these was the Ignacy Paderewski collection, which was donated by Paderewski's sister after the death of the pianist in 1941. Following the outbreak of World War II in 1939, much of the content of the Polish pavilion of the New York World's Fair was acquired by the PRCUA and also found a home in the museum.

Over the decades, the museum also acquired a significant collection of Polish and Polish American art, including works by Olga Boznańska, Jan de Rosen, Maria Werten, Władysław Benda, Wojciech Kossak, and Stanisław Kaczor-Batowski. The PMA is also the most significant repository of Polish Art Deco outside of Poland.

By the start of World War II, Chicago was the unquestioned "capitol" of American Polonia. New York City, New Jersey, Detroit, Buffalo, Cleveland, and Milwaukee could all claim large Polish populations with an impressive range of organizations and talents, but none came close to the size and scope of Chicago. Yet, the sheer size of the city's Polish population made organizing and communicating among its many organizations and factions difficult. Ironically, the institutional complexity and completeness of the successful parish-community model developed by Chicago's Resurrectionists created self-contained urban villages that did not need much from each other. Despite that, the Polish influence was a decisive factor in shaping the social and physical landscape of America's second city.

# 7

# KULTURA: POLISH AND POLISH AMERICAN CULTURE IN ILLINOIS

Poles came to Illinois not merely to settle and work but also to imagine and create. Since their arrival in the state, Poles have been deeply involved in a wide range of artistic and cultural endeavors. Count Tadeusz Zukotyński, a student of the famous painter Jan Matejko, relocated to Chicago in the late nineteenth century among the first wave of many Polish artists, musicians, and writers who made the city their home. They were soon joined by American-born Poles, often pupils of the first immigrant artists and musicians. For example, Zukotyński trained Sister Mary Stansia (née Monica Kurkowska) a noted painter of church frescos. Stansia in turn was the teacher of Harriet Krawiec, who, along with her husband, Walter, were among the country's best-known artists in the 1930s and 1940s.[1] Through their creativity, Poles enriched their home state in a variety of media.

## Music

With Polish immigrants' deep ties to their local Roman Catholic parishes, it is no surprise that Polish parishes were among the earliest musical centers in Polonia. They hosted many dances and banquets at which orchestras and folk ensembles performed Polish music. From tavern entertainment to lavish banquets with full orchestras in the most elegant ballrooms, Polish life was centered on music. Polish documents from the Century of Progress date the first local Polish musician on record as Sylvester Lawinski, an accomplished violinist who opened a music store on State Street and Twelfth in 1860. Another leading Pole was composer Dr. Felix Borowski, who began teaching composition, violin, and music history at the Chicago Musical College in 1897, becoming president of the college in 1916. In 1870, Count Napoleon

Ledochowski, a pianist and teacher as well as a graduate of the Sorbonne, came to Chicago and founded a conservatory of music.[2]

Among the earliest Polish musical groups in Illinois, which first emerged in the 1870s, were the hundreds of choirs based in Polish parishes and fraternal organizations. They were (and to this day remain) affiliated through the Polish Singers Alliance of America (PSA), founded in 1899 and led by Anthony Mallek, the pioneering church organist of Holy Trinity Church. Mixed, children's, men's, and women's choirs performing secular and sacred Polish music were a central feature of life for the Poles of Illinois. Named for historical figures, composers, characters in Polish operas, and Polish saints and heroes, groups such as Chopin's Choir (Group Number 1 of the Polish Singers Alliance of America), the Women's Alliance Choir, the Halka Choir, and Paderewski's Choir preserved and shared Polish language and song throughout Illinois and neighboring states. In addition to these members of the PSA, each parish sponsored at least one parochial choral group. Dozens of these choral groups performed

Ignacy Jan Paderewski in recital at the Auditorium Theatre, Chicago, March 1929. This is one of the few photos of Paderewski taken during a recital in his long international career. Courtesy of Polish Museum of America Archives.

in a massive Polish singing spectacle at the World's Fair of 1893 and the Chicago World's Fair of 1933 in conjunction with the Polish Week of Hospitality at the Century of Progress. The PSA has had hundreds of Polish choirs with thousands of members in Illinois in the past century, and many of those choirs continue today.[3]

The visit of Ignacy Jan Paderewski—pianist, composer, philanthropist, statesman, signer of the Treaty of Versailles, and, briefly, prime minister of Poland during its independence between the World Wars—to Chicago in 1891 was one of the most significant Polish musical events in Illinois. His performance at the World's Fair of 1893 included appearances of the United Polish Singers of America under Mallek's direction. His first Chicago performance with the Chicago Symphony was followed by many others over a forty-year span. Wildly popular and deeply admired, Paderewski was an international emissary for Polish music as well as Polish independence, and was without a doubt the most famous pianist in the world for many decades. Greeted by adoring fans around the world, Paderewski was in many ways the first global rock star and a central figure of Polish culture in Illinois.

Chicago legend links Paderewski to a Victorian home at 2138 W. Pierce Avenue in Chicago. It is said that in the 1920s, at the home of Jan F. Smulski—a lawyer who served as a city alderman, state treasurer, founder of Northwestern Trust and Savings Bank, and a leader in Chicago's financial affairs, as well as chairman of the National Polish Committee during World War I, a committee of which Paderewski was also a member—Paderewski is said to have given an outdoor concert for the Wicker Park community from the building's spacious veranda. Ever since, it has been known as the Paderewski House. In 1939, the *Chicago Tribune* described Paderewski as the "young pianist with the great head of hair" who "caught America's imagination." Known for his wild mane of red locks, he has been referred to as the "original long hair" and was met with adoring throngs wherever he toured. Paderewski was also a key supporter and sponsor of the Polish Museum of America. His legacy of advocacy and extensive fundraising for Poland is preserved in a special way for the Poles of Illinois through the museum's Paderewski Room, which contains the maestro's possessions that were donated by his sister shortly after his death in 1941. Among the entrusted objects are Paderewski's last practice Steinway piano, the pen that Paderewski used to sign the Versailles Treaty, jewelry, letters, documents, everyday objects, and furnishings of his last living place, the suite at the Buckingham Hotel in New York City.

In the early 1900s, numerous Polish musicians and singers were active in Chicago with performances at Orchestra Hall, Ravinia, the Chicago Symphony Orchestra, and other music institutions of Illinois. The famous Holy Name Cathedral Quartet in the 1900s was composed of Polish operatic singers. In 1926, the Polish Arts Club of Chicago was founded, marking another significant movement in Polonia's musical development. Under the direction of its first music chairman, Anthony Milewicz, the club organized lectures and opera and concert parties. Polish Symphony concerts at Orchestra Hall were sponsored by the Polish American Philharmonic Society of Chicago. Through the club's promotion, concerts at Ravinia Park in Highland Park featured prominent musicians of Polish ancestry, including the annual Ravinia Polish Day concerts beginning in 1926. Poles also featured in Chicago's lively jazz scene in the interwar and postwar era. Gene Krupa set the standard for jazz drummers and became the most famous percussionist of his day, going on to tour nationally and appear in Hollywood films.[4]

Organized in 1922, the Polish Musicians Club in Chicago extended mutual aid to professional musicians in the Polish community. Polonia's important links to organized labor were also evident within the music community. Affiliated with the American Federation of Labor, the club was Local No. 10 in the Chicago Federation of Musicians. Already in the 1920s it boasted over one hundred members. Well-trained musicians offered lessons and classes to the Polish community. The Jasinski School of Music on South Ashland Avenue in Chicago, headed by the director of the Polish-American Symphony Orchestra, was well established by the 1930s. The Polish Symphony Orchestra debuted at the Goodman Theater in 1930 under the direction of Casimir Jasinski.[5]

### The Business of Music

Among the earliest advocates of music in the Polish American communities of Illinois were music publishers and distributors who printed and sold extensive collections of sheet music. The earliest publishers were located on Chicago's Polish Triangle, the Southwest Side of Chicago, and Downers Grove, Illinois.[6]

The first of these publications preserved and circulated an impressive array of classical and popular music, including violin instruction in Polish language, piano accordion arrangements of Polish classical songs, full orchestra arrangements for Polish dance music, folios of Polish national dances arranged for various band and orchestral instruments, Polish Christmas carols arranged for choir, trios for piano and violin for Polish song in the home, and Polish dance collections for accordion. A catalog of musical offerings from 1900 printed by B. J. Zalewski had an impressive range of Polish music pedagogy, including theoretical and practical courses in violin, singing, flute, organ, and numerous instruments reproduced from Poland. Catalogs of Polish opera (Moniuszko, in particular), Polish national anthems, Polish orchestral music arranged for Americans, Polish composers (such as Chopin), music for children and young people, Polish theater music, hundreds of four-part singing arrangements with piano accompaniment of Polish art songs, mazureks, obereks, waltzes, krakowiaks, patriotic songs, and melodies were printed. Illinois publishers and distributors at the dawn of the twentieth century were central in preserving and sharing a wide variety of Polish musical culture in the United States. They continued their influence into the twentieth century by recording local artists and helping to create a cornerstone of ethnic recordings in America.

One of the most influential forces in Polish music in America was W. H. Sajewski, who is considered the first Polish music publisher in the United States and is central to the history of ethnic recordings. Generations of Poles in Illinois first bought sheet music, piano rolls, and records in his shop at the Polish Triangle of Chicago, beginning in 1897. In those early years, the inventory included theatrical books, sheet music, instruments, piano rolls, and recordings. In time, the store flourished, and its mail-order business reached the farthest corners of rural and urban America. In the 1910s, Sajewski entered a contract with the United States Music Roll Company (located on Lake Street, Chicago), which produced music rolls for player pianos, in which they became exclusive producers of Polish music rolls. In the 1920s when their contract ended, the Victor Roll Company (organized

Władysław Sajewski standing in front of his music store on Milwaukee Avenue, 1911. The family-owned store operated from 1897 to 1981 as the largest Polish music specialty store in the United States. Courtesy of Polish Museum of America Archives.

by professional musician and former Sajewski music arranger, Frank Przybylski, among others) manufactured rolls until the industry was supplanted by vinyl records.

By the 1910s, the production of Polish-language records was in full force, but the Victor and Columbia record labels catered to more formally arranged orchestrations and classical music of a type not as familiar to working-class Poles, as these more formal recordings failed to recall the music of the towns and rural villages of their homeland. Sajewski was central in responding to this dilemma. Using print advertisements in well-established Polish American newspapers, and splitting the advertising cost with the Columbia record company, Sajewski began selling recordings made by Columbia and Victor right in his establishment in 1915. The first Chicago recordings made by Columbia in 1915 were by a group led by Frank Przybylski performing "The Laughing Polka" and the "Dziadunio Polka" (an ancestor of the "Clarinet Polka") under the name Orkiestra Columbia. Though Przybylski's professional orchestrations relied on folk music sources, he and Sajewski began actively recruiting the performers more in line with the tastes that local Polish markets demanded. Seeking folk songs and vernacular music performed by ordinary singers rather than trained musicians, Sajewski's shop would often record folks who came into the store, with Przybylski backing them up. Polish people who walked into the store and sang often wound up on records—a basic source for Sajewski finding recording artists. By the 1930s, Columbia was recording a specially numbered Polish series with accordionists and the newer Polish orchestras. Following the trend of Pawlo Humeniuk's Ukrainian recordings of folk music in a livelier and less formal style, Victor recorded the village music of Chicago's Franciszek Dukla, which, according to music historian Richard Spottswood, seems to have been the first Polish American recorded dance music in a real village style utilizing lead fiddle, clarinet, two harmony fiddles, and bowed cello or bass. His recording brought a genuine excitement and an authentic touch that paved the way for many good village music groups on Victor. It can definitely be argued that these early village groups performing in a new style laid the foundation for polka recordings in Illinois. Meanwhile, not all the ethnic recordings in Illinois Polonia featured folk or village bands, but they also included Polish crooners such as Władysław Ochrymowicz and Paweł Faut singing topical songs, as well as innovative accordionists such as the popular Jan Wanat. Also crucial to the history of ethnic recordings in America were albums of music of the Polish highlanders. This ancient, dissonant, and distinctive Polish music was recording by Columbia and Victor, with fiddler Karol Stoch being a key player.[7]

Music and instrument shops were found throughout Polonia, with local businesses such as the Polonia Sewing Machine and Music Company (founded in 1909) selling furniture, radio, and musical instruments to patrons throughout Illinois. Throughout the twentieth century, Polish newspapers advertised numerous Polish businesses selling musical instruments. A 1928 Polish Roman Catholic Union Daily survey of Polish commercial enterprises lists thirty music stores—estimated at a net worth of $250,000—in Chicago alone. During the 1930s, *Dziennik Chicagoski* carried advertisements for concertinas, sheet music, records, and related materials from scores of Polish American music shops. The ads promote the sale of radios, Victrolas, gramophones, and sheet music, boasting complete catalogs of Polish records. A number of these businesses thrived into the late twentieth century.

When radio arrived in the 1920s, record sales declined, but not as rapidly in the ethnic markets. In fact, those recording Polish artists such as Sajewski and Bolesław J. Zielinski, often listed as B. J. Zielinski on sheet music, saw the new technology as a way to expand their audience. The legacy of ethnic radio and Polish radio in Illinois in particular requires historical scholarship. Suffice it to say, from the 1920s onward, Polish radio programs in Illinois had a long, robust history. On WKBI, concertina players such as Rudy Patek and Ben Ray played Polish music live on air. An overview of Polish American newspapers from the 1930s through the present includes numerous Polish radio programs of all sorts. By the 1940s, Polish programs were advertised on WEDC, WGES, WHFC, WHIP, WIND, WSBS, and WWAE in Illinois. In the 1950s, WLEY FM offered Polish programming for listeners who "love Polish music, Polish song and the living Polish language." WPNA radio (originally WBES), owned by the Polish National Alliance and based in Oak Park, Illinois, first broadcast in 1951. In the 1960s, well-known Polish American radio personality Sig Sakowicz, who had a column in the *Polish Daily News*, was heard daily on WHFC, while radio station WOPA presented the Voice of Polonia and extensive Polish programming from its California Avenue studios. Chicago Polka legend Li'l Wally presented a show on WSBC and WTAQ, while Chet Gulinski offered Sunday polka programming from WOPA in Oak Park. Founded in 1971 by longtime Polonian broadcasters Józef and Sława Migala, WCEV (Chicagoland's Ethnic Voice), was the first ethnic concept station in the United States. It continues to be headquartered in Cicero, Illinois.

Sajewski's son Alvin, who began in his father's shop as a child and continued the business after his father's death in 1948 well into the late 1980s, was a publisher, talent scout, and owner of the oldest and largest polka music store in the United States, eventually recognized by the Library of Congress as a leading authority of ethnic folk songs and polka music. By donating over four hundred rare 78-rpm records to the Library of Congress, he helped lay a foundation on which to build an authentic chronological library of recorded Polish folk and polka music. Many of his papers, sheet music, and recordings are now part of the Sajewski Collection in the Polish Museum of America's archives. The Sajewski music shop on Milwaukee continued to be an epicenter of Polish music in Illinois. Branching off from their early ethnic recordings, the Sajewskis continued as local talent scouts in Polonia, signing many of the artists who would develop and pioneer polka music.

## Polka

Polish American polka is not Polish but a uniquely American cultural hybrid of ethnic styles and popular forms. As early as the 1840s in Europe, polka began as a working-class rebellion against the elitist minuet before racing around the globe. Polish American polka was born when turn-of-the-century North American Polish immigrants blended this lively dance with folk melodies and jazz, inventing a dynamic participatory art form that was Polish *and* American. Thus, polka was not a transplant of a preexisting Polish folk form to America but an amalgam of ethnic styles and mass-mediated popular music that emerged from America's multiethnic urban milieu. The Poles of Illinois were central players in the invention and development of Polish American polka, with two of the three primary styles of polka music (Honky or Dyno and Push) having deep roots in the state. And many of those innovators began through Sajewski's early intervention.

Following the smash hit "Beer Barrel Polka" in the 1930s on Victor Records, polkas became big business, with new polka styles developing in various ethnic groups. A host of new polka bands sprang up, with the Sajewskis recording many of them. Alvin Sajewski signed many of the pioneers of Polish American music, including Marisha Data, Steve Adamczyk, and Eddie Zima. Data was also well known in the radio and stage field as an announcer, operatic and concert singer, and a comedienne, as well as for her extensive charitable work.

Alvin Sajewski connected artists such as Data, Johnny Bomba, and the Polkateers with East Coast musician and producer Walt Dana, who wanted to break in to the Midwestern market. Dana, an accomplished pianist and composer, had a strong sensibility for producing successful records in the Polish American market. This collaboration laid the groundwork for the biggest names and pioneers in the new field of Polish American polka.

Throughout the twentieth century, Polish American polka developed a diversity of styles and instrumentations, including piano accordions, concertinas, fiddles, horns, and clarinets, in lineups ranging from three-piece combos to orchestras. Polish American polka is a hybrid of styles. The definitive Chicago approach, often called Honky or Dyno, originated on the North Side on Division Street, the so-called "Polish Broadway," in the early to mid-twentieth century. Illinois innovators included Eddie Zima, Marion Lush, and Li'l Wally, who used blues-like soulful jams in their Honky sound.

Push style in the mid- to late twentieth century incorporated the horns of neighboring Latino immigrants and the influence of country and western with *Górale* melodies of Polish highlanders. Push style emerged from working-class Polish American enclaves, such as those of Chicago's South Side, which included large communities of Polish highlanders. Push was developed and promoted by Illinois natives such as Lenny Gomulka (of the Chicago Push) and Eddie Blazonczyk Sr. and Eddie Blazonczyk Jr. (of the Versatones). The latter described the style as a driving rhythm that is anchored by a heavy accordion bellows-shake and pushing drum, which is then amplified by heavy brass and soulful polka vocals. Eastern style—less represented in Illinois—melded big-band sounds with Polish folk tunes. Polka was grounded in communal cultural rituals; it continues to be heard at weddings, parish picnics, and neighborhood dances, on the radio, and at national festivals.

By the mid-twentieth century, another generation of Polonians purchased their records at Sajewski's shop, first hearing the Polish

American hits in its large listening booths. Those hits stemmed in part from the early village music groups recorded at Sajewski's music shop and also from entrepreneurial Polish Americans like Walter Jagiello (Li'l Wally), who got his musical start in the picnic groves and taverns on Division Street in Chicago. Polka music exploded in the Chicago area. This younger generation of musicians sought Alvin Sajewski's counsel and assistance, and by the 1950s many of them were running their own record labels, music shops, publishing companies, radio shows, and more. Li'l Wally Jagiello operated Jay Publishing. Chet Schafer's Chicago Polkas record label recorded the 47th Street Concertina Band and reissued early polka music from old 78s. Marion Lush founded the Dyno Record Company in 1955 and became the owner of Lu-Mar Publishing Company. Eddie Blazonczyk Sr. also founded a wide range of polka-related businesses and promotion and was a model for the polka entrepreneur.

The Poles of Illinois developed an entire economy and infrastructure of Polka music, with Polka promoters, publishers, musicians, and performers founding dance halls, bars, orchestras, bands, festivals, publishing houses, radio shows, music shops, and recording labels. The biography of Polka Hall of Fame artist Eddie Blazonczyk Sr. typifies the network of the polka economy of Illinois. Eddie's parents, Fred and Antoinette Blazonczyk, operated the Pulaski Ballroom and later the Club Antoinette in Chicago. In the 1950s, Eddie began as a songwriter and recording artist for Mercury Records under the name Eddie Bell and the Bel-Aires. In 1962, Eddie founded the polka band the Versatones, which toured worldwide, recording many albums under the Bel-Aire Publishing Label and winning the Grammy Award in the polka category. Eddie Blazonczyk was also a polka promoter, a disc jockey heard on WTAQ, WCEV, and WNPA, and the president of the Bel-Aire Record Company. Eddie Blazonczyk's extensive influence and superb artistry in a unique genre of American music was recognized by the National Endowment for the Arts National Heritage Fellowship in 1998. Bel-Aire Enterprises, based in Bridgeview, Illinois, continues to host Polka festivals, dances, and numerous polka radio shows, even though its founder passed away in 2012. This entrepreneurial engagement with music publishing, production, promotion, radio, and festivals is typical of the Poles of Illinois.

Illinois is home to the International Polka Association (IPA), founded largely by Polish Americans, which continues to promote polka. The first Polka Convention was held by the group in 1963, and in 1968, under the steering committee of Johnny Hyzny, Leon Kozicki, Joe and Jean Salomon, Eddie Blazonczyk, and Don Jodlowski, the association was officially chartered by the State of Illinois as a nonprofit corporation. It was registered with Cook County, serving as an "educational and charitable organization for the preservation, promulgation and advancement of polka music and; to promote, maintain and advance public interest in polka entertainment; to advance the mutual interests and encourage greater cooperation among its members who are engaged in polka entertainment; and to encourage and pursue the study of polka music, dancing and traditional folklore." The IPA continues to host the Polka Hall of Fame and Museum and the annual Polka Music Awards. Its members were central to the successful lobbying effort that led to the creation by the National Academy of Recording Arts and Sciences of the polka category at the Grammy Awards, which was given from 1986 to 2009.

Illinoisans were also central to the development of the Polka Mass, a Roman Catholic liturgy using polka music. Chicago native Father Wally Szczypula, a concertina player with the 47th Street Concertina Band who served as chaplain of the IPA from the 1970s through the 1990s, initiated the Polka Mass at IPA Festivals.

Polka music, according to one critic, "continues to be performed by skilled musicians who are continually incorporating new influences. . . . By any reasonable criterion, then, the polka ought surely to be regarded as among the most dynamic and innovative participatory art forms this country has ever produced."[8] Polka is a phenomenally resilient and creative hybrid musical form. This unique American musical style is just one—but an important one—of Polish America's musical contributions in Illinois and is most closely aligned with the descendants of the great wave of Polish immigration to Chicago in the later 1890s.

## Polish Music Today

Since Illinois is home to a wide and culturally diverse Polonia from various immigration cohorts, it continues to host and nurture a wide range of musical activities. The diversity includes choirs from Polish American Saturday schools, Polish ethnic dance troupes,

Polish radio programs, ensembles such as the Lira Singers, the Polish American Symphony Orchestra, Polish DJs, and Polish American artists in all genres: from opera, pop, rock, and rap to polka and jazz, all contributing to the musical culture of America.

Polish American music continues to thrive in Illinois in the twenty-first century. The Lira Ensemble, the nation's only professional performing arts company specializing in Polish music, brings the best of Polish culture into American life. Founded in 1965 as the Lira Singers, an amateur youth group, by Alice Stephens and her student, Lucyna Migala (the daughter Polish radio pioneers Józef and Sława Migala, founders of WCEV radio), the company now consists of a professional symphony orchestra, chamber ensembles, singers, and dancers who perform classical, folk, and popular Polish dance and music. It is headed today by Lucyna Migala, its artistic director and general manager. Lira's repertoire includes Polish popular and folk songs and dances, traditional court dances, as well as classical music—Polish opera, ancient Polish music, sacred music, music of various historic periods, new music of Poland, works by Polish American composers, and Polish compositions rarely heard in the United States. The Lira Ensemble, which tours the Midwest, the United States, and Poland, has won numerous awards for its work, and it performs as the artist-in-residence at Loyola University Chicago.[9]

In 1999, the Paderewski Symphony Orchestra was founded in Chicago, and it is now the largest professional musical institution dedicated to the popularization of Polish music and culture outside of Poland. The organization has gone from a small chamber ensemble to a large cultural organization with permanent staff, over forty volunteers, its own choir, and an academy of music for children and youth.[10]

Harpist Regina Niemirska, Chicago, circa 1920s. Courtesy of Polish Museum of America Archives.

### Theater and Radio

From the beginning, every Polish community of any size had an amateur theater troupe, and larger communities and parishes might support several companies.

Even smaller communities in rural Illinois had Polish drama clubs.[11] There were children's theater groups organized by schools and young adult and adult drama circles created by parishes, fraternal societies, and political organizations. For example, one newspaper account noted,

> St. Casimir's Young Men's Society staged an amateur Play last night at the Polish hall on Bradley Street. The audience was large, and it enjoyed a very pleasant pastime. Well learned roles, properly arranged scenery; audible, distinctive, and beautiful diction; attractive costumes, and artistic decorations, suitable to the occasion, made a very good impression as a whole, and revealed the theatrical tendencies of the young society. Most of the members of this society are very young, yet for a long time they have proved how fervently they love their native land, how patriotic are their feelings, and also how they strive to remain Poles on American soil. . . . It would be impossible to describe all the characters of the Play as presented. The Play, "Four Episodes from the Life of Thaddeus Kosciuszko," depicts the moments in which this great Polish hero had some of the most thrilling experiences, patriotic as well as personal. . . . We should not overlook here the Polish orchestra which moved the public to almost continuous applause by playing beautiful Polish selections between the acts.[12]

Plays put on by Polish drama circles were often written by immigrant playwrights. Szczesny Zahajkiewicz, for example, wrote numerous plays for amateur drama clubs in Illinois, and some of his plays were performed in other Polish communities. Zahajkiewicz was a particularly prolific playwright: at least four of his plays appeared on stage in Chicago between February 1892 and January 1893.[13] Nuns teaching in parochial schools often wrote plays for school drama groups. The majority of Polish plays performed in Chicago prior to World War II appeared to have been patriotic productions based on figures and events in Polish history, though plays with religious and moral themes were also well known. Comedy and satire also appeared on some stages. From existing newspaper accounts, it seems that Zahajkiewicz and other Polish playwrights in Chicago drew heavily on mid-nineteenth-century Polish and European Romanticism. Polish plays appearing on Illinois stages mirror these artistic preferences, including those by Józef Ignacy Kraszewski, Aleksander Fredro, Juliusz

Słowacki, Adam Mickiewicz, and others. Though the majority of plays were by Polish authors, Polish drama clubs did translations of well-known work by other playwrights including Shakespeare and Friedrich Schiller.[14] Most amateur plays were performed in parish halls, though there was a short-lived socialist theater that operated in Chicago in 1915.[15]

Although the majority of Polish immigrant theater activity was undertaken by amateur companies, the mass immigration to Illinois also brought professional artists and actors who developed permanent professional theaters in Chicago prior to World War I. By the end of the war, there were eight Polish theaters in Chicago.[16] Kazimierz Majewski attended the Academy of Fine Arts in Warsaw and acted in plays in Poland's largest city before leaving for Chicago to avoid the Russian military draft. He and his father-in-law managed Chicago's Premier Theater, which was considered one of the best in town, its content closely reflecting what appeared on the contemporary Warsaw stage.[17]

Polish newspapers of the period before World War II record the existence of dozens and perhaps hundreds of cultural groups that combined theatrical skits, music, dramatic readings, speeches, and comedy. A report from the St. John Cantius Circle noted, "Yesterday's program was quite varied. Besides solos, duets, and choir singing, there were recitations, speeches, a comical recitation, etc. Especially noteworthy were the speeches by F. Osuch (on education), F. Gibasiewicz (on the need of organizing societies for the young people), and Chmielewski (on the patriotism of our forefathers). A member of the Circle, Rydwelski, entertained the audience with his tricks and jokes. Some of the songs and recitations were not bad. All of the amateurs in yesterday's celebration showed evident improvement."[18] By the 1920s, Poles in Chicago established a number of cultural societies, such as the Polish Arts Club, that promoted the study and appreciation of fine art, literature, and music. These not only included appreciation of Polish culture but also encouraged group attendance at events offered by the Chicago Art Institute. Although the Art Institute did not feature a great deal of Polish-themed programs, it did sponsor occasional lectures on Polish topics.[19]

By the late 1920s, changing technology and tastes began to put professional theaters out of business, though amateur drama continued, especially at the parish level. Theaters were increasingly replaced by radio and movies. The first Polish-language broadcasts began around 1927 on Chicago radio stations, often sponsored by Polish organizations and businesses. The newspaper *Dziennik Chicagoski* sponsored a regular radio hour:

> Tonight at eight o'clock, another Polish program will be presented over station WCFL under the auspices of *Dziennik Chicagoski*. This evening's radio presentation will be a variety show. . . . One of the attractions of this evening will be the appearance of the popular Polish tenor, John Krawiec. This artist will sing fragments from the opera, *Halka*. Another feature will be the presentation of the well-known singer of national songs, Miss Kulczycka-Obrzut. A comedy will also be presented on this evening's program. The title role will be played by Thaddeus Kantor. He will be supported by Miss Pedecini and M. Marski. Miss Kulczynska-Obrzut will take the role of a servant. Besides this, Alexander Bonczkowski, pianist, and Miss Mary Gruszczynska, singer, will appear. If time permits Christmas carols will also be sung.[20]

By the early 1930s, Polish-language programming was widely available in Chicago. East St. Louis also had a weekly Polish radio

Theater troupe performing *The Arsonist's Daughter*, Chicago. Courtesy of Polish Museum of America Archives.

show, featuring polka, classical music, and Polish comedy skits, beginning in 1935.[21]

The most notable feature of Polish-language radio in Chicago and beyond was the creation of long-running situation comedies, a brand new type of theater. Actors such as Majewski transitioned from the stage to this new medium, which emphasized settings familiar and relevant to Polish Americans. As one historian noted, "Far from being imitative of American radio comedy, [Polish radio performers] were a decade ahead of it. Except for the popular serial *Amos n' Andy* (which peaked in 1930–32), American radio comedy in the 1930s ran in a vaudeville rut, consisting largely of gag routines and one liners. Not until *Fibber McGee and Molly* made the top five list in 1940 did English language radio situation comedies begin to develop into the genre which would dominate American radio comedy."[22] Actors such as Majewski and Kantor hung out in Polish bars and neighborhoods, picking up immigrant dialect and amusing stories to add to their repertoire. They created memorable characters such as the wily but slightly foolish Bartek Bieda and the "greenhorn" Walenty Gomuła. Humor on Polish radio drew on the disconnections, misunderstandings, and absurdities of immigrant life. In one show, Gomuła (played by Majewski), gets increasingly incensed as an American waiter refers to him as "sir," which he misunderstands for the Polish word for cheese (*ser*). So popular were these programs that Chicago's Polish radio actors developed a fan base all across the Midwest.[23]

## Dance

Dancing accompanied many aspects of Polish immigrant life in Illinois, being a prominent feature at parties, weddings, and informal gatherings. But Polish dance also reflected an emerging ethnic identity and helped Poles find their place in a multicultural society. Early dances were adapted from village forms, and they reflected the music that accompanied them: obereks or mazureks, as well as more formal waltzes and later polkas. Polish organizations sponsored dancing classes and dances for young people. Lillian Cwik recalled, "I did the Krakowiak, the Troiak, Mazur . . . we used to have a class, and every Sunday at the Falcons, we'd gather together and we had an instructor."[24]

Many dances were hosted in taverns, with the tables and chairs cleared away, or in private homes. In good weather, dances could be held outdoors in the backyard or in parks, and during summer weekends, Polish neighborhoods were filled with the sounds of music, laughter, and dance. By the 1930s and 1940s, middle-class Polish families could attend balls hosted by Polish fraternal groups. One, the Red and White Ball, began in 1939 at Lenard's restaurant in the Lewis Hotel, located at the Polish Triangle in Chicago. "The daughters of Chicago's best Polish families . . . gowned like princesses, with their fathers in tails, wearing elaborate sashes and decorations of a quasi-knightly import, danced an aristocratic, carefully choreographed grand polonaise."[25]

Poles, especially young ones, adopted American dance forms such as the fox-trot and the Charleston. Such dancing met with a mixed reception by Polonia leaders, as second-generation young people found dance venues outside of their parents' community where they met, danced with, and dated young people from Chicago's other ethnic groups. Chicago's infamous "taxi dances," where young women were paid by the dance (and turned over part of the proceeds to the hall owners), were heavily attended by Poles but were also attended by Irish, Greeks, Italians, Filipinos, and others.[26]

A very different type of dance movement began in the interwar years—Polish folk dance. Early waves of immigrants came to escape village life and evinced no desire to retain regional folk dress or reproduce any sort of formal folk dancing. Although the early history of Polish dance in America is sketchy, the first efforts at folk dancing did not occur until the late 1920s or early 1930s, roughly coinciding with increasing interest in folk culture in independent Poland. The first folk dance classes were either held at settlement houses or sponsored by Polish fraternal societies. Non-Polish settlement house workers were often instrumental in the early development of interest in folk dance, as they tried to promote a positive vision of assimilation to their diverse clientele. Folk dance provided a way for immigrant youth to participate in activities that did not obliterate their home culture but still provided unthreatening examples of the "many gifts" of the city's immigrant communities. In the years after World War II, folk dance instruction and performance was taken over entirely by Polish organizations, with the first known group in Illinois forming in 1946. Folk dance and the folk dress that went with it (most often derived from the Kraków region of southern Poland) became a marker of Polish ethnicity that was shared across generations and also readily accessible and accepted both inside and outside of the Polish community.

## Food

The Poles of Illinois have contributed to America's multicultural eating habits by making "pierogi" a household word and contributing the popular street food "the Polish" to the American vernacular. The Poles in Illinois have a rich history that can be found in recipes and restaurants, preserving Polish culture through food production and family traditions. The Poles of Illinois have expressed Polishness in private kitchens, restaurants, and taverns, adding to the local culture with distinctly Polish flavors such as pierogi and kiełbasa. Examining foodways requires us to understand the complex ways in which social norms, cultural meanings, historical contexts, and economic realities underlie food habits. As scholars have argued, food is more than a matter of physical sustenance. It is also a system of communication, a type of language through which we express identities and relationships, including gender, ethnicity, nationality, festivity, and sacrality. The Poles of Illinois have a rich culinary tradition that continues to thrive.

Among the very earliest food-related services in Polonia were the home-cooked meals of Polish women who ran boardinghouses in the 1800s for Polish immigrants, mostly men, who had traveled alone to work in Illinois. These women cooked, cleaned, and did laundry for their boarders, running labor-intensive family businesses serving the new immigrant population. These boardinghouses were particularly popular among the immigrant workers of Illinois's largest industries, such as meatpacking and steel. They provided familiar Polish foods for the workers before they could set up their own homes or send for their family members back in Poland. This work was difficult and dreary, but it often provided new immigrants with their only connection to Polish foodways and customs.

In the major wave of nineteenth-century Polish immigration to Illinois, taverns, bars, cafes, banquet halls, and restaurant businesses were established by enterprising Poles who labored in the food and beverage industries as soon as they arrived. Of course, many Illinois Poles were employed in the Union Stock Yards, making a significant labor contribution to the meatpacking capital of the world. Already by the turn of the twentieth century, Poles were well-established small business owners. The 1903 Polish Directory for the City of Chicago had pages of listings for Bakers, Butcher Shops, Groceries, Dry Goods purveyors, Milk & Cream deliveries, and Barkeepers. The 1903 publication noted that there were too many Polish taverns to list, estimating over five hundred Polish barkeepers in Chicago alone.

The 1903 directory listed almost forty Polonian milk and dairy providers in the region. The Boyda Dairy Company, organized in 1919 on West Superior Street, was one of many Polish-owned dairy concerns offering milk to the city and suburbs. In the mid-twentieth century, numerous others founded and directed by Polish Americans flourished, among them the White Eagle Dairy Company, the Douglas Dairy Company, the Polonia Dairy Company, and the West Side Dairy Company.

By the 1930s, Polish American trade and commerce in Chicago alone was estimated by the Polish Roman Catholic Union of America as totaling over $16 million in value, documenting small grocers, large grocery stores, meat markets, sausage stores, soft drink shops, dry goods, and peddlers employing over fifteen thousand Polish Americans. One chain of forty-five stores, the Novak Meat Markets, was estimated at an annual operations budget of $150,000. Polish Americans sought advancement in high schools, evening schools, colleges, academies, and universities. They developed a number of large Polish commercial enterprises in wholesale meats, flourmills, wholesale groceries, and breweries. A list of commercial trade enterprises compiled by the Polish Roman Catholic Union of America in 1933 listed 500 bakeries and 150 restaurants valued at over a half a million dollars and employing several thousand Illinois Poles.

Polish American restaurateurs were evident at the 1933 Chicago World's Fair where the Warszawski Bufet operated at the Polski Pawilon on Enchanted Island. The commemorative souvenir books that Poles in America compiled and published for the Century of Progress chronicled many food and beverage concerns in 1930s Polonia. These included small storefronts such as the Gydnia Lunch Room on South Commercial Avenue and the Warsaw Restaurant's "Beautiful Beer Roof Garden," where patrons could "Dine and Dance" on North Ashland Avenue.

Major food and beverage wholesalers also blossomed under the innovation of Illinois Poles. The National Cordial Company liquor wholesaler was founded Western Avenue in Chicago by Polish immigrant M. F. Struzynski, who began manufacturing the Polish honey wine, *miód*, in a small shop on Oakley Avenue in Chicago. This expanded after prohibition to a twenty-thousand-square-foot facility on Division Street, which included a factory and a fleet of delivery trucks. The White Eagle Brewing Company, founded in 1902 at 38th and Racine in Chicago, survived Prohibition and continued in operation until the 1950s.[27]

The Novak Milling Corporation, founded by Albert Novak in 1901, produced livestock feed from its locations in South Hammond and Chicago. The Pasier Products Company, Inc., was founded in 1921 and produced a line of pickles and sauerkraut at facilities in Crystal Lake, Illinois; Division Street, Chicago; and Genoa City, Wisconsin.[28] From a tiny delicatessen store on Commercial Avenue in South Chicago, Joseph Slotkowski founded the Slotkowski Sausage Company in 1918, which by 1935 was a leading manufacturer of Polish sausage from its factory at West 18th Street in Chicago.[29] The Chicago Flour Company was founded in 1920 by the Dombrowski brothers, who supplied flour to the Polish bakeries in Illinois. John Dziurgot and Sons of West North Avenue produced over eight thousand pounds of egg noodles and macaroni products per day by 1937, claiming to be "the only Polish American concern in the United States that manufactures the entire line of macaroni products and egg noodles."[30]

Both wholesale and retail food operations flourished in Polonia, with bakeries, millers, dairies, food processing plants, and sausage makers thriving throughout Illinois. Such businesses continue to the present day, with numerous grocery stores in the North and South Sides of Chicago and throughout Illinois serving the Polish population. The 1903 Guide to Polish Chicago listed well over 250 Polish grocers in Chicago alone. Larger trade groups such as the Polish Bakers Union and the Polish Bakery Owner's Club were established in the early twentieth century. So numerous were these businesses that they organized regional trade organizations, such as the Butchers and Grocers Association of South Chicago, which boasted over sixty members in the 1930s. Meat and sausage companies such as Andy's Deli & Mikołajczyk (founded in 1918 on Chicago's North Side) and Bobak's Sausage Co. (founded in 1967 on Chicago's South Side) continue to sell their wares wholesale, but they also run their own retail grocery stores offering hot and cold prepared Polish foods, full-service meat and sausage counters, and entire grocery lines of house-made and imported Polish items.

Among the most prevalent food-related businesses owned and operated by Illinois Poles were the many bakeries beginning in the late 1800s, some of which still operate to this day. Bakers in every

neighborhood and town proffered Polish rye breads and special-
ties such as *pączki* and *mazurki* at local shops like the Avondale
Bakery, the Krispy Roll Bake Shop, Kleczewski's Bakery, Majew-
ski's Confections, the Mil-Mont Bakery, Home Bakery, Cortland
Bakery, Neighborhood Bakery, Village Bakery, New Century
Bakeries, Forest View Bakery, Ideal Pastry, and Oak Mill Bakery.
A common practice in Chicago's taverns and bakeries was to name
the establishment after the street of the nearest intersection on
which it was located. Thus, a bakery at Milwaukee Avenue and
Montclare in Chicago was christened Mil-Mont. A bakery on
Oakton and Milwaukee Avenues in Niles was named Oak Mill
Bakery, an example whose numerous locations continue today in
Chicago, Niles, and Mount Prospect. These bakeries provided a
daily connection to Polish foodways, with many Polish Americans
enjoying the cuisine of their homeland without interruption across
oceans and generations.

Cafés and restaurants were a central business enterprise for the
Poles of Illinois and remain so to the present day, with numerous restaurants and banquet halls serving the Polish American
community throughout Illinois. Local businesses included lunch
counters, taverns, cafés, restaurants, and banquet halls, and they
promised home-cooked Polish cuisine. Polish-owned taverns
and banquet halls were central meeting places for Illinois Poles.
Taverns represented a central locale of community life, offering
informal meals, neighborhood socialization, family celebrations,
and live music. Polish American entrepreneurs built catering and
banquet halls, which hosted parish events, civic celebrations,
balls, and dinner dances, as well as familial milestones such as
weddings, First Communions, and funeral luncheons. Community cornerstones, such as Stanisław Michalski's Oaza Catering
founded in 1922 on Milwaukee Avenue, operated banqueting halls
that were "the scene of many social activities," such as banquets
in honor of General Haller, affairs for the Kosciuszko Foundation, and "practically all the most important affairs in Polish
American social and civic life." These food-based businesses in
the hospitality industry were well established by the late nineteenth century, and they continue to serve Polish Americans in
the twenty-first century. Mid-century icons of Polonia included
Syrena Restaurant on West 47th Street and the Orbit Restaurant
on Milwaukee Avenue. Generations of Polish Americans have
marked weddings, funerals, and other rites of passage with Polish

cuisine and hospitality in the halls of Polonia Banquets, the Jolly Inn, Sawa's Old Warsaw, the Dom Podhalan (Polish Highlanders Club), the Red Apple, the House of the White Eagle, and the Lone Tree Manor.

The third wave of Polish immigration to Illinois saw many entrepreneurs and chefs bring new energy to the dining scene in the 1980s and 1990s. A wide range of businesses were founded by newcomers from modest homestyle Polish buffet restaurants such as the Red Apple or Staropolska to the more gourmet sensibilities of immigrant Richard Zawadzki, whose show *Cooking with Chef Ryszard* appeared on local television. Zawadzki ran the Pierogi Inn and Chopin Mon Ami in Jefferson Park. Another pioneer in Polish fine dining was the Lutnia Restaurant on Belmont Avenue. In multiethnic Chicago, Polish food can mix freely with other cuisines. For example, in the Bridgeport neighborhood, the restaurant Kimski mixes Polish and Korean foods, including kiełbasa topped with kimchi.

While Polish food traditions have been preserved in commercial enterprises and parish hall kitchens, these traditions have also persisted in the private homes of Polish Americans, where mothers and grandmothers have persisted in practicing their heritage long after immigration. These Polish foodways often are the most persistent legacy of Polish culture, even when third-, fourth-, and fifth-generation Polish Americans have lost the Polish language and a direct connection to Poland itself. Poles in Illinois have preserved foodways in connection to holidays and domestic celebrations linked to the Roman Catholic calendar. Pączki Day, for example, is a homegrown American holiday created by Polish immigrants that mirrors the Polish tradition of Fat Thursday. In Poland, the Thursday before Ash Wednesday, when Lenten sacrifice begins, is celebrated with the puffy, round, jam-filled, deep-fried pastries called *pączki*. In Polish America, this pre-Lenten excess relocated to the Tuesday before Ash Wednesday. Pączki Day is widely celebrated in Illinois, with Polish bakers and grocers preparing hundreds of thousands of the namesake delicacy for sale across the region. This tradition, though Polish in origin, is widely known by all people in Illinois, especially Catholics of other ethnic groups; television reporters annually document lines at local bakeries and happy customers with boxes of pastries.

One of the most enduring and beloved food-based customs of Illinois Poles is the *Święcone*, or "Blessing of the Food," linked to

Polish Easter customs. Polish Roman Catholic parishes in America remain dedicated to preserving this distinctive celebration, where each family brings a carefully decorated basket of symbolic Easter foods to the church on Holy Saturday to be blessed. The basket is traditionally lined with a white linen or lace napkin and decorated with sprigs of boxwood, flowers, and ribbon. Observing the beautiful foods and creations of other parishioners is one of the special joys of the event. The Blessing of the Food is a festive occasion. The three-part blessing specifically addresses the various contents of the basket, with special prayers for the meats, eggs, and cakes and breads, giving each a symbolic significance. Some foods, such as butter and cakes, are shaped like lambs, signifying Jesus, the Sacrificial Lamb. These blessed foods are then shared at the Easter breakfast. The most common foods at the meal are ham, kiełbasa, hard-boiled eggs, salads, and beet and horseradish relish, followed by such holiday cakes as *babka, mazurek*, and *sernik*. The breakfast often starts with a tart soup containing eggs and kiełbasa, known as *biały barszcz* in eastern Poland and *żurek* elsewhere. Even for Polish Americans of the fifth generation and beyond, these food practices are treasured and preserved with great persistence.

Another persistent food tradition in Illinois Polonia is the Wigilia, or Vigil meal on Christmas Eve. The Poles of Illinois widely continue to observe this traditional meatless meal at the center of the holiday. The Wigilia table is set with a white tablecloth, under which hay is placed. The hay represents the manger, and the cloth is a symbol of Mary's veil, used to swaddle the infant Jesus. The family's best china and crystal grace the table, as this is a sacred night. The Wigilia dishes are prepared according to beloved family recipes. The foods represent the four corners of the earth: the mushrooms from the forest, grain from the fields, fruit from the orchards, fish from the lakes and sea. The meatless meal is said to honor the animals who were first to see baby Jesus in the manger. The meal always begins with a special soup, such as a *barszcz wigilijny z uszkami* (Christmas borscht with mushroom dumplings) or a mushroom soup. The soup course is followed by many elegant fish preparations, vegetables, and the beloved Polish pierogi. Typical dishes include carp in aspic, herring (*śledźe*), breaded whitefish, meatless cabbage rolls (*gołąbki*), noodles with poppy seed (*kutia*), kluski noodles with cabbage, and Polish mushrooms. A list of tempting special desserts is also required, the favorites being nuts and fruits, *kompot* (fruit compote), *makowiec* (poppy seed roll), *pierniki* (honey spice cakes), and *Mazurka*.

Of particular symbolic and emotional significance in the Christmas Wigilia meal is the enduring tradition of the *Opłatek*, or Christmas wafer, which is shared in Polish homes around the world. Since the 1800s, the wafers—often impressed or embossed with religious designs—have been baked by Polish monasteries and convents, as well as imported directly from Poland to parishes and grocers across Illinois. In the center of the table the *Opłatek* is often placed in a bed of hay, sometimes also with a representation of the baby Jesus. The candles are lit after the youngest child has spotted the first evening star. The wafer is then shared with the family members in an emotional exchange, during which each person breaks off a part of the other's wafer and gives wishes for the future and apologizes for the past. Family members now gone are recalled in these moments. Tradition also dictates that an empty place be set for an unexpected guest, for an ancestor (in their memory, or for their spirit to occupy), or perhaps for Jesus himself. This is in keeping with the core Polish adage, "*Gość w dom, Bóg w dom*" (Guest in the home is God in the home). While these are deeply private moments celebrated within the family, many Polish churches and cultural groups also conduct celebratory Wigilia events during the Christmas holiday.

More publicly, Polish Americans have made a distinctive contribution to local American cuisine, where many entrepreneurs and family cooks have made "pierogi" a household word. Many Illinois businesses, such as Kasia's Deli or Alexandra's Pierogi, founded by third-wave Polish immigrants who saw the opportunity for mass marketing this Polish staple, have a wide customer base that extends well beyond Polonia. The boiled pockets of dough are traditionally filled with meat, sauerkraut, mushrooms, cheese, or fruit and then baked or fried. In Illinois, the "Chicago Polish" or "Maxwell Street Polish" is a well-known street food initially offered by vendors in the Maxwell Street market, which began on Chicago's near West Side in the mid-1800s. This Polish kiełbasa served on a bun—often with grilled onions and mustard—is a staple of Illinois street food known across all ethnic groups. The Chicago-specific variation of kiełbasa is distinguished by its additional seasoning and its composition of both beef and pork. The Chicago Polish is a quintessential Chicago food.[31]

The preservation of Polish food traditions has continued in homes, in Polish civic organizations and Saturday schools, in parishes, and in the Polish press. Recipes were a regular feature in the *Dziennik Chicagoski*, with regular columns such as "Obiad Na Jutro" (Dinner for Tomorrow) that would provide menu ideas for a complete Polish meal. In February 1940, the paper recommended *Zupa Grzybowa* (mushroom soup), *Kotlety cielęce* (veal cutlets), *Kartofle* (potatoes), *Szpinak* (spinach), *Strudel z Jabłek* (strudel with apples), and *Kawa* (coffee) for dinner. In 1950, recipes *Na Kawkę Popułudniowa* (for afternoon coffee) included a streusel cake made with poppy seeds (*Ciasto z Kruszanką*). Contemporary cookbooks have documented Illinois's Polish cooking, Polonian restaurants, and bakeries for an English-speaking audience, such as Chef Michael Baruch's *The New Polish Cuisine* and Joseph W. Zurawski's *Polish Chicago: Our History, Our Recipes*. The newspapers, newsletters, and bulletins of churches, fraternal, organizations and the larger Polonia continue to preserve Polish recipes and traditions.

## Street Processions and Parades

From spring through fall, the streets of American Polonia are home to a series of sacred processions honoring the Virgin Mary and significant feasts of the Roman Catholic calendar. With the city streets temporarily blocked by police, parishioners perform an elaborate public display of faith, ethnic affiliation, and neighborhood identity. Curious onlookers gaze from cars, congregate on street corners, and lean off the porches of apartment buildings as parishioners sing, pray, and chant. Throughout their history, the Poles of Illinois have celebrated religious and civic holidays through public processions and parades.

One segment of Polish street processions are linked to religious events in the Roman Catholic calendar. The first of these processions takes place on Good Friday, the most somber day of the Christian year, as it commemorates the death of Christ. As evening falls, the parish recreates a kind of funeral cortege in the darkening streets. The crucifix borne by men of the parish is carried throughout the streets, followed by mourners. This funeral procession is accompanied by altar boys wielding special wooden clappers (*klekotki, grzechotki*), which rhythmically represent the nailing of Jesus to the Cross. The sorrowful mood is enhanced by such plaintive hymns as "*Ludu, mój luud*" and "*W krzyżu cierpienie."* These laments are not accompanied by musicians—which would be featured in other processions—as this would be considered vulgar at a time of such sorrow. The funeral cortege returns to the church and then inaugurates many hours of veneration at a tableau of Christ's Tomb called the *Bozy Grób.* Throughout Polonia, as in Poland, a life-size figure of Christ lying in his tomb is widely visited by the faithful, especially on Holy Saturday. Each parish creates an artful display of Christ's dead body, flowers, candles, fabrics, and a monstrance exposing the Blessed Sacrament. On Good Friday, many Polish parishes in Illinois have historically dramatized the Lord's Passion and reenacted the Stations of the Cross.

Another major procession in Polonia that is celebrated with great pomp and solemnity is Corpus Christi (*Boże Ciało*), which commemorates the institution of the Holy Eucharist. The important rituals that form the core of Polish Roman Catholic Corpus Christi devotions are the Corpus Christi Altars (*Bozy Domek*) and the Processions (*Procesja*). For this event, the entire parish assembles in finest dress. Often children in First Communion attire precede the Blessed Sacrament, dropping rose petals or petals of another flower to create a carpet for the approaching Eucharist. Altar boys, clergy, prominent citizens with guild and society banners of silk, and others process. The Holy Eucharist is transported in a processional monstrance, carried by the priest or bishop. The monstrance is further protected by an embroidered silk canopy held by four posts, which is borne by parishioners or altar servers. Publicly proclaiming and reaffirming their devotion to the Holy Eucharist, the entire congregation walks through the neighborhood to the sound of bells and voices singing sacred hymns. The procession then walks and sings its way to the first of the altars. There the Blessed Sacrament rests while the assembled faithful kneel to pray and sing in adoration of the Holy Eucharist. The procession then continues on in the same manner to the other altars. Central to the feast is the building and decorating of four special altars away from the confines of the church building. Decorated with statues, holy pictures, cloth, and flowers, these usually resemble small chapels. Traditionally, these are erected at four centers of a Polish town square, four points in a village, or four homes in a Polish American neighborhood.

Molded in the traditions, iconography, languages, and religious vernacular of Polish ancestors, these events function as acts of cultural identification and preservation for the Poles of Illinois. Religious processions are dramatic demonstrations and confirmations of Polish Catholic identity organized around the display of a central religious icon. Anthropologists argue that these processions not only express preexisting community affiliations but also represent collective experiences that create a heightened sense of community belonging in Polonia.

In addition to religious processions, the Poles of Illinois have long celebrated their civic and ethnic pride in secular parades. Numerous events have marked Polish pride and heritage in large displays on Poland's May 3 Constitution Day and Pułaski Day. Kazimierz Pułaski, who is a famous freedom fighter in both Poland and the United States, has been particularly celebrated in Illinois, where a main street in Chicago was named for him in 1935 and a public holiday in his honor is celebrated on the first Monday of every March. Floats, bands, Polish schools, dance groups, civic organizations, and politicians have been part of these celebrations for well over a century, allowing the larger community to see Polish American identity affirmed and acclaimed.

Perhaps the most famous Polish parade in Illinois occurred on October 7, 1893, in conjunction with the Chicago's Columbian Exhibition. Tens of thousands of the city's Polish Americans from fraternal societies, parishes, and community groups marched through downtown Chicago. The parade was seen by hundreds of thousands of spectators and greeted by the mayor and prominent city officials. At the heart of the parade were sixteen elaborate floats illustrating major themes and events in Polish history and culture. Around them massed ranks of Polish societies dressed in uniforms and other fine clothes.[32]

The May 3 Parade for Polish Constitution Day was first celebrated in Chicago in 1892 as a commemoration of the

Young woman wearing a historic dress for the Polish exhibition float at the Columbian Exhibition and World's Fair, Chicago, 1893. The exhibition provided a brief opportunity for Illinois's Polish immigrants to highlight their history and culture before an international audience. Courtesy of Polish Museum of America Archives.

ratification of Poland's constitution of 1791. The parade continues to the present day with a large event in downtown Chicago. The Association of Polish Clubs organizes the event, which is locally televised.

In both in formal and informal settings, the arts and culture provided creative expression for Illinois Polonia. During the first several decades of Polish settlement, artistic and cultural endeavors existed mainly within Polonia and for Poles themselves. Churches, parish halls, homes, and saloons were the main venues for artistic expression. Internationally known performers like Paderewski helped to bring some awareness of the richness of Polish culture to the larger community but also signaled to Poles that their culture could be a bridge beyond the bounds of the parish-community. Even though Catholic parishes were strictly divided by ethnicity, artists such as Sister Mary Stansia were also able to go beyond the confines of Polonia due to their clerical status. In 1927, Stansia was commissioned to execute a series of paintings for the Stations of the Cross at the German and Irish parish of St. Margaret of Scotland in South Chicago.[33] While Poles would not have felt welcome in the parish, her work was seen as that of a member of her religious order rather than as a member of a rival ethnic group. In the years following World War I, an increasing number of Polish American artists and performers successfully ventured beyond Polonia, though their work did not necessarily reflect their culture. Folk dancing by contrast was an acceptable "Polish" art that could transcend the community even though it was largely developed just prior to the Second World War. Illinois's Polish and Polish American artists, actors, and musicians would build on this legacy and gradually find greater acceptance and prominence.

# 8

# PO WOJNIE: POLES IN ILLINOIS DURING THE COLD WAR ERA

On September 1, 1939, Adolf Hitler launched the full might of Nazi Germany against Poland, beginning the Second World War in Europe. On September 17, Hitler's communist ally, Josef Stalin, attacked Poland from the east. Despite ferocious resistance, Poland, in the space of five weeks and after only twenty-one years of freedom, was partitioned by two of the most murderous dictatorships the world had yet known. The country was the scene of brutal fighting and equally brutal occupation for over five years. Polish underground resistance forces relentlessly struck back at the invaders, and, in 1941, the Nazis and their erstwhile Soviet allies went to war against each other. Hitler's genocidal policies virtually wiped out Poland's ancient Jewish community, and his regime murdered millions of Polish gentiles, while Stalin deported large numbers of Poles to the gulags and murdered many of Poland's best and brightest leaders.

For Poles in Illinois, the fate of the homeland again rose to the fore. Despite the lingering impact of the Depression, Polish communities across the state again raised funds for civilian relief and aid for the Polish forces in exile as they fought alongside the Allies in France, England, Norway, Africa, and Italy. Although relatively few of the state's Polish men of military age were non-citizens and thus eligible to join a foreign army), some two thousand Poles from Illinois and other states volunteered for the Polish army, air force, and navy based in England.[1] By 1940, Polish organizations from Illinois had equipped a small fleet of ambulances for the Polish army in the west and donated at least $200,000 for Polish relief.[2] By the war's end, American Polonia would raise $1.6 million for Polish relief.[3] Polish organizations lobbied the U.S. government on Poland's behalf, including the new Polish American Congress, an umbrella group representing most major Polish American organizations founded in 1944 and naturally headquartered in Chicago.

As America entered the war in December 1941 following the Japanese attack on Pearl Harbor, Poles responded to the call of America's armed forces in massive numbers. In addition to other eastern and southern European Americans, there was an unusually large percentage of young Polish men of military age, thanks to the "baby boom" years of 1916 to 1925. A survey taken in 1944 showed that as much as 40 percent of members of some Polish parishes were in the armed services.[4]

The war had a tremendous impact on Polish communities in Illinois. The large cohort of young men and women who joined the armed services had transformative experiences outside the confines of family and parish. The postwar years would open new opportunities for some. They also saw the arrival of a new wave of Polish immigrants, victims of Nazi and communist terror and veterans of the Polish armed forces who were forced into exile by the communist takeover of their country.

### War and Its Impact

For Polish communities, the experience of World War II outweighed every other conflict due to its duration, the sheer number

Polski Fundusz Ratunkowy

Polish Relief Fund

LEGION MŁODYCH POLEK

**Your donation will save a starving war victim**

Flyer for Polish Relief Fund, Legion of Young Polish Women (Legion Młodych Polek), Chicago, circa 1940. Flyers like these were used to raise money for Polish refugees displaced by Nazi and Soviet terror. Courtesy of the Women and Leadership Archives, Loyola University Chicago, Legion of Young Polish Women Collection.

of Polish Americans involved, and the central place of Poland's tragedy in the war's history. Every single Polish parish had its own service flag, with a blue star for each parishioner in service and a gold star for each member killed. Blue Star and Gold Star Mothers clubs formed in many parishes to support families of service members and continued to be important organizations long after the war had ended. During the war, men too old to serve almost invariably worked in factories to produce war material. Retired workers were called back to their factories to assist and to train new hires. They were joined in factories and farms by large numbers of women, both married and single, who filled all the gaps left behind by men in the armed services. Civilians not engaged in war-related work often volunteered in other ways, including joining the Red Cross or the United Service Organizations (USO). Young women members of the Polish Roman Catholic Union of America (PRCUA) opened and ran a Polish American USO club in Chicago for the many servicemen passing through the city on the way to training or deployment.[5]

The war cemented an enduring patriotism for America throughout the state's Polish communities. They would no longer see themselves as "newcomers" but as a vital part—regardless of how others saw them or how economically or socially marginalized they were—of the very fabric of the country that their families journeyed to a generation before. Nothing demonstrated this better than the attention accorded to Illinois Poles who had distinguished themselves in combat. In 1942, Marine Leo Lopacinski, born in Argo-Summit, was honored with a citywide parade after he was credited with killing thirty-six Japanese soldiers on Guadalcanal. Still limping from wounds suffered in the battle, the quiet young marine was the star attraction as the mayor closed schools and city offices to allow people to attend the parade.[6] Two Poles from Chicago were posthumously awarded the Congressional Medal of Honor, the nation's highest decoration for valor. Army private Edward Moskala received the medal for defending and rescuing wounded comrades on Okinawa in 1945. When marine private Frank Witek's unit was ambushed on Guam in August 1944, the Chicago man launched a lone counterattack that destroyed the enemy position and covered the withdrawal of his comrades. He then remained behind to rescue a wounded Marine. Later, he singlehandedly attacked and destroyed a Japanese strongpoint before being killed.[7] Witek's mother, Nora, accepted her son's medal from Marine Corps commandant general Alexander Vandergriff at Soldier Field on "I Am an American Day" with fifty thousand fellow Chicagoans in attendance.[8]

Commemorating the war, remembering the veterans, the fallen, and their families, became a central part of the collective memory of virtually all Polish communities in the state. St. James Parish in Chicago commissioned a memorial painting with four scenes from the war. The first was the storming of the Nazi fortress of Monte Cassino by soldiers of the Polish Second Corps. The second was the raising of the flag on Iwo Jima by a party of Marines led by a Slovak American sergeant, Michael Strank. The third was the sinking of the German battleship *Bismarck*, which had eluded Allied forces until it was spotted and attacked by the Polish destroyer *Piorun*. The fourth showed American forces seizing the bridge over the Rhine at Remagen, Germany, a coup that allowed the Allies to break the last line of Nazi defense. The first American soldier to cross the bridge had been Sergeant Alexander Drabnik, the son of Polish immigrants from Toledo, Ohio.[9] The memorial thus linked the service of Polish Americans in both the Pacific and European theaters with the larger national narrative of the war and the role of the Polish armed forces (some of whose veterans had also joined the parish). The names of parishioners killed in the conflict were often enshrined in plaques in the church as well as in parish history books.[10]

### Polish American Congress

Given Chicago's centrality to American Polonia, it was understandable that the city would be at the heart of efforts to aid the cause of Poland both during and after the war. In 1944, efforts to form a broad coalition of Polish American organizations bore fruit in the creation of the Polish American Congress (PAC). The PAC's first task was to lobby the U.S. government to support a restoration of Polish independence based on the country's prewar boundaries and without Soviet intervention in the country's internal affairs. By early 1945, following the Yalta Conference, it was clear that this effort had failed due to the willingness of American and British leaders to give the Soviets a free hand in postwar east-central Europe. Despite this, the PAC continued to advocate on behalf of a free Poland and to provide assistance to Polish refugees and military personnel in the west following the end of hostilities against Germany.[11] This initial focus on Polish affairs would be supplemented by actions on behalf of the Polish community in the United States, especially from the 1960s to the 1980s. During this period, as an umbrella organization representing the major Polish organizations in the United States, it served as the most visible agent of the Polish community before national and international audiences until the end of the Cold War. Although the PAC had chapters throughout the country and for many years maintained an office in Washington, DC, the structure of the organization made Chicago its logical headquarters. The PAC was made up of constituent organizations rather than individual members.[12] Thus, the president of the PAC was also the head of the Polish National Alliance (PNA), the largest single fraternal Polonia organization, while its vice president was president of the Polish Women's Alliance and its treasurer headed the PRCUA. The organization focused on national and international affairs, while organizing locally within Illinois was handled by the Illinois chapter of the PAC, one of the original and enduring chapters of the congress.[13]

## Refugees

The twin invasions of Poland and the subsequent occupations by Nazi and Soviet forces resulted in unprecedented human catastrophe. Millions were killed by the occupiers, and millions more were displaced from their homes and deported to concentration and slave labor camps. Families were broken apart, and countless children were orphaned or involuntarily separated from their kin. In 1939 and 1940, Stalin ordered the mass deportation of Poles from the regions of eastern Poland that he controlled. The communists sent hundreds of thousands of Poles in the dead of winter to gulags in Siberia and northern Russia where many were executed, starved, tortured, or worked to death. With the German invasion of the USSR in 1941, the Polish survivors were allowed to leave the camps, and those that were able made their way out of the Soviet Union via Iran. Men of military age joined the Polish army in the west, but tens of thousands of civilians, many of them suffering from disease, malnutrition, and months of brutal mistreatment, were displaced to refugee camps in the Middle East, Africa, and India. One group, with a large number of orphaned children, was sent to Mexico when the government there agreed to host them at Colonia Santa Rosa. Poles from Chicago made a special effort to assist the refugees in Mexico. The Women's Department of the PRCUA visited the camp several times, bringing care packages with clothes, books, food, and school supplies. Polish Felician Sisters from Illinois went to Santa Rosa to open a school for the Polish orphans. After years of neglect and minimal adult attention, many of the children suffered from post-traumatic stress, often acting out of control. Tadeusz Pieczko, who had been separated from his parents in Russia, recalled,

> The orphanage was in a state of total chaos. There was no discipline, and if any rules existed they were completely ignored. . . . Given this state of affairs, it was decided to send for the Felician Sisters from Chicago to look after us. At first we did not like this. . . . One Sunday we were ordered to go to church to greet the nuns. They arrived in our settlement the previous day so they knew what a wild bunch we were. As they entered the church, the crowd parted to let them through and some of the kids quietly hissed and booed. This was meant to give them a taste of what to expect. These nuns were small in stature but tough and they shaped us up in no time. . . . Before the nuns came, reading materials were very scarce. Now there was a library stocked with Polish books. I read, or tried to read, anything I could get my hands on.[14]

By late 1940, the U.S. government began to allow some of the refugees to settle in the United States, and many came to Chicago.

Polish American nurses in Chicago making bandages during World War II. Courtesy of Immigration History Research Center Archives, University of Minnesota.

Some of the refugees found jobs, and those who did not were supported by Polish organizations. Groups of orphans were sponsored by associations such as the PNA to come to Chicago. In some cases, young people were given scholarships to attend high school in Chicago. Children whose parents could not be located were sent to orphanages run by Polish religious orders, including one hundred children who went to St. Hedwig orphanage in Niles.[15]

As the war ended, governments, the Red Cross, and churches and private welfare agencies struggled to resolve the unprecedented refugee problem, spending years trying to do so. With the communist takeover of Poland, many Poles who had been deported to Germany were unable to return. Likewise, veterans of the Polish armed forces who had fought alongside the Allies in every campaign, as well as members of the underground Polish Home Army, which had resisted the Nazis during the occupation, faced persecution, arrest, torture, and execution in socialist Poland. With widespread devastation in Europe and the threat of a postwar economic downturn in America, few governments were interested in accepting this mass of people who were termed "Displaced Persons" or DPs. In many cases, Polish and other refugees were not allowed to resettle until 1948. In America, an intense lobbying effort by Jewish, Catholic, and Polish organizations eventually resulted in the United States accepting some of the refugees. Polish organizations in Chicago such as the PNA and the PAC were at the forefront, and many later acted as sponsors for Polish refugees. Between 1948 and 1953, between 110,000 and 155,000 Polish DPs came to the United States along with about 10,000 veterans of the Polish armed forces.[16] A large number would ultimately settle in the greater Chicago area.

Many Polish Americans gave selflessly of their time and money to help the newcomers. Especially noteworthy was the work of Wanda Rozmarek, the wife of PAC and PNA president Charles Rozmarek. One historian noted,

Over a period of four years, Wanda Rozmarek devoted all of her time and energy to the resettlement cause. She met DPs personally at the train stations at all times of the day and night, drove them around the city to their sponsors, cooked for them, ran errands, and actively looked for jobs [for them]. Rozmarek's house accepted about four hundred DP families for a temporary stay. Her private phone number was passed around among DPs waiting for resettlement in Germany. All the expenses Wanda Rozmarek covered herself; and on top of this, she and her husband donated two thousand dollars to DP funds.[17]

Refugees fortunate enough to have relatives in Illinois had a somewhat easier time transitioning to their new lives. Wesley Adamczyk's father had been executed along with other Polish officers by Stalin's NKVD in 1940, and his mother had died from exhaustion, hunger, and mistreatment in Iran, leaving him, his sister, and his older brother without parents. In 1949, he was allowed to join his aunt and uncle in Chicago, which seemed like coming to a second home. After years in refugee camps, Chicago's abundance with its cars, lights, stores, and even air conditioning was stunning: "I could hardly take it all in."[18]

For other refugees, the transition to a new life was hard, and even Illinois's large Polish community did not always seem fully welcoming. New arrivals were unused to the hybridized culture and language of their new home. Those from educated backgrounds in Europe looked with disdain on the mass of working-class Polish Americans. For their part, Polish Americans failed to realize fully the extent of the trauma and dislocation felt by the new arrivals. In some instances, the horrors some of the refugees had experienced seemed too fantastical to believe. While Poles from Europe were initially welcomed, some refugees needed more than just a set of clothes and a hot meal, and over time, some of the DPs were viewed as lazy and ungrateful for the help extended to them.

Refugees faced significant discrimination. Antonette Brusik Metelski recalled,

> I have to say that in the eyes of the American people, we looked like poor, homeless, Polish immigrants. . . . It was so difficult to rent a room or small apartment especially with a child. The truth is, we had no money, all we needed was a spoon and plate to eat from and a bed to sleep in. [W]hat kept us going was hope and confidence, because we didn't fear any tyranny and we appreciated our freedom. . . . It was those times that I wish I had someone to talk to and a shoulder to cry on. It was very difficult to get decent paying job. We had to wait five years to get citizenship papers. Discriminations were quite obvious, not only in housing, but in work too.[19]

Poet John Guzlowski, whose parents survived Nazi slave labor camps, came to Chicago as a child:

We eventually settled in an immigrant neighborhood around Humbolt Park. . . . There I met Jewish hardware-store clerks with Auschwitz tattoos on their wrists, Polish cavalry officers who still mourned for their dead horses, and women who had walked from Siberia to Iran to escape the Russians.

It was a tough neighborhood, where I grew up, and our lives were hard: America then—like now—didn't much want to see a lot of immigrants coming over and taking American jobs, sharing apartments with two or three other immigrants families, getting into the trouble immigrants get into. We were regarded as Polacks—dirty, dumb, lazy, dishonest, immoral, licentious, drunken Polacks.

I felt hobbled by being a Polack and a DP—a Displaced Person. It was a hard karma.[20]

In the face of hardships and the trauma they had experienced, the new Polish immigrants in Illinois persevered. Like earlier generations of arrivals, they created and joined organizations, clubs, and groups. They usually joined existing Polish parishes and religious orders but formed a host of new organizations reflecting their own interests, backgrounds, and concerns.[21] Among the most prominent of these were groups belonging to Stowarzysze-nie Polskich Kombatantów (SPK or the Association of Polish Combatants), as well as other groups representing Polish veterans, many of which were associated with individual combat units. For example, Chicago had organizations representing the 5th Borderlands Rifle Division (veterans of the Italian campaign), the 1st Armored Division (veterans of battles in Normandy, Holland, and Germany), and the National Armed Forces (a right-wing resistance movement that had fought both Nazis and communists). In addition, there were groups formed from refugees from the towns and regions of eastern Poland given to the Soviet Union in 1945, such Wilno (now Vilnius, Lithuania), Lwów (now Lviv, Ukraine), and Wołyn (Volhynia). For the children of these new immigrants, a new and very active scouting organization, Związek Harcerstwa Polskiego w Chicago (Polish Scouting Alliance in Chicago), was founded in 1949.[22]

One of the most significant institutions developed by the new immigrants was Polish Saturday schools. Having spent a great deal of time in refugee camps in Europe, Polish émigrés were already used to creating and operating their own schools for children who had been caught up in the refugee crisis as well as those born to refugee parents. Early schools were ad hoc affairs, but in 1951 the Circle of Teachers and Students of Polish Schools in Exile was founded in Chicago, and by 1959 over seven hundred students were enrolled in two schools. By the 1960s and 1970s, as Poles increasingly moved to the suburbs, the number of Saturday schools grew, so that by the early 1980s there were fifteen schools in operation in and around Chicago with three thousand students each year. The majority of the students were children of Polish immigrants, but classes were open to any students aged five to nineteen, and classes for non-Polish speakers were also held. Although quite a few students knew at least some Polish, the schools helped to develop reading and writing skills, and they also taught Polish history and culture. Since most of the schools were associated with Catholic parishes, they usually offered catechesis and sacramental preparation in Polish as well.[23]

As time went on, the shared experience of living in Illinois brought the existing Polish communities closer to the new arrivals. One scholar noted that "cooperation between the organizations of Old Polonia and the New Emigration grew slowly, but steadily, as they often shared common space and resources. Observances of national holidays became an especially fruitful common ground. . . . Special gestures of good will further fostered the cooperative spirit prevalent in many localities. For instance, Chicago's Legion Młodych Polek (Legion of Young Polish Women), which distinguished itself in its work for Polish refugees both during the war and the resettlement, funded a banner for Chicago's Armia Krajowa [Home Army veterans] in 1950."[24] Cooperation and friendships emerged on a personal level as well. Mary Janka noted that her neighbor, a DP, helped her retain her fluency in Polish: "Thank God. . . . She almost forces me to speak Polish to her and I enjoy it otherwise I think I'd forget a lot of it."[25]

### Changes in the City

Although significant divisions had formed between the new arrivals and the state's existing Polish American communities, Polish institutions in Illinois, in some respects, were at the height of their powers in the years following the war. Membership in core Polish parishes remained strong, and most parochial schools experienced growing enrollments, though few regained the numbers they had seen during the boom years of early 1920s (see appendix 2). Yet significant developments inside and outside Polonia were bringing major changes to Polish communities. Three interlocking developments began to disrupt the coherence of the parish-communities. The first was growing prosperity and economic opportunities for English-speaking children and grandchildren of Polish immigrants, which drew young people out of the old neighborhoods and into suburban areas, even to places as far afield as Arizona or Florida. The second was so-called urban renewal and freeway construction projects, which physically disrupted Polish neighborhoods, reduced existing housing stock, and threatened small businesses and other institutions. The third was increasing ethnic and racial tension as Chicago's African American population grew dramatically due a new wave of migration, putting pressure on working-class ethnic neighborhoods and their institutions.

The experience of the war—especially for veterans—opened up new possibilities. The GI Bill allowed some veterans to attend college who otherwise would not have had the opportunity. It also allowed veterans easier access to home and business loans. While

Members of the Legion of Young Polish Women meeting with servicewomen of the American forces and the Polish armed forces in exile during World War II. Courtesy of the Women and Leadership Archives, Loyola University Chicago, Legion of Young Polish Women Collection.

many young people stayed within the communities in which they were born, others moved out. This movement was abetted by a strong postwar economy and both blue- and white-collar jobs that provided stable or growing income. Polish settlement in Chicago expanded further into suburban areas. North Side Polish communities, for example, gradually moved north and west. The new areas where Poles settled were often heavily Polish American, but the new parishes they joined were territorial rather than ethnic, and the new communities rarely sustained the same density of Polish institutions that had characterized the original core communities. In addition, existing Polish institutions often found themselves under pressure to reduce the use of the Polish language, as the younger generation felt more comfortable speaking English. Parents who spoke Polish as their first language perceived heavily accented English as a barrier to their children's future success and began to pressure parochial schools to drop bilingual curricula. Although many of the nuns teaching in these schools sought to retain Polish instruction, all-English curricula were increasingly the norm by the mid-1950s.

Pressure to reduce the use of Polish came from above as well as from below. The non-Polish bishops of the Catholic Church and the increasingly numerous and influential corps of lay employees of the dioceses had always viewed national or ethnic parishes with trepidation, and they disliked the independent nature of the informal circle of Polish clergy that had run Polonia's parish-community system in Chicago during the first half of the twentieth century. Although leaders like Chicago auxiliary bishop Alfred Abramowicz kept strong connections to the Polish community, there was little interest in ministering to Polish-speaking Catholics by the 1960s among most of his fellow bishops. Following the changes in the Catholic liturgy after the Vatican II Council, American Catholic reformers sought to discourage or eliminate many of the traditional devotions and paraliturgical practices that had sustained Polish American culture and language at the parish level (even though the Vatican II Council neither forbid nor discouraged such practices).

Although use of Polish declined, it did not disappear. It remained strong and even increased in some core parishes. Holy Trinity, one of the first Polish parishes in the state, became a center for pastoral care to new immigrants, and there Polish was spoken more frequently, especially in 1980s.[26] A survey of Polish parishes in 1969 showed that inner-city parishes that had not been the victims of urban renewal or highway construction retained a relatively robust Polish culture, including weekly Polish Masses, sacraments, and other ministries. Nevertheless, the survey also indicated an aging population in the core parishes, and many pastors were skeptical about the possibility that their parishes would need Polish-speaking clergy a decade hence. A number of territorial parishes that had become heavily Polish due to post-war migration contained younger populations, but these offered limited ministry in Polish. With few exceptions, parishes with the youngest populations used Polish the least, a situation that would not change until the 1980s and 1990s (table 8.1).[27]

Outmigration from Polish parish-communities was evident by the 1950s. The author of the seventy-fifth-anniversary history of St. Josephat Parish in 1959 was unusually blunt: "Since World War II [the] Lake View neighborhood has changed much of its face. More factories were opened, with the result that many of the fine people have moved to nicer localities and suburbs (we hate to lose them!!), and the so-called 'white trash' element replaced it. The number of families in the parish has greatly dwindled. Within recent years the decline was slowly (perhaps imperceptibly) accomplished."[28]

Even more damaging was the process of urban renewal and highway construction, which, while benefitting downtown Chicago, damaged functional working-class neighborhoods, including those of African Americans and eastern and southern European groups. New eminent domain laws allowed the city to condemn and buy out private property before giving it to developers or taking it for public projects. Polish neighborhoods were especially hard hit by highway construction, and rumors abounded that the city was targeting the Polish communities and other marginal groups. Major expressways, such as the Kennedy, cut through the heart of core parish-communities, destroying or reducing the value of housing stock, furthering out migration, and often bringing blight in its wake. The history of St. Hedwig Parish noted that "the new expressway cut through the heart of the parish and forced hundreds of parishioners to move to other parts of the city. The decline of parishioners was evident. St. Hedwig lost its standing as one of the largest parishes in the Archdiocese. . . . School enrollment dropped from 1300 students to 700 students. This was the beginning of a changing era."[29] The historian of St.

Table 8.1. Survey of Select Polish Roman Catholic Parishes, Illinois, 1969

| Parish | City | 1960 | | 1969 | | Polish Masses (per week) | Parishioners over age 50 (%) |
|---|---|---|---|---|---|---|---|
| | | Members | Polish | Members | Polish | | |
| Sts. Peter and Paul | Chicago | 1,300 | 1,040 | 1,300 | 1,040 | 4 | 40 |
| St. Valentine | Chicago | 400 | 325 | 300 | 250 | 4 | 50 |
| Our Lady of Częstochowa | Cicero | 1,500 | 1,450 | 1,400 | 1,350 | 2 | 50 |
| St. William | Chicago | 3,200 | 1,000 | 3,200 | 1,000 | 0 | 25 |
| OL Queen of Heaven | Elmhurst | na | na | 600 | 20 | 0 | 20 |
| St. Francis of Assisi | Chicago | 1,000 | 950 | 1,200 | 1,000 | 4 | 50 |
| St. Joseph | Chicago | 1,800 | 1,750 | 1,600 | 1,500 | 4 | 70 |
| St. Camillus | Chicago | 1,000 | 950 | 1,500 | 1,300 | 4 | 25 |
| Holy Family | Oglesby | 680 | 65 | 780 | 60 | 0 | na |
| Our Lady of the Snows | Chicago | 1,200 | 600 | 1,200 | 600 | 0 | 10 |
| St. Stanislaus | Posen | 700 | 650 | 1,050 | 750 | 4 | 10 |
| Our Lady of Knock | Calumet City | 900 | 500 | 1,200 | 700 | 0 | 5 |
| St. John of God | Chicago | 2,200 | 2,178 | 2,000 | 1,980 | 4 | 20 |
| St. Casimir | Streator | 100 | 96 | 125 | 100 | 0 | 20 |
| St. Pancratius | Chicago | 1,500 | 1,350 | 1,350 | 1,200 | 4 | 25 |
| St. Mary Magdalene | Chicago | 1,643 | 1,600 | 1,500 | 1,500 | 4 | 34 |
| Blessed Agnes | Chicago | 1,700 | 600 | 1,500 | 600 | 0 | 30 |
| St. Roman | Chicago | 2,100 | 1,110 | 1,400 | 560 | 2 | 35 |
| St. Turibius | Chicago | 2,300 | 1,200 | 2,600 | 1,110 | 2 | 25 |
| St. Barbara | Scheller | 65 | 60 | 65 | 60 | 4 | 60 |
| St. Ladislaus | Chicago | 1,800 | 1,600 | 1,800 | 1,600 | 2 | 30 |

*Source:* "Preliminary Study of the Use of Polish, Orchard Lake Center for Polish Studies and Culture, Orchard Lake, Mich.," Central Archives of Polonia, Orchard Lake Schools, Orchard Lake, Mich.

Boniface echoed this sentiment: "With the coming of the Kennedy Expressway many of the parishioners were forced to leave the area."[30] Nicolas Leffner, who had been involved in North Side real estate since the 1937, noted, "The Poles are moving out. The majority of the Poles moved when they were building the Kennedy Expressway . . . because they took the land [and] properties down for the highway. . . . That ran right through the Polish section up here."[31]

The loss of manufacturing jobs also resulted in a decline in some Polish communities. East St. Louis underwent deindustrialization in the 1970s, and the Polish community faded as younger people moved out and African Americans moved in; however, this latter group did not enjoy the same employment opportunities as earlier residents did, as jobs left the area. The Polish parish there was forced to consolidate in 1979, eliminating the place where parishioners gathered and spoke Polish together.[32]

### Poles and Blacks in Chicago

One of the most complex and misunderstood aspects of Polonia's story in the decades after the war was the often tense relationship with Chicago's growing black population. African Americans had a modest presence in the city until the 1910s when the first major

Girl Guides belonging to the Związek Harcerstwa Polskiego (ZHP, or Polish Scout and Guide Association) abroad, on parade in Chicago, early 1950s. The children of post–World War II émigrés carried on the traditions of prewar Polish scouts and guides in their new homeland. Courtesy of Immigration History Research Center Archives, University of Minnesota.

migration from the rural South began (which brought not only blacks but also a considerable number of poorer whites). The end of mass immigration from Europe and industry's steady demand for labor in the 1920s resulted in a second wave of black migration to Chicago, while World War II and the 1950s increased the African American presence even more. Initially, Poles and African Americans had only limited interaction. Poles stayed out of the 1919 Chicago race riot, despite some Polish neighborhoods being attacked by Irish gangs seeking to incite Poles to join the mayhem. Polish participation in other race riots in Illinois was negligible. Polish newspapers and community leaders frequently denounced violence against blacks.[33] At the same time, however, there had often been tension between Poles and blacks over labor disputes and strikebreaking.[34] The Lamont Canal Strike Massacre and use of African Americans to break strikes in which Poles were among the greatest number of participants were long remembered in Polonia. Oddly enough to modern eyes, this led Poles to view African Americans as tools of the factory owners and the city's white Anglo-Protestant elite. To this image were added stereotypes picked up from the deep racial divisions in American society.

By the 1940s, the growing incorporation of blacks into unions muted conflicts over job competition and strikebreaking, but they did not completely disappear. Instead, new clashes emerged over housing and urban space, often abetted by cynical politicians and industrialists who often played different groups against each other.[35] As Chicago's black population grew, many areas once home to working-class whites slowly became African American neighborhoods, as groups like the Irish and Germans moved out. Although some Poles moved beyond the old neighborhoods, Poles were far more likely to remain in their core communities than other "white ethnics" were, a condition reinforced by postwar immigration and by the high level of home ownership in many Polish enclaves. For Poles, particularly older immigrants, movement to suburbs was not always an option since these locations were often more expensive, and in some cases restrictive housing covenants aimed at Poles and other eastern and southern European remained in force until the early 1970s. Working-class immigrants and their children had poured a lifetime of resources earned through tough factory jobs into their homes, and they could not easily sell that property and move. In addition, rebuilding ethnic institutions at the same density, which had given immigrant life its meaning and shape, was often impossible in the new suburban locations.

The intensively internal focus of Polish communities and their institutions also made it hard for them to adapt as neighborhoods underwent cultural and racial change. Created for an era in which ethnic groups fenced each other out, Polish institutions struggled in ethnically mixed neighborhoods and often were not able to represent Poles effectively to other groups or public institutions, such as the city housing authority.[36] The signal failure of Chicago's Polish leaders to build political coalitions across ethnic lines left the community adrift in the face of racial conflict and an era in which keeping African Americans at arm's length was viewed in the most negative terms by society at large. Poles were increasingly stereotyped by elite opinion makers as racist "hard hats."

The result was a festering conflict over urban spaces that often took on ugly racial overtones. Polish neighborhoods felt themselves under siege, especially as crime rates rose and riots became regular stories in national news. Poles viewed urban elites as taking the part of blacks, and they frequently pointed to politicians and liberal elites who lived in all-white neighborhoods while criticizing Poles as racists. African Americans, for their part, viewed Poles in light of the centuries of racial discrimination and abuse they had experienced. Poles seemed no different from other whites who had constantly sought to restrict their housing options and keep them out of better employment. As white elites used their wealth and status to insulate themselves from the consequences of rapid urban change, blacks increasingly encountered Poles and other eastern and southern Europeans who became a proxy for white racism. Many Poles deeply resented Anglo elites. In 1963, Andrzej Filipowski wrote to *Ameryka-Echo*:

> To us, the white race, it is not about skin color [but] the Person! What great difference is there between a Japanese person and—a Negro person? A Japanese in dirty shoes will not enter into a room. . . . But a Negro? God have mercy! . . . Here our authorities have to . . . teach them to how they are to live, like people, give schooling, hygiene, human custom, and only then call for uniting with whites. . . . I have taken a voice in this matter because I see so much lying about unity and coming together. All the higher-ups are crying to the heavens: Unite! Out with segregation! But look more closely at these

great Gentlemen. . . . Every Senator, Congressman, Prosecutor, Judge flees far from Negroes, does not want to reside in Negro districts, does not want to invite Negroes as friends, does not want to give their—daughters in marriage to Negroes. . . . I know personally such Gentlemen who also speak about equality but they themselves sold their homes to Negroes and fled far to the west of Chicago so as not to see them.[37]

While Polish voters consistently rejected candidates like George Wallace, their attitudes toward blacks hardened into outright racism in many cases. After the assassination of Dr. Martin Luther King Jr., when flags across the country were lowered to half-staff in mourning, the head of a Chicago Polish homeowner's association along with about fifty supporters went to a local school and raised the flag back to full staff while singing "America." The man was arrested, but the incident symbolized the intensity of the resentment felt in many Polish neighborhoods.[38]

## Polonia and the "New Ethnicity"

The civil rights and black power movements and the growing attention paid to racial and ethnic discrimination in America had a profound impact on Polish American communities in other ways. Poles had been long aware of the negative stereotypes held by those outside of their community. Informal but very real discrimination in employment and housing were widely recognized if rarely discussed in public, creating a defensive mentality among Polish Americans that was not lessened by the racial conflicts of the period. In the early 1970s, a study of the ethnicity and race of directors and officers of Chicago's largest publicly held companies showed that Poles, as well as Italians, Hispanics, and African Americans, were virtually nonexistent in the boardroom. While such results had been expected for blacks, the complete lack of progress for "white ethnic" groups like Poles surprised most observers.[39]

As Polish Americans moved into ethnically mixed suburbs and out of the cocoon of largely Polish neighborhoods and parishes, they encountered negative stereotypes more commonly, especially in schools and workplaces. The growing stigma attached to verbal expressions of racism among educated liberal-minded Americans—which the black power movement confronted most forcefully—ironically contributed to an increasing acceptance of anti-Polish bigotry. Racist jokes about blacks were recycled as "Polack jokes," and indeed the negative stereotype of Poles closely paralleled that of African Americans. Literary elites joined in, and authors like Nelson Algren, who wrote *Never Come Morning* and *The Man with the Golden Arm*, made a career picturing Poles as debased subhumans.[40] When celebrity Chicago interior designer and novelist Richard Himmel celebrated his birthday at his posh Northbrook summer home, he chose the theme "Polish picnic." According to the *Chicago Daily News*, Himmel's ultra-wealthy friends arrived in a U-Haul truck dressed in overalls and undershirts. "Polish presents" were distributed out of a garbage can. The story circulated widely in Polish communities across United States, painfully demonstrating how the country's elite viewed them.[41] In the past, Poles had responded to negative stereotypes by hunkering down in their parish-communities, but in the 1960s and 1970s, they began to respond publicly. Polish organizations like the Polish American Congress and the Chicago-based Polish American Guardian Society wrote letters, organized boycotts and held public protests against shows such as *Laugh-In* or the *Carol Burnett Show*, which regularly featured demeaning caricatures of Poles, while at the same time seeking to promote Polish contributions to American and world history, culture, and science as a counternarrative to the negative portrayals. These efforts slowly paid off, helped greatly by the election of Polish cardinal Karol Wojtyła as Pope John Paul II in 1978 and the subsequent rise of the Solidarity trade union movement in Poland. The celebration of America's bicentennial in 1976 also provided Polish Americans with the opportunity to highlight Polish contributions to American history.

The late 1960s and 1970s saw a revival of interest in ethnic heritage among many second- and third-generation descendants of immigrants, many of whom had become separated from their ancestral background thanks to economic and residential mobility. Poles in Illinois created new cultural organizations, and younger (often college-educated) people helped to sustain older groups. Folk dance and folk art, exhibits of Polish art, and interest in Polish literature and history were key parts of this cultural revival.[42]

The ethnic revival of the 1970s also sparked the creation of outdoor Polish festivals, the largest being the Taste of Polonia held annually since 1979 over the Labor Day weekend at the grounds of the Copernicus Center in Chicago. At summer's end, the festival offers four days of live entertainment, food vendors serving Polish cuisine, over thirty local and international bands playing a variety of genres, performances by ethnic dancers and musical groups, original arts and crafts, handiwork, imported items, and exhibits familiarizing festivalgoers with many aspects of Polish customs, culture, traditions, and language. It has grown to be the largest Polish festival in the country; visited by over thirty thousand people annually.

A special highlight in the history of Illinois Polonia was the massive celebration in 1979 for the visit of Pope John Paul II. The first Polish pope was welcomed to Chicago in October 1979 by thousands of people lining the route from O'Hare Airport to Milwaukee Avenue. During his stay, the pope visited St. Peter's Church in Chicago's Loop, Holy Name Cathedral, and Five Holy Martyrs Parish, where he celebrated an outdoor Mass in Polish. The central public event of the Holy Father's visit was the massive outdoor Mass in Chicago's Grant Park, with crowds estimated at over 1.2 million worshippers.

President of the Polish National Alliance and Polish American Congress, Al Mazewski (*left*); Alderman Roman Pucinski (*center*); and Congressman Frank Annunzio with booklets about the 1940 Katyn Forest Massacre, 1988. Poles in Chicago played an important role in informing the American public about the Soviet massacres and repression of Poles. Copelin Commercial Photographers, JPCC_02_0001_0004_0007_0038, James Parker Collection, Special Collections, University of Illinois at Chicago Library.

## "Solidarity" Immigrants and *Wakacjusze*

A small but steady trickle of immigrants left communist-controlled Poland during the 1960s and 1970s. Some were political dissidents, others economic immigrants. Poles were allowed to visit the United States and reunite with families, and many did. More than a few worked illegally while in the United States on tourist visas, and some ended up staying. Regular ship and later air travel between Poland and the United States made this process much easier. Illegal immigrants who came to work on tourist visas were known as *wakacjusze* (literally "vacationers"). Political repression and the bad state of Poland's socialist economy, which experienced a series of crises in 1968, 1973, and 1975–76, contributed to this phenomenon. The U.S. dollar became a widely used black market currency. A common joke in Poland was, "What is the same in Poland and in America? In America you can buy anything with dollars and nothing with *złoty*. In Poland it is the same." As one *wakacjusze* put it, "I arrived on Sunday [in Chicago] with a job waiting for me and by noon on Monday had earned a month's salary."[43]

In 1978, the election of Karol Cardinal Wojtyła of Kraków as Pope John Paul II sent shockwaves around the world and began the process of unraveling communist power in Poland and its neighbors. In Chicago, the news was greeted with joy and wonder. Emboldened by the first papal visit in 1979 and facing grim economic prospects, Polish workers in the summer of 1980 created the first independent trade union movement in the communist bloc: Solidarity. Solidarity's success at winning concessions from the government created a brief "springtime" of freedom in Poland, which was snuffed out by a brutal crackdown and the imposition of martial law in December 1982. As a result of the repression, a new wave of political emigrants left Poland for West. Many were dissidents active in Solidarity who were pressured by the government to leave as a way to undermine the movement. Approximately sixty thousand Poles came to the United States during the 1980s. As in times past, many came to Chicago; but unlike previous waves, the "Solidarity" immigrants spread themselves out across the country. Many were educated professionals, professors, engineers, and doctors. Chicago's large Polish community—and the fact that many émigrés had friends or relatives there—allowed newcomers to access networks of contacts in order to find jobs quickly. But those jobs were often blue-collar positions: janitors, house cleaners, construction workers, and home healthcare aides. While the newcomers did well financially, their new jobs rarely matched their skills and education. Over time, some of the immigrants, after improving their English and learning the intricacies of the American economy, were able to resume their previous occupations, but others never did so.

As the Polish economy continued to deteriorate throughout the 1980s, more Poles left their country to find opportunity elsewhere. While many went to Western Europe, America and Chicago again attracted a significant number. Far fewer new immigrants went to other parts of state, though some could be found in university towns such as Urbana-Champaign or Evanston. By the late 1980s and early 1990s, as communist rule finally imploded in Europe, Polish immigrants (both legal and illegal) helped make Chicago one of America's main gateways for immigrants once again. Unlike in previous waves, however, a significant number of Poles were *wakacjusze*. By 1992, an estimated 27 percent of all illegal immigrants in Chicago were Poles.[44] The new arrivals experienced both the advantages and hardships of immigration and work that earlier generations of immigrants had known, albeit in less grueling circumstances. One newspaper in southern Poland commented on residents who had gone to Chicago to work and returned home with money in their pockets: "It would not be exaggerating to say that several thousand houses and as many cars in Podhale, Tarnów, Kraków, and tens of other places are a result of this cleaning business [in Chicago] . . . Iwona, a young Polish wife and school teacher from Nowy Targ, bought her Toyota with the money she earned cleaning floors, porches, and restrooms." Yet Chicago, the newspaper warned in another article, was no bed of roses: "The tempo of work is high and you do not have time for cultural activities; and so as these needs disappear the people become flat and primitive. They are able only to count their dollars. . . . Of course, they have a car and savings in the bank. However, they do not have any time to spend this money because they spend all their time working."[45]

Although Chicago remained the first stop for many recent arrivals in the 1980s and 1990s, the newest wave of Poles also found homes in the suburbs, sometimes coming directly to join relatives or to take jobs, or as a secondary move after being in the country for a period. One scholar noted, "The number of new arrivals listing a suburban zip code as their intended residence more than doubled, from 16 to 36 percent, between 1983 and 1998. In addition, more immigrants buy homes in suburban areas five to ten years after their arrival." In 1983, of eighteen Polish Saturday schools in the metro area, only one was in the suburbs. By 2002, fourteen of twenty-seven schools were suburban.[46]

Like the World War II generation that had preceded them, the new arrivals of the 1980s, especially the educated, politically active Solidarity émigrés, did not mesh well with the existing Polonia on arrival. Although there was general agreement on the notion of freeing Poland from the communist yoke, many new immigrants viewed Polish Americans (including the World War II generation) as crude, overly Americanized, and far too willing to compromise with elements of the Warsaw regime. The Polish communities of Illinois, for their part, often saw the new arrivals as pushy, lazy, ungrateful products of communism. It did not help matters when new Polish immigrants penned derisive commentary on Polonia that often mimicked the anti-Polish stereotypes the community had spent so much effort combating.[47] The new immigrants, like their World War II–era counterparts, often formed new organizations reflecting their common experiences and providing space to both organize and socialize. These groups included Pomost (Bridge), founded in the late 1970s, which published a quarterly journal with a circulation of two thousand and provided financial support for anticommunist groups in Poland. Also active were Freedom for Poland, Brotherhood of Dispersed Solidarity Members, and the Polish-American Economic Forum.[48] Despite differences, as in the past, areas of common agreement could also be found, and the use of shared space and institutions such as parishes helped to bridge some of the divides. The economic immigrants of the late 1980s and 1990s that immediately followed the Solidarity newcomers were less politically active and less likely to take issue with the state of Polonia or engage in conflicts over Polonia politics.

The highly visible and politically active post–World War II waves of Polish immigration significantly changed the nature of

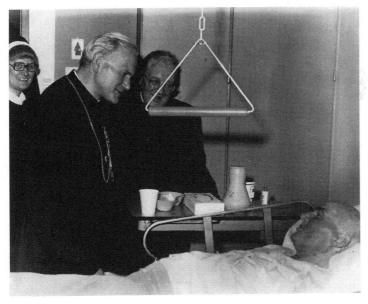

Karol Cardinal Woytła, cardinal archbishop of Kraków, Poland (Pope St. John Paul II), visiting patients at St. Mary's Hospital, Chicago, 1976. Courtesy of Polish Museum of America Archives.

Polish American communities in Illinois. Unlike many other eastern and southern Europeans in the state, Poles in Illinois represent both an ethnic group and an immigrant group. Contemporary Polish usage (as opposed to a more Americanized dialect spoken in many mid-twentieth-century neighborhoods), modern Polish culture, and homeland events continue to play an important role in Polonia. In Chicago, a thriving Polish business and professional community with its own telephone directory of over fifteen hundred pages and blocks of commercial real estate with signage largely in Polish are evidence of this impact. These developments have significantly counterbalanced the Americanization of earlier waves of immigrants and kept the state's Polish presence far more contemporary. Yet, periodic ethnic revivals and the continued vitality of older Polish parishes and cultural organizations have also been due to the abiding interest and vitality of Polish identity among third- and fourth-generation Polish Americans. These varied elements, while not always in harmony with each other, are signs of a hybrid ethnic/immigrant group that is simultaneously a long-standing element of Illinois history and culture and also a new element in the state's story.

# 9

# DZIŚ I WCZORAJ: POLES IN ILLINOIS, TODAY AND YESTERDAY

Poles in Illinois are a living part of the state's past, present, and future. Illinois continues to be shaped in multiple ways by its large Polish community. The history of Poles in the Land of Lincoln is the raw material with which Polish Americans—both recent arrivals from Europe and the descendants of the original nineteenth-century pioneers—shape their future. Even for many fourth-generation Poles, ethnicity continues to be an important, if not always immediately visible, part of their heritage and identity.[1]

## Illinois Polonia in a New Millennium

The Polish population of Illinois reached a peak in the year 2000, with just under one million people. Of these, the vast majority—over eight hundred thousand—lived in the greater Chicago area. About 15 percent of the state's Poles were foreign born. While three-quarters of all Chicago Poles lived in the suburbs, the city of Chicago itself remained a gateway for new immigrants, with almost half of all foreign Poles in the metro area residing in the city.[2]

After 2000, Polish immigration to the United States began to slow due to improved economic conditions in Poland and, more importantly, Poland's accession to the European Union in 2004. Young Poles looking for work began to travel to the United Kingdom and Ireland,

Dankowski sisters, Wicker Park neighborhood, Chicago, 1937 A. Gunkel.

171

countries that provided jobs closer to home. In addition, the older generations of Polish immigrants and Polish Americans began to pass away, while many of the children born to the recent wave of Polish émigrés have yet to reach childbearing age. Despite the decrease in the Polish population as reported by the census between 2000 and 2010, Poles remain a significant presence in the state, especially in Chicago, and are one of its largest ancestry groups (table 9.1).

Table 9.1. Poles in Illinois, 1980–2010

| Year | Number | Percentage of State Population |
|------|--------|-------------------------------|
| 1980 | 890,009 | 7.8 |
| 1990 | 962,827 | 8.4 |
| 2000 | 995,445 | 8.0 |
| 2010 | 924,762 | 7.2 |

*Note*: Numbers represent Illinois residents reporting Polish ancestry.
*Source*: U.S. Census.

Although the ratio of Poles in Illinois remains between 7 and 8 percent of the population, the social and economic characteristics of the demographic have undergone a significant change since the 1970s. New economic and educational opportunities for the descendants of Polish immigrants and recent waves of émigrés made of up of well-educated people means that "Polish American" is no longer synonymous with "blue collar." Overall, the median income of Polish Americans in 2010 was well above the state average, with the exception of recent immigrants from Poland. Whereas Poles were once the dominant group in fields like manufacturing, in 2010 less than one in five of the state's Poles worked in factories or in construction. The children and grandchildren of Polish factory workers and miners clearly preferred jobs related to education, healthcare, and social work, as well as the professions and administrative and managerial occupations (table 9.2).

Although the original parish-communities of the first generation have largely dissolved, many of the parishes founded in the initial wave of settlement continue to be important centers of faith and culture. Holy Trinity, for example, serves a hub for Polish-language ministry in Chicago almost 140 years after its founding.[3]

Table 9.2. Occupations of Polish Americans, by Selected Industry, 2010 (%)

| | |
|---|---|
| Education, healthcare, social assistance | 21.7 |
| Professional, scientific, managerial, administrative | 12.9 |
| Manufacturing | 12.1 |
| Retail trade | 11.3 |
| Finance, insurance, real estate | 7.8 |
| Arts, entertainment, recreation, food service | 7.6 |
| Construction | 6.9 |

*Source*: U.S. Census figures, courtesy of Piast Institute.

Membership at Holy Trinity peaked in the years between 1910 and 1925 due to the baby boom of the first generation. The parish aged in spite of the postwar population increase, and the coming of the Kennedy Expressway caused a serious decline by the 1960s and 1970s. Yet the parish revived in the 1990s with a new wave of immigrants, and though it did not return to its first-generation peak, its continuing vitality can be seen in an increase in baptisms (table 9.3). Its parishioners are no longer necessarily living in the immediate area, but many often commute from suburbs. Parishioners maintain connections through parish associations or electronic media, rendering the physical parish-community of old as a virtual parish-community—one that encompasses less of everyday Polish life but still plays an important role in the lives of its members.

Although the Polish community as a whole remained vibrant, the role of traditional organizations such as fraternal societies or the PAC declined. With the fall of communism, organizations that focused on the Polish cause overseas struggled to find relevance to their members. The PAC emerged as a particular concern, as its leaders were drawn exclusively from the ranks of Polish fraternals and it struggled to adjust to new political and social realities. A series of public relations gaffes by PAC leaders was compounded by a failure to develop any sort of grassroots political organization or even to stand up forcefully for the rights of Poles. In 2000, a group of Chicago police officers was charged with extorting money and jewelry from Polish immigrants.[4] The immigrant workers were often intimidated with threats of deportation. Organizations such as the PAC did little to help the

Table 9.3. Life Cycle of Polish American Parish-Communities, Chicago, 1877–2005

| | Holy Trinity | | | St. Hyacinth | | |
|---|---|---|---|---|---|---|
| Year | Baptisms | Weddings | Funerals | Baptisms | Weddings | Funerals |
| 1877 | 55 | 0 | 0 | | | |
| 1880 | 80 | 0 | 0 | Parish founded 1894 | | |
| 1889 | 67 | 0 | 0 | | | |
| 1895 | 446 | 90 | 140 | 25 | 2 | 0 |
| 1900 | 448 | 117 | 130 | 72 | 3 | 22 |
| 1905 | 617 | 160 | 174 | 182 | 23 | 37 |
| 1910 | 978 | 315 | 318 | 328 | 52 | 111 |
| 1915 | 1271 | 407 | 440 | 294 | 75 | 11 |
| 1920 | 972 | 276 | 296 | 360 | 127 | 145 |
| 1925 | 678 | 166 | 251 | 379 | 108 | 105 |
| 1930 | 362 | 161 | 189 | 196 | 74 | 108 |
| 1935 | 222 | 126 | 169 | 150 | 128 | 125 |
| 1940 | 171 | 148 | 170 | 187 | 155 | 140 |
| 1945 | 223 | 100 | 175 | 224 | 109 | 144 |
| 1950 | 239 | 131 | 168 | 274 | 109 | 150 |
| 1955 | 145 | 71 | 167 | 250 | 93 | 174 |
| 1960 | 84 | 45 | 150 | 226 | 80 | 186 |
| 1965 | 79 | 33 | 132 | 206 | 95 | 228 |
| 1970 | 80 | 35 | 118 | 215 | 119 | 236 |
| 1975 | 4 | 9 | 84 | 154 | 117 | 205 |
| 1980 | 6 | 4 | 56 | 157 | 108 | 209 |
| 1985 | 9 | 9 | 35 | 203 | 115 | 191 |
| 1990 | 56 | 41 | 22 | 237 | 138 | 239 |
| 1995 | 70 | 48 | 20 | 182 | 94 | 172* |
| 2000 | 101 | 67 | 23 | na | na | na |
| 2005 | 89 | 47 | 23 | na | na | na |

*In this row, figures for St. Hyacinth are for 1994.
Source: Urszula Piątek, "Polonia w Chicago," master's thesis, Akademia Pedagogiczna im. Komisji Edukacji Narodowej w Krakowie, 2008.

victims and lodged no protest with city hall, further contributing to the impression that the organization had lost touch with the needs of the people it had been founded to serve.[5]

## Arts

Vibrant artistic culture continues to flourish in Illinois Polonia. One such venture is the Chicago-based Society for Arts, head-quartered on Milwaukee Avenue. The society runs two nonprofit art galleries, hosts visiting artists and scholars, publishes art books and exhibition catalogs, runs educational programming, and hosts two major film festivals, the Chicago International Documentary Festival, established in 2002, and the Polish Film Festival in America, established in 1989.

The Polish Film Festival in America is the world's largest festival of Polish cinema and holds branch events in twelve U.S. cities. The annual event runs every November at multiple venues in Rosemont and Chicago and screens films by Polish and European filmmakers. In its first twenty-five years, the festival has presented over fifteen hundred films by filmmakers of Polish descent from across the globe. Hailed as the most extensive showcase of Polish film outside of Poland, the festival has won numerous awards worldwide, has appeared in celebratory articles by the *New York Times* and the *Chicago Tribune*, and has persevered to become one of the largest and oldest film events in the Midwest.

Founded in 1990, the Chopin Theatre has grown into one of America's most active arts centers, producing, coproducing, or presenting over five hundred theater, music, film, literary, and social events each year. With approximately eighteen hundred unique events over its twenty-five-year history, its mission is to promote enlightened civic discourse through a diverse range of artistic offerings. Chopin Theatre is also the producer of I-Fest: Ideas in Motion, an international festival of solo performances that has brought international artists to Chicago. Originally constructed in 1918 by M. F. Strunch Architects as a 987-seat nickelodeon, today it houses the Main Stage, a cabaret studio with a lounge, the Nelson Algren Café, and the East Wing Art Gallery.

The Chopin Theatre is also host to the All Souls Jazz Fest, a center for Polish and American jazz in Chicago. The Poles in Illinois play a significant role in the jazz culture of the region. Polonia has deep ties to the jazz scene, perhaps none more so than drummer Gene Krupa. Today, numerous Polish and Polish

American artists, such as noted jazz vocalist, composer and arranger Grażyna Auguścik, reside in Illinois. The All Souls Jazz Fest mirrors an annual jazz festival of the same name that has been held for over fifty years in the historic city of Kraków, Poland. This Polish American music festival showcases internationally renowned jazz artists and talented young performers. Over time, the Chicago counterpart has grown to become a popular event with both the local Polish community and American music connoisseurs. Held in early November, the all-night event includes over fifty musicians.

Polish art and artists gradually found a place in Chicago's classical music and arts scenes. A visit from the Krakow Philharmonic Orchestra, conducted by Gilbert Levine, paved the way for other artists and engendered a greater acceptance of Polish music. In the summer of 1999, with the sponsorship of the PNA, the Chicago Art Institute hosted the very successful exhibit "Land of the Winged Horseman," at which was displayed a wealth of Polish art from early modern Poland, a period of art history heretofore little appreciated in the United States.

Illinois Polonia has a vibrant musical culture ranging from folk groups to polka bands, jazz musicians, classical performers, rap artists, and DJs performing at a wide range of venues in Illinois, from large theater spaces such as the Copernicus Center to

Three young women at the Polish Constitution Day parade, Chicago, May 2000. Photo by Zbigniew Bzdak; copyright © 2000.

banquet halls and nightclubs throughout Polonia. Visual arts and theater have proven enduring as well and have found a growing acceptance in the mainstream of Chicago life. Specifically Polish cultural institutions such as the Polish Museum of America and the Chopin Theatre remain important in bringing Polish culture to the region, though performances and exhibitions increasingly find homes in mainstream venues. While parishes are no longer the dominant venues for art and music that they were throughout much of the community's history, they continue to play a big role in the community's cultural life. The parish of St. John Cantius, for example, has reinvented itself as a citywide center for traditional Catholic arts and liturgy. In 1989, a new order of canons was founded in the parish, dedicating itself to restoring beauty in sacred liturgy, with a special emphasis on music and visual art.[6]

When the first descendants of Antoni Sądowski reached Illinois shortly after the start of American settlement, they would have had little sense that they were at the forefront of a migration that would be a vital part of their new home state. If Illinois cities, like Chicago, were said to have sprung up almost overnight, so too Illinois Polonia. A few hundred scattered immigrants in the 1860s became hundreds of thousands a few decades later. The state's development as the industrial and agricultural center of America's heartland drew upon the labor and ingenuity of a massive wave of immigration, and Poles were central to that tide of newcomers. They were the human component of the state's industrial might, but they were far more than cogs in the machinery of economic progress. A bitter and polluted industrial landscape was made into neighborhoods, marked by church spires pointing heavenward, schools, hospitals, theaters, and social halls. While Polish immigrants toiled in often dehumanizing conditions, their aspirations for their children and grandchildren ultimately came to pass after generations of sacrifice, as their descendants reaped the fruits the original generations had been denied. They were joined by new waves of Poles, escaping the horrors of war, genocide, and political repression. Today the Polish communities of Illinois are a living kaleidoscope reflecting a past that is both fully American yet abidingly Polish.

Appendixes
Notes
Further Reading
Index

# APPENDIX 1: POLISH PARISHES IN ILLINOIS, BY DATE OF FOUNDING

| Parish | Town | County | Location | Founding |
|---|---|---|---|---|
| St. Stanislaus Kostka | Chicago | Cook | Noble St. & Evergreen Ave. | 1869 |
| Holy Trinity | Chicago | Cook | Noble St. | 1873 |
| St. Adalbert | Chicago | Cook | 17th St. (between Paulina & Ashland) | 1874 |
| St. Hyacinth | LaSalle | LaSalle | Tenth St. & Tonti St. | 1875 |
| St. Michael | Radom | Washington | 52 S. 3rd St. | 1876 |
| St. Charles | DuBois | Washington | 223 S. 3rd St. | 1877[a] |
| Our Lady of Perpetual Help | Chicago | Cook | 32nd St. (between Aberdeen & Morgan) | 1882 |
| Immaculate Conception BVM | Chicago | Cook | 88th St. & Commercial Ave. | 1882 |
| Sts. Cyril & Methodius | Lemont | Cook/ DuPage | Sobieski St. & Czacki St. | 1883 |
| St. Josephat | Chicago | Cook | Belden Ave. & Southport Ave. | 1883 |
| St. Joseph | Chicago | Cook | 48th St. & Hermitage Ave. | 1886 |
| St. Hedwig | Chicago | Cook | Webster Ave. & Hoyne Ave. | 1888 |
| St. Casimir | Chicago | Cook | Cermak Rd. & Whipple St. | 1890 |

[a] Mixed German and Polish.

| Parish | Town | County | Location | Founding |
|--------|------|--------|----------|----------|
| St. Mary of Gostyn | Downer's Grove | DuPage | Douglas St. & Wilson St. | 1891 |
| Sts. Peter & Paul | Spring Valley | Bureau | 220 N. Terry St. | 1891 |
| St. Valentine | Peru | LaSalle | 1109 Pulaski St. | 1891 |
| St. Andrew | Calumet City | Cook | 155th Pl. & Lincoln Ave. | 1892 |
| St. Michael | Chicago | Cook | 83rd St. & South Shore Dr. | 1892 |
| Holy Cross | Joliet | Will/ Kendall | 901 Elizabeth St. | 1893 |
| St. John Cantius | Chicago | Cook | Carpenter St. (between Fry & Chicago) | 1893 |
| St. Stanislaus Bishop & Martyr | Chicago | Cook | Belden Ave. & Lorel Ave. | 1893 |
| St. Hyacinth | Chicago | Cook | George St. & Lawndale Ave. | 1894 |
| St. Stanislaus | Posen | Cook | 14430 S. McKinley Ave. | 1894 |
| Our Lady of Czestochowa | Cicero | Cook | 30th St. & 49th Ave. | 1895 |
| Sts. Peter & Paul | Chicago | Cook | 38th St. & Paulina St. | 1895 |
| All Saints PNCC | Chicago | Cook | 9201W. Higgins Rd. (2019 W. Charleston St.) | 1897 |
| St. Barbara | Scheller | Jefferson | | 1898 |
| St. Salomea | Chicago | Cook | 118th & Indiana Ave. | 1898 |
| Our Lady of the Angels | Chicago | Cook | 3808 W Iowa St. | 1899 |
| Sacred Heart | Oglesby | LaSalle | | 1900 |
| St. Barbara | Minonk | Woodford | Washington St. | 1900 |

| Parish | Town | County | Location | Founding |
|---|---|---|---|---|
| St. Isadore | Blue Island | Cook | Burr Oak Ave. & Wood St. | 1900 |
| Our Lady of Perpetual Help | Posen (Nashville) | Washington | | 1901 |
| Assumption BVM | Chicago | Cook | 123rd St. & Parnell Ave. | 1903 |
| St. Ann | Chicago | Cook | 18th Pl. & Leavitt St. | 1903 |
| Immaculate Conception | Tamaroa | Perry | 533 W. 2nd St. N. | 1904 |
| Our Lady of the Rosary | North Chicago | Lake | 14th St. & Victoria St. | 1904 |
| St. Adalbert | East St. Louis | St. Clair | 7th Ave. & Pennsylvania Ave. | 1905 |
| Holy Innocents | Chicago | Cook | Superior St. & Armour St. | 1905 |
| St. Joseph | Chicago Heights | Cook | 15th St. | 1905 |
| St. Florian | Chicago | Cook | 131st St. & Houston Ave. | 1905 |
| St. John of God | Chicago | Cook | 52nd St. & Throop St. | 1906 |
| St. Stanislaus | Kewanee | Henry | 10th St. & Main St. | 1906 |
| Good Shepherd | Chicago | Cook | 28th St. & Kolin Ave. | 1907 |
| Five Holy Martyrs | Chicago | Cook | 43rd St. & Richmond St. | 1908 |
| Our Lady of Czestochowa | De Pue | Bureau | Park Addition | 1908 |
| St. Francis of Assisi | Chicago | Cook | Augusta Blvd. & Kostner Ave. | 1909 |
| St. Barbara | Chicago | Cook | Throop St. South of Archer Ave. | 1910 |
| St. Mary Magdalene | Chicago | Cook | 84th St. & Marquette Ave. | 1910 |

| Parish | Town | County | Location | Founding |
|--------|------|--------|----------|----------|
| Ascension | Evanston | Cook | Washington St. & Ridge Ave | 1911 |
| St. Valentine | Cicero | Cook | 13th St. & 50th Ave. | 1911 |
| Transfiguration | Chicago | Cook | Carmen Ave. & Rockwell St. | 1911 |
| Immaculate Heart of Mary | Chicago | Cook | Byron St. & Spaulding Ave. | 1912 |
| Our Lady of Czestochowa | Madison | Madison | 1621 10th St. | 1912 |
| St. Stanislaus | Rockford | Winnebago | 201 Buckbee St. | 1912 |
| St. Wenceslaus | Chicago | Cook | Roscoe St. & Lawndale Ave. | 1912 |
| St. Helen | Chicago | Cook | Augusta Blvd. & Oakley Blvd. | 1913 |
| St. John the Baptist | Harvey | Cook | Cary Ave. (between 157th & 158th) | 1914 |
| St. Ladislaus | Chicago | Cook | 3435 N. Lawndale Ave. | 1914 |
| St. James | Chicago | Cook | Fullerton Ave. & Menard Ave. | 1914 |
| St. Casimir | Streator | LaSalle | 401 South Illinois St. | 1916 |
| St. Constance | Chicago | Cook | Strong St. & Marmora Ave. | 1916 |
| St. Camillius | Chicago | Cook | 55th St. & Lockwood Ave. | 1921 |
| St. Blaze | Argo | Cook | 61st Pl. & 75th Ave. | 1924 |
| St. Pancratius | Chicago | Cook | 40th Pl. & Sacramento Ave. | 1924 |
| St. Boniface | Chicago | Cook | Chestnut St. & Noble St. | 1925[b] |
| St. Bruno | Chicago | Cook | 48th St. & Harding Ave. | 1925 |

[b] German parish founded 1864; Polish by c. 1925.

| Parish | Town | County | Location | Founding |
|--------|------|--------|----------|----------|
| St. Thecla | Chicago | Cook | Devon St. & Oak Park Ave. | 1925 |
| St. Fidelis | Chicago | Cook | 1405 N. Washtenaw Ave. | 1926 |
| St. Priscilla | Chicago | Cook | 6949 W Addison St. | 1926 |
| St. Susanna | Harvey | Cook | 14931 Lincoln Ave. | 1927 |
| St. Thaddeus | Joliet | Kendall | Columbia St. | 1927 |
| St. Turibius | Chicago | Cook | 57th St. & Karlov Ave. | 1927 |
| Good Shepherd PNCC | Chicago | Cook | 2564 W. Cortez | 1925–27? |
| Holy Trinity PNCC | Kewanee | Henry | 716 N. Tremont St. | 1928 |
| St. Bronislawa | Chicago | Cook | 87th St. & Colfax Ave. | 1928 |
| St. Roman | Chicago | Cook | 23rd St. & Washtenaw Ave. | 1928 |
| St. Hedwig Mission | Chicago | Cook | 2445 N. Washtenaw Ave. | 1939 |
| Sts. Cyril & Methodius PNCC | Chicago | Cook | 5744 W. Diversey Ave. (2241 N. Major Av.) | 1939 |
| St. Hedwig PNCC | Chicago | Cook | 3320 East 134th St. | 1940 |
| San Juan Baptista PNCC | Chicago | Cook | 4555 Kedzie Ave. | 1953[c] |
| St. Steven | Tinley Park | Cook | 17500 South 84th Avenue | 1999[d] |
| Sacred Heart | Rutland | LaSalle | | Unknown |
| St. Francis Mission PNCC | McHenry | McHenry | 5345 W. Flanders Road | Unknown |
| Divine Word PNCC | Chicago | Cook | 3842 West 57th St. | Unknown[e] |
| St. Mary's PNCC | Chicago | Cook | 2235 S. Damen St. | Unknown |

[c] Now a Spanish-language parish of the PNCC.

[d] Has Polish-language Mass & ministry.

[e] Mixed Polish and Spanish parish.

| Parish | Town | County | Location | Founding |
|--------|------|--------|----------|----------|
| Holy Family PNCC | Chicago | Cook | 5201 S. Justine St. | Unknown |
| Holy Spirit PNCC | Chicago | Cook | 8152 S. Saginaw St. | Unknown |
| Polish Baptist Church | Chicago | Cook | Unknown | Unknown |

*Sources*: Archdiocese of Chicago Polish Parishes (online database), Polish Genealogical Society of America, www.pgsa.org; Wacław Kruszka, *A History of Poles in America to 1908*, part 2: *The Poles in Illinois*, ed. James S. Pula (Washington, DC: Catholic University of America Press, 1994); *Srebny Jubileusz parafii św. Wojciecha w East Louis, Illinois* (East St. Louis: n.p. [1929]); *Golden Jubilee 1916–1966 Saint Casimir's Church, Streator, IL* (Streator: n.p., 1966), accessed online at http://www.liturgicalcenter.org/media/parish_pdf/PEO/peo-15.1.pdf; *St. Charles Borromeo Church, DuBois, Ill.: Centennial 1877–1977* (DuBois: n.p., 1977); Diocese of Belleville, Illinois, Papers, Central Archives of Polonia, Polish Mission, Orchard Lake Schools, Orchard Lake, Michigan; Diocese of Peoria, Illinois, Papers, Central Archives of Polonia, Polish Mission, Orchard Lake Schools, Orchard Lake, Michigan; Niklewicz, *Polacy w Stanach Zjednoczonych* (Green Bay, 1937).

# APPENDIX 2: POLISH SCHOOLS IN ILLINOIS, 1946 AND 1959

| | |
|---|---|
| Br. Holy Cross | Brothers of the Holy Cross |
| CR | Congregation of the Resurrection |
| CSFN | Sisters of the Holy Family of Nazareth |
| Felicians | Sisters of St. Felix of Cantalice |
| OFM | Order of Friars Minor |
| OSF (Bl. Kun.) | Franciscan Sisters of the Blessed Kunegunda |
| OSF (Imm. H.) | Franciscan Sisters of the Immaculate Heart |
| OSF (Perp. Help) | Franciscan Sisters of Our Lady of Perpetual Help |
| Resurrectionists | Sisters of the Resurrection |
| SSJ | Sisters of St. Joseph |
| SSJ-TOSF | Sisters of St. Joseph, Third Order of St. Francis |
| SSND | School Sisters of Notre Dame |

A. Polish Elementary Parochial Schools in Illinois, 1946 and 1959

| Parish | City | Teaching Sisters, 1946 | Teaching Sisters, 1959 | Students, 1946 | Students, 1959 | Order |
|---|---|---|---|---|---|---|
| St. Bronislava | Chicago | 10 | 7 | 305 | 383 | Felicians |
| St. Bruno | Chicago | 8 | 11 | 370 | 609 | Felicians |
| Good Shepherd | Chicago | 9 | 7 | 287 | 418 | Felicians |
| St. Helen | Chicago | 24 | 26 | 840 | 1,328 | Felicians |
| Holy Innocents | Chicago | 27 | 21 | 742 | 1,184 | Felicians |
| St. James | Chicago | 12 | 12 | 437 | 512 | Felicians |
| St. John of God | Chicago | 25 | 20 | 771 | 1,025 | Felicians |
| St. Joseph | Chicago | 27 | 16 | 812 | 917 | Felicians |

| Parish | City | Teaching Sisters, 1946 | Teaching Sisters, 1959 | Students, 1946 | Students, 1959 | Order |
|---|---|---|---|---|---|---|
| OL of the Gardens | Chicago | n/a | 8 | n/a | 349 | Felicians |
| St. Mary Magdalene | Chicago | 18 | | 713 | | Felicians |
| Sts. Peter & Paul | Chicago | 16 | 11 | 681 | 611 | Felicians |
| Sacred Heart | Chicago | 16 | 12 | 510 | 607 | Felicians |
| St. Stephen | Chicago | 7 | | 113 | | Felicians |
| St. Turibius | Chicago | 8 | 20 | 265 | 956 | Felicians |
| St. Wenceslaus | Chicago | 12 | 12 | 467 | 568 | Felicians |
| St. Wenceslaus | Chicago | 2 | | 21 | | OSF (Imm. H.) |
| St. Adalbert | Chicago | 16 | 21 | 503 | 629 | CSFN |
| St. Ann | Chicago | 13 | 18 | 523 | 616 | CSFN |
| Assumption BVM | Chicago | 10 | 10 | 328 | 384 | CSFN |
| St. Camilius | Chicago | 6 | 8 | 183 | 393 | CSFN |
| St. Francis | Chicago | 4 | | 145 | | CSFN |
| St. Hedwig | Chicago | 29 | 40 | 1,139 | 1,112 | CSFN |
| Holy Trinity | Chicago | 14 | 24 | 501 | 938 | CSFN |
| St. Hyacinth | Chicago | 29 | 33 | 1,170 | 1,163 | CSFN |
| Imm. Heart of Mary | Chicago | 11 | 14 | 526 | 638 | CSFN |
| St. Josephat | Chicago | 11 | 12 | 355 | 475 | CSFN |
| St. Joseph | Chicago | n/a | 6 | n/a | 500 | CSFN |
| St. Ladislaus | Chicago | 7 | 9 | 222 | 370 | CSFN |
| St. Michael | Chicago | 18 | 23 | 768 | 876 | CSFN |
| St. Barbara | Chicago | 21 | | 460 | | SSJ-TOSF |
| St. Fidelis | Chicago | 16 | | 456 | | SSJ-TOSF |
| Immaculate Con. | Chicago | 23 | | 653 | | SSJ-TOSF |

| Parish | City | Teaching Sisters, 1946 | Teaching Sisters, 1959 | Students, 1946 | Students, 1959 | Order |
|---|---|---|---|---|---|---|
| OL Perpetual Help | Chicago | 20 | | 673 | | SSJ-TOSF |
| St. Roman | Chicago | 20 | | 604 | | SSJ-TOSF |
| St. Salomea | Chicago | 9 | | 300 | | SSJ-TOSF |
| Transfiguration | Chicago | 5 | | 129 | | SSJ-TOSF |
| St. Casimir | Chicago | 24 | 22 | 700 | 732 | Resurrectionists |
| OL of the Angels | Chicago | 16 | 22 | 670 | 835 | Resurrectionists |
| St. Thecla | Chicago | 11 | 12 | 250 | 474 | Resurrectionists |
| Resurrection | Chicago | 5 | 3 | 102 | 62 | Resurrectionists |
| Five Holy Martyrs | Chicago | 19 | 24 | 750 | 871 | OSF (Bl. Kun.) |
| St. Florian | Chicago | 9 | 14 | 418 | 535 | OSF (Bl. Kun.) |
| St. Pancratius | Chicago | 11 | 13 | 460 | 491 | OSF (Bl. Kun.) |
| St. Stanislaus | Chicago | 18 | 22 | 700 | 871 | OSF (Bl. Kun.) |
| St. Constance | Chicago | 21 | | 346 | | SSND |
| St. John Cantius | Chicago | 11 | | 344 | | SSND |
| St. Stan. Kostka | Chicago | 15 | | 610 | | SSND |
| Holy Rosary | N. Chicago | 11 | 7 | 230 | 353 | Felicians |
| St. Joseph | Chi. Heights | 6 | | 207 | | OSF (Perp. Help) |
| St. Linus | Oak Lawn | n/a | 8 | n/a | 264 | Felicians |
| St. Bede | Fox Lake | n/a | 3 | n/a | 104 | Resurrectionists |
| St. Adalbert | East St. Louis | 6 | 6 | 173 | 189 | OSF (Bl. Kun.) |
| St. Andrew | Christopher | 2 | | 44 | | OSF (Perp. Help) |
| St. Paul | Johnston City | 2 | | 48 | | OSF (Perp. Help) |
| OL Perpetual Help | Posen | 2 | | 42 | | OSF (Perp. Help) |

| Parish | City | Teaching Sisters, 1946 | Teaching Sisters, 1959 | Students, 1946 | Students, 1959 | Order |
|---|---|---|---|---|---|---|
| St. Barbara | Scheller | 2 | | 20 | | OSF (Perp. Help) |
| St. Mary Magd. | Todd's Mill | 2 | | 44 | | OSF (Perp. Help) |
| St. John the Baptist | W. Frankfort | 3 | | 107 | | OSF (Perp. Help) |
| St. Michael | Radom | 3 | | 108 | | SSND |
| St. Charles | Dubois | 2 | | 64 | | SSND |
| St. Isadore | Blue Island | 4 | 6 | 153 | 258 | Felicians |
| St. Mary of Gostyn | Downer's Grove | 2 | 7 | 49 | 350 | Felicians |
| Ascension | Evanston | 8 | 4 | 143 | 163 | Felicians |
| St. Thaddeus | Joliet | 7 | 8 | 207 | 252 | Felicians |
| Holy Cross | Joliet | 3 | 3 | 88 | 117 | Felicians |
| St. Stanislaus | Rockford | n/a | 4 | n/a | 176 | Felicians |
| Sts. Cyril & Method. | Lemont | 6 | 5 | 157 | 237 | Felicians |
| St. Hyacinth | LaSalle | n/a | 7 | n/a | 281 | Felicians |
| St. Valentine | Peru | n/a | 5 | n/a | 196 | Felicians |
| St. Stanislaus | Posen | 7 | 7 | 227 | 352 | Felicians |
| Holy Family | Oglesby | n/a | 8 | n/a | 398 | Felicians |
| St. Mary | Centralia | n/a | 5 | n/a | 216 | Felicians |
| St. Blasé | Argo | 10 | 16 | 380 | 708 | CSFN |
| St. Valentine | Cicero | 6 | 8 | 108 | 211 | CSFN |
| St. John the Baptist | Harvey | 7 | 10 | 173 | 296 | CSFN |
| St. Susanna | Harvey | 6 | 7 | 170 | 218 | CSFN |
| St. Stanislaus | Kankakee | 4 | 6 | 129 | 164 | CSFN |
| St. Andrew | Calumet City | 11 | | 462 | | CSFN |

| Parish | City | Teaching Sisters, 1946 | Teaching Sisters, 1959 | Students, 1946 | Students, 1959 | Order |
|---|---|---|---|---|---|---|
| OL Czestochowa | Cicero | 14 | | 403 | | SSJ-TOSF |
| St. Stanislaus | Kewanee | 2 | | 35 | | FSSJ |

## B. Polish Catholic High Schools, Illinois, 1946 and 1959

| School | City | Teachers, 1946 (Clergy) | Teachers, 1946 (Lay) | Sisters, 1959 | Students, 1946 | Students, 1959 | Order |
|---|---|---|---|---|---|---|---|
| St. Ann | Chicago | 8 | 2 | 16 | 215 | 268 | CSFN |
| St. Barbara | Chicago | 5 | 1 | | 88 | | SSJ |
| St. Constance | Chicago | 11 | 2 | | 278 | | SSND |
| St. Joseph | Chicago | 19 | 0 | 23 | 458 | 518 | Felicians |
| OL Perpetual Help | Chicago | 16 | 1 | | 349 | | SSJ |
| St. Michael (girls) | Chicago | 11 | 3 | 10 | 255 | 651 | CSFN |
| Holy Family (girls) | Chicago | 40 | 5 | 35 | 628 | 584 | CSFN |
| St. Josephat (girls) | Chicago | n/a | n/a | 2 | n/a | 72 | CSFN |
| Resurrection (girls) | Chicago | 15 | 2 | 13 | 170 | 315 | Resurrectionists |
| Lourdes | Chicago | 28 | 2 | | 281 | | SSJ |
| St. Stan K. (girls) | Chicago | 13 | 0 | | 322 | | SSND |
| Good Counsel (girls) | Chicago | 18 | 0 | 23 | 342 | 517 | Felicians |
| Villa Nazareth (girls) | Des Plaines | 12 | 0 | | 150 | | CSFN |
| St. Hedwig Ind. (girls) | Niles | 15 | 0 | 6 | 209 | 26 | Felicians |

Appendix 2

| School | City | Teachers, 1946 (Clergy) | Teachers, 1946 (Lay) | Sisters, 1959 | Students, 1946 | Students, 1959 | Order |
|---|---|---|---|---|---|---|---|
| Madonna | Chicago | n/a | n/a | 20 | n/a | 310 | OSF (Bl. Kun.) |
| Holy Trinity (boys) | Chicago | 18 | 0 | | 558 | | Br. Holy Cross |
| Polish Manual Training School (boys) | Chicago | 20 | 0 | | 248 | | Felicians |
| St. Mary's (boys) | Crystal Lake | 8 | 0 | | 42 | | OFM |
| Weber HS (boys) | Chicago | 11 | 0 | | 310 | | CR |
| HS of the Missionaries (boys) | Olivet | 8 | 0 | | 32 | | Missionaries of Our Lady of La Salette |

*Sources*: Rev. Francis Bolek, *The Polish American School System* (New York: Columbia Press Corp., 1948); *Sacrum Poloniae Millenium* (1959).

# APPENDIX 3: POLISH NEWSPAPERS IN ILLINOIS

Poles in Illinois published a great number of periodicals. This listing, while not comprehensive, provides some indication of the number as well as the breadth of what has been and continues to be published. Given the fact that many publications were short-lived or of limited circulation, a complete list of all Polish periodicals is not possible. The list does not include more recent, web-based Illinois publishing. Any errors or oversights are the fault of the author.

| Title | Translation | Founded | Closed | Type | Affiliation |
|---|---|---|---|---|---|
| Gazeta Polska | Polish Gazette | 1873 | 1913 | Weekly | |
| Gazeta Polska Katolicka Gazeta Katolicka | Polish Catholic Gazette Chicago Gazette | 1874 | 1887? | Weekly | PRCUA (unofficial)/ Catholic |
| Ziemianin | The Landowner | 1874 | 1874 | Agricultural | |
| Zgoda | Harmony | 1881 | Open | Varies | PNA/Nationalist |
| Gazeta Chicagoska | Chicago Gazette | 1882 | 1884 | Weekly | |
| Rodzina Polska | The Polish Family | 1882 | 1918? | Weekly | Catholic |
| Ziarno | Grain | 1886 | 1903 | | |
| Tygodnik Naukowo-Powieściowy | News and Science Weekly | 1873 | 1914 | Weekly/ literary | |
| Dzień Święty | Holy Day | 1880s? | 1910s? | Weekly | Catholic |

| Title | Translation | Founded | Closed | Type | Affiliation |
|---|---|---|---|---|---|
| Lekarz Domowy | Home Doctor | 1886 | 1886 | Home medicine | |
| Dziennik | The Daily | 1887 | 1887 | Daily | |
| Kuryer Chicagoski | Chicago Courier | 1887 | 1887 | | |
| Czas w Chicago | Times in Chicago | 1887 | 1887 | | |
| Kropidło | Aspergillum | 1887 | 1888 | Weekly | Catholic |
| Wiara i Ojczyzna | Faith and Fatherland | 1887 | 1899 | Weekly | PRCUA/Catholic |
| Głos Wolny | Free Voice | 1889 | 1890 | | |
| Nowe Życie | New Life | 1890 | 1896 | Weekly | |
| Polacy w Chicago | Poles in Chicago | 1890 | 1890 | | Catholic |
| Dziennik Chicagoski | Chicago Daily | 1890 | 1971 | Daily | Catholic (Resurrectionist) |
| Reforma | The Reform | 1891 | 1892 | | |
| Telegraf | The Telegraph | 1892/96 | 1939 | Weekly | Democratic |
| Gazeta Handlowa | Commercial Gazette | 1892 | 1892 | Business | |
| Nowy Świat | New World | 1892? | 1922 | Weekly | |
| Przegląd i Tygodnik | Review and Week | 1892 | 1892 | Weekly | |
| Sztandar | The Standard | 1893 | 1902 | | |
| Gazeta Robotnicza | Worker's Gazette | 1894 | 1894 | | Socialist |
| Dziennik Polski | Polish Daily | 1895 | 1896 | Daily | |
| Przyjaciel Młodzieży | The Friend of Youth | 1895 | 1897 | Children /Youth | |
| Naród Polski | The Polish Nation | 1897 | Open | Weekly | PRCUA/Catholic |
| Dziennik Narodowy | National Daily | 1899 | 1923 | Daily | Republican |

| Title | Translation | Founded | Closed | Type | Affiliation |
|---|---|---|---|---|---|
| Macierz Polska | Polish Alma Mater | 1899 | | Youth | Polish Alma Mater/Catholic |
| Komar | The Gnat | 1900 | 1900 | Satire | |
| Kurjer Świąteczny | Sunday Courier | 1900 | 1922 | Weekly | Catholic (had several names) |
| Głos Polek | Polish Women's Voice | 1900 | 2016 | Women's | PWA/Nationalist |
| Promien | The Beam | 1901 | 1907? | | (LaSalle) |
| Polonia | Poland | 1904 | 1916? | | |
| Gospodarz | The Squire | 1905 | 1908? | Agricultural | |
| Tygodnik Katolicki | Catholic Weekly | 1902 | 1905 | Weekly | Catholic (LaSalle) |
| Lud | The People | 1905? | | | |
| Robotnik | The Worker | 1903 | 1908 | Monthly | Socialist |
| Perły Humoru | Pearls of Humor | 1906 | 1907 | | Humor |
| Kumoszka | The Gossip | 1907 | 1918 | | |
| Słowo Polskie | The Polish Word | 1907? | ? | | Republican |
| Dzwon Niedzielny/ Dzwon/ Nowy Dzwon/ Kropidło | Sunday Bell/ Bell/New Bell/ Aspergillum | 1904 | 1922 | Weekly | Catholic |
| Dziennik Ludowy | The People's Daily | 1907 | 1922 | Daily | Socialist |
| Filomat | Lover of Learning | 1907 | 1909? | | Science and learning |
| Rodzina | Family | 1908? | | | Catholic (LaSalle) |
| Dziennik Zwiąkowy | Alliance Daily | 1908 | Open | Daily | PNA/Nationalist |
| Odgłos Trójcowa | Trinity Echo | 1909 | 1940s? | Monthly | Local/Catholic |
| Abstynent | The Abstainer | 1911 | 1915 | Weekly | Dry/Catholic |

| Title | Translation | Founded | Closed | Type | Affiliation |
|---|---|---|---|---|---|
| Młotek Duchowny | Spiritual Hammer | 1911 | 1912? | Weekly | Protestant |
| Bicz Boży | Scourge of God | 1912 | ? | Weekly | Socialist/ anti-Catholic |
| Kantowiak | The Kantovian | 1912 | 1940? | Weekly | Parish/Catholic |
| Przegląd Polsko-Amerykański/ Przegląd Kościelny | Polish-American Review/ Eccesiastical Review | 1912 | 1936? | Clerical | Catholic |
| Wici | Clarion | 1912 | 1918 | | KON |
| Głos Ubogich | Voice of the Poor | 1913 | 1914 | | |
| Free Poland/ Wolna Polska | | 1914 | 1919 | English | Wydzial Narodowy |
| Ekonomija | The Economy | 1915 | ? | | Pub. in Poland from 1920 |
| The Polish Cause | | 1915? | 1915? | Irregular | |
| Kurjer Narodowy | National Courier | 1916 | 1920 | | |
| Nowiny Handlowe | Commercial News | 1915 | 1919? | Monthly | Business |
| Podaniec Serca Jezusa | Sacred Heart Messenger | 1917 | 1970s? | | Catholic (moved from NY) |
| Figlarz Illustrowany | Illustrated Joker | 1918 | 1922 | Humor | |
| Gazeta Handlowa | Commercial Gazette | 1918 | 1918 | Business | |
| Gość Niedzielny | Sunday Guest | 1918 | 1948? | Weekly | Catholic (Niles) |
| Kurjer Niedzielny | Sunday Courier | 1918 | 1920 | Weekly | Catholic |
| Technika Popularna | Popular Mechanics | 1918 | 1921 | Monthly | Science/ Technology |
| Helenowianin | The Helenian | 1918 | | Weekly | Local/Catholic |
| National Polish Committee of America | | 1918 | 1921 | Semi-monthly | |

| Title | Translation | Founded | Closed | Type | Affiliation |
|-------|-------------|---------|--------|------|-------------|
| Okólnik Wydzialu Narodowego Polskiego | Circular of the Polish National Department | 1919 | 1920 | Bi-weekly | Wydzial Narodowy |
| Monitor Polski | The Polish Monitor | 1919 | ? | | |
| Palatyniec | The Palatine | 1919 | 1919 | | |
| Szewc | The Shoemaker | 1919 | 1919 | | |
| Rozwój | Development | 1920 | 1920 | | |
| Dziennik Zjednoczenja | Union Daily | 1921 | 1939 | Daily | PRCUA/Catholic |
| Kupiec Polski | The Polish Merchant | 1921 | 1922? | Monthly | Commercial |
| Czyn | The Deed | 1921 | 1921 | | |
| Chicago Society News | | 1921? | 1970s? | Monthly | PNA |
| Wojciechowianin | The Adelbertian | 1924 | | Weekly | Local/Catholic |
| Głos Polski/ Niedzielny Głos Polski | The Polish Voice/ Sunday Polish Voice | 1924? | 1929 | Weekly | |
| Przegląd Polski | Polish Review | 1929 | ? | | |
| Przegląd Polonji | Polonia Review | 1929 | ? | | |
| Przebudzenie | The Awakening | 1929 | 1951? | Weekly | |
| National Medical & Dental Assoc. of America Bulletin | | 1929 | 1970? | Monthly | Professional |
| Polski Student | The Polish Student | 1930 | ? | | Youth |
| Dziennikarz | The Journalist | 1930s? | 1930s? | Monthly | |
| Nasze Jutro | Our Future | 1930s? | 1930s? | Monthly | |
| The New American | | 1930s | 1940s? | Monthly | |
| Morze | The Sea | 1930s? | 1960s? | Quarterly | Polish Sea League |

| Title | Translation | Founded | Closed | Type | Affiliation |
|---|---|---|---|---|---|
| Prawda/Prawda dla ludu | The Truth/ Truth for the People | 1935 | ? | Weekly | |
| Polish American Review | | 1935 | 1950s? | Monthly | Originally pub. in Cleveland |
| The Chicagoan | | 1936 | ? | Weekly | Bilingual |
| Sw. Jadwiga Biuletyn | St. Jadwiga Bulletin | 1930s? | ? | | Local/Catholic |
| Polamerican Law Journal | | 1938 | 1941 | Semi-annual | Legal |
| Skarb Rodzinny | Family Treasure | 1939 | ? | Monthly | (Techny) |
| The Kapustkan | | 1941 | 1940s? | Monthly | Literary |
| Polish War Relief | | 1943? | 1945? | Irregular | |
| Promien | Sunbeam | 1943 | 1980s? | Quarterly | |
| Liga | The League | 1940s | 1940s? | Monthly | Previously pub. in Detroit |
| Przyszłość | The Future | 1943? | 1943? | | |
| Okno na Świat | Window on the World | 1940s? | 1940s? | Monthly | |
| Polish American Congress Bulletin/Newsletter | | 1945 | 2000s? | Quarterly | PAC |
| Nowe Drogi | New Roads | 1950s? | ? | Monthly | |
| Orleta | Eaglets | 1950s? | 1950s | Monthly | |
| Zew Młodych | Youth Call | 1952 | 1954 | Monthly | Youth |
| Orka Biuletyn Informacyjny | Plow Information Bulletin | 1955 | 1969 | Irregular | |
| Quarterly of the Polish Western Association of America | | 1960 | 1992? | Quarterly | Scholarly |
| Extension | | 1960s? | 1960s? | Monthly | |
| Ameryka-Echo | America-Echo | 1961 | 1971 | | In Chicago, 1961–71 |

| Title | Translation | Founded | Closed | Type | Affiliation |
|---|---|---|---|---|---|
| Walka | Struggle | 1961 | 1969 | Monthly | |
| Wspólnymi Silami ku Wolnej Polsce Biuletyn | Mutual Effort for Free Poland Bulletin | 1962? | ? | Monthly | |
| Wiadomości | News | 1966? | ? | | |
| Jedność | Unity | 1971 | ? | Weekly | |
| Polonia | | 1971? | 1976? | Weekly | |
| Polish-American | | 1960s? | 1960s? | Weekly | |
| Bulletin of Polish Medical Science and History | | 1967 | 1971 | Quarterly | Medicine and science |
| Polish American Educators' Assn. Newsletter | | 1973 | 1979 | Monthly | |
| Echo | | 1970s? | 1970s? | Bi-monthly | Bilingual |
| Pancerniak | The Tankman | 1970s? | 1970s? | | Veterans |
| Przegląd Polski | Polish Review | 1970s | 1970s | Quarterly | |
| Po Prostu | Simply | 1970s? | 1970s? | Irregular | |
| Szaniec | Rampart | 1972 | 1973 | Monthly | |
| Studium | | 1977 | 1980 | Quarterly | News extracts from Poland |
| Polish Genealogical Society Bulletin/Newsletter | | 1979 | Open | Semi-annual | |
| POMOST | Bridge | 1979 | 1984 | Quarterly | |
| Panorama | | 1980s? | 1990s? | | |
| Relax | | 1984 | 2000s? | Weekly | |
| Nowy Dziennik | Polish Daily News | 1986 | | | |
| Dziennik Chicagowski | Chicago Daily | 1990 | ? | Daily | |
| Express: Chicago Polish Daily News | | 1992 | Open | Daily | |
| Monitor | Monitor | 1993 | Open | Free Weekly | |

| Title | Translation | Founded | Closed | Type | Affiliation |
|---|---|---|---|---|---|
| 2B: A Journal of Ideas | | 1994 | 2000s? | | Art and literary journal |
| Tygodnik Program | Weekly Polish Program | 1999 | Open | Free Weekly | |
| Czas na Biznes | Time for Business | 2002 | 2004? | Monthly | |
| Polonia Magazyn | Polonia Magazine | 2002 | Open | Print/Web | |

*Sources*: Edmund G. Olszak, *The Polish Press in America* (Milwaukee: Marquette University Press, 1940); *Thirty Third Annual Report of the Board of Directors of the Chicago Public Library* (Chicago: 1905); *N.W. Ayer and Son's American Newspaper Annual* (Philadelphia: 1905–22); Polish Periodicals, Immigration History Research Center Archives, University of Minnesota, https://www.lib.umn.edu/ihrca/periodicals/polish (accessed April 11, 2017); Radzilowski, *Eagle and the Cross*; Cygan, "Political and Cultural Leadership"; Erdmans, *Opposite Poles*.

# NOTES

## Preface

1. Anna D. Jaroszyńska-Kirchmann, *Letter from Readers in the Polish American Press, 1902–1969: A Corner for Everybody*, trans. Theodore Zawistowski and Anna D. Jaroszyńska-Kirchmann (Lanham, MD: Lexington Press, 2014).

## Introduction

1. Thaddeus C. Radzilowski and Dominik Stecula, "Polish American Today," Piast Institute Research Report, Piast Institute, Hamtramck, MI, 2010, accessed at http://piastinstitute.org/assets/library/Polish%20Americans%20Today%20Survey%20Book%202012.pdf.

2. See Wojciech Materski and Tomasz Szarota, *Polska 1939–1945: Straty osobowe i ofiary represji pod dwiema okupacjami* (Warsaw: Institute of National Remembrance, 2009).

## 1. Na Początku: Settling in Illinois

1. James D. Lodesky, *Polish Pioneers in Illinois, 1818–1850* (Bloomington, IN: Xlibris, 2010), 29–32.

2. *Portrait and Biographical Album of Vermilion and Edgar Counties, Illinois* (Chicago: Chapman Bros., 1889), 493–95.

3. James S. Pula, *The Polish Americans: An Ethnic Community* (New York: Twayne, 1995), 4–5.

4. Florian Stasik, *Polish Political Émigrés in the United States of America, 1831–1864* (New York: East European Monographs/Columbia University Press, 2002), 61–64.

5. Ibid., 65.

6. Ibid., 65–78.

7. Lodesky, *Polish Pioneers*, 13–16.

8. Ibid., 360.

9. Ibid. In 1860, the couple was living in Warren (Lake County) with three teenage children.

10. Ibid.; J. Fletcher Williams, *A History of the City of St. Paul to 1875* (1876; St. Paul, 1983), 121–22, 199; Matthew Cecil, "Justice in Heaven: The Trial of Ann Bilansky [*sic*]," *Minnesota History* 55 (Winter 1997–98): 350–63.

11. *Poles of Chicago, 1837–1937* (Chicago: Polish Pageant, 1937), 2.

12. See William Cronon, *Nature's Metropolis: Chicago and the Great West* (New York: Norton, 1991), 104.

13. Rev. Francis Bolek, ed., *Who's Who in Polish America* (New York: Harbinger House, 1943).

14. Dominic A. Pacyga, *Polish Immigrants and Industrial Chicago: Workers on the South Side, 1880–1922* (Columbus: Ohio University Press, 1991), 127.

15. Mieczysław Haiman, *Historja udziału Polaków w amerykańskiej wojnie domowej* (Chicago: Dziennik Zjednoczenia, 1928), 35–36.

16. Alfred T. Andreas, *History of Chicago from the Earliest Period to the Present Time*, vol. 2, *From 1857 until the Fire of 1871* (Chicago: A. T. Andreas Company, 1885), 261; *Supplement to the Official Records of the Union and Confederate Armies*, part 2 (Wilmington, NC: Broadfoot Publishing, 1994–2001), 7:695, 697, 710–11.

17. Helen Busyn, "Peter Kiolbassa: Maker of Polish America," *Polish American Studies* 8, no. 3–4 (July–December 1951): 65–84.

18. Bureau of the Census, Manuscript Census, 1860, Illinois. Accessed online.

19. Bureau of the Census, Manuscript Census, 1870, Illinois, Cook County, Chicago, Ward 15, p. 392, online; Sister M. Inviolata, SSJ, "Noble Street in Chicago," *Polish American Studies* 11, nos. 1–2 (January–June 1954): 1–8.

20. Bureau of the Census, Manuscript Census, 1870, Illinois, Cook County, Chicago, Ward 15, pp. 392–98, online; Ibid., Ward 2, p. 130.

21. Bessie Leniak interview transcript, Oral History Archives of Chicago Polonia, Box 5, Fl. Len-014, Chicago History Museum, p. 5.

22. Thaddeus Radzilowski, "Immigrant Women and their Daughters," The Fiedorczyk Lecture in Polish American Studies, Polish Studies Program, Central Connecticut State University, 1990, pp. 10–11.

23. Angela Mischke autobiography, p. 2, The Angela Mischke Papers, 1908–69, Polish American Collection, Immigration History Research Center, University of Minnesota.

24. Witold Kula et al. *Writing Home: Immigrants in Brazil and the United States, 1890–1891* (Boulder/New York: East European Monographs/Columbia University Press, 1986), 213.

25. Ibid., 341. For John Lubienski, see Bureau of the Census, Manuscript Census, 1900, Illinois, Cook County, Chicago, Ward 15, p. 16, online; For Ignatius, see ibid., Ward 16, p. 44.

26. Oral History Archives of Chicago Polonia, quoted in Thaddeus Radzilowski, "Reinventing the Center: Polish Immigrant Women in the New World," in Thomas and Rita Gladsky, eds., *Something of My Very Own to Say: American Women Writers of Polish Descent* (New York: EEM/Columbia University Press, 1998), 13.

27. Catherine Kozik interview transcript, Oral History Archives of Chicago Polonia, Box 3, Fl. Koz-113, Chicago History Museum, p. 3.

28. Wacław Kruszka, *A History of Poles in America to 1908*, part 2: *The Poles in Illinois*, ed. James S. Pula (Washington, DC: Catholic University of America Press, 1994), 259–67; *Historja Parafji św. Michała Arch. i Poświęcenia Nowege Kościoła w Radomiu, Ill.* (Radom: n.p., 1924), 8–11.

29. *Historja Parafji*, 8–11; Bureau of the Census, Manuscript Census, 1880, Illinois, Washington County, Dubois Township, online; Joseph F. Martin, "Early Polish Immigrants Settled in Southern Illinois," *Illinois State Genealogical Quarterly* 41, no. 3 (Fall 2009). See also https://en.wikipedia.org/wiki/Radom,_Illinois.

30. Quoted in Kruszka, *History of Poles in America to 1908*, part 2: *The Poles in Illinois*, 259.

31. *Srebny Jubileusz parafii św. Wojciecha w East Louis, Illinois* (East St. Louis: n.p. [1929]), 11–14; Anthony M. Golec, *Polonia in St. Clair County: 101 Years of Polish Immigrant History in East St. Louis, Illinois* (Belleville, IL: Golec Corp., 1997), 71–73.

32. See Paula Angle, *A Biography in Black: A History of Streator, Illinois* (Streator, IL: Weber Publishing Co., 1962); *Golden Jubilee 1916–1966 Saint Casimir's Church, Streator, IL* (Streator, IL: n.p., 1966) accessed online at http://www.liturgicalcenter.org/media/parish_pdf/PEO/peo-15.1.pdf.

33. Edward R. Kantowicz, "Polish Chicago: Survival through Solidarity," in *Ethnic Chicago: A Multicultural Portrait*, ed. Melvin G. Holli and Peter d'A. Jones, 4th ed. (Grand Rapids, MI: William B. Eerdmans Publishing Company, 1995), 175.

34. See Kruszka, *History of Poles in America to 1908*, part 2: *The Poles in Illinois*, 259–67.

35. *Annual Report of the Year 1939: St. Blase Parish, Argo, Illinois* (copy in the Archives of the Polish Museum of America, Chicago).

36. Thaddeus C. Radzilowski, "Patterns of Slavic Secondary Migration as Reflected in Fraternal Records, 1895–1905," paper given at the Symposium on a Century of European Migration, November 6–9, 1986, Minneapolis, MN, p. 16, n. 20 (copy in the author's possession).

37. Kruszka, *History of Poles in America to 1908*, part 2: *The Poles in Illinois*, 253, 256.

38. *Diamond Anniversary St. Josephat Church, 1884–1959* (Chicago: n.p., 1959), 22.

39. Ethnic parishes serve a particular ethnic or language group. Territorial parishes serve a geographic area. The former were largely done away with after World War II.

40. See http://www.stgall.org/history, accessed February 23, 2016.

41. *St. Charles Borromeo Church, DuBois, Ill.: Centennial 1877–1977* (DuBois, IL: n.p., 1977); Diocese of Belleville, Illinois. Papers. Central Archives of Polonia, Polish Mission, Orchard Lake Schools, Orchard Lake, Michigan, file: "St. Barbara Catholic, Scheller, IL" from *Centennial St. Barbara Catholic Church, 1898–1998*.

42. *125th Anniversary, St. Boniface Church* (Chicago: n.p., 1989), 4–7; F. L. Kalveage, *The Annals of St. Boniface Parish, 1862–1926* (Chicago: n.p., 1926), 108–9.

43. John Radzilowski, "A New Poland in the Old Northwest: Polish Farming Communities on the Northern Great Plains," *Polish American Studies* 59, no. 2 (Autumn 2002): 79–96; idem, "Born a Gypsy: Secondary Migration and Spatial Change in Two Polish Immigrant Communities, 1880–1925," *Polish American Studies* 66, no. 2 (Autumn 2009): 73–85.

## 2. Rodzina: Family Life

1. Carole Haber and Brian Gratton, *Old Age and the Search for Security: An American Social History* (Bloomington: Indiana University Press, 1994), 68–81.
2. Kozik interview transcript, p. 4.
3. John Bukowczyk, *And My Children Did Not Know Me: A History of the Polish Americans* (Bloomington: Indiana University Press, 1986).
4. Mischke Papers, 3–4.
5. Ibid.
6. Radzilowski, "Reinventing the Center," 11.
7. Bessie Leniak interview transcript, Oral History Archives of Chicago Polonia, Box 5, fl. Len-014, Chicago History Museum, pp. 3–4.
8. Kula et al., *Writing Home,* 364.
9. Golec, *Polonia in St. Clair County,* 66.
10. Kula et al., *Writing Home,* 364.
11. Ibid., 263–64.
12. *Naród Polski,* March 15, 1916, CFLPS.
13. John Radzilowski, "Fecund Newcomers or Dying Ethnics? Demographic Approaches to the History of Polish and Italian Immigrants and Their Children," *Journal of American Ethnic History* 27, no. 1 (Fall 2007): 60–74.
14. Kula et al., *Writing Home,* 298–99.
15. Ibid., 385.
16. Frank Kozik interview transcript, Oral History Archives of Chicago Polonia, Box 3, fl. Koz-114, Chicago History Museum, p. 17.
17. *Naród Polski,* June 14, 1914.
18. *Naród Polski,* March 12, 1902, CFLPS.
19. *Dziennik Związkowy,* November 21, 1911, CFLPS.
20. *Dziennik Związkowy/Zgoda,* March 15, 1910, CFLPS.
21. *Naród Polski,* June 19, 1901, CFLPS.
22. Radzilowski, "Immigrant Women and Their Daughters," 9–10; *Narod Polski,* August 7, 1912, CFLPS
23. *Dziennik Chicagoski,* August 7, 1896, CFLPS.
24. See *Dziennik Chicagoski,* February 26, 1907, CFLPS.
25. Roman Lapkiewicz interview transcript, Oral History Archives of Chicago Polonia, Box 5, fl. Lap-048, Chicago History Museum, p. 2.
26. *Naród Polski,* December 13, 1905, CFLPS.

27. Kantowicz, "Polish Chicago," 177.

28. Joseph C. Bigott, *From Cottage to Bungalow: Houses and the Working Class in Metropolitan Chicago, 1869–1929* (Chicago: University of Chicago Press, 2001), 120–145.

29. Marta Leszczyk, interview transcript, Oral History Archives of Chicago Polonia, Box 5, fl. Les-032, Chicago History Museum, p. 29.

30. Lillian Cwik, interview transcript, Oral History Archives of Chicago Polonia, Box 2, fl. Cwi-072, Chicago History Museum, p. 26.

31. Mary Hojnacki, interview transcript, Oral History Archives of Chicago Polonia, Box 3, fl. Hoj-066, Chicago History Museum, p. 6.

32. Ibid., 6–7.

33. Catherine Kozik, interview transcript, Oral History Archives of Chicago Polonia, Box 3, fl. Koz-113, Chicago History Museum, p. 6.

### 3. Praca: Poles in Industrial Illinois

1. Kula, et al. *Writing Home*, 363–64.

2. Pacyga, *Polish Immigrants in Industrial Chicago*, 50, 52.

3. Ibid., 48. See also "Meatpacking," *Encyclopedia of Chicago*, www.encyclopedia.chicagohistory.org/pages/804.html.

4. "Iron and Steel," *Encyclopedia of Chicago*, www.encyclopedia.chicagohistory.org/pages/653.html.

5. Pacyga, *Polish Immigrants in Industrial Chicago*, 82.

6. Ibid., 89–95.

7. For a description of the disaster and a list of victims, see http://hinton-gen.com/coal/bureau_cherry.html.

8. William Galush, "Journeys of Spirit and Space: Religion and Economics in Migration," *Polish American Studies* 59, no. 2 (Autumn 2002): 5–16.

9. Pacyga, *Polish Immigrants in Industrial Chicago*, 78.

10. Ibid.,109; *Wages and Hours of Labor in the Iron and Steel Industry: 1907–1924* (Washington, DC: GPO, 1925), 10, 19, passim.

11. *History of Wages in the United States from Colonial Times to 1928. Revision of Bulletin No. 499 with supplement, 1929–1933* (Washington: GPO, 1934), 332.

12. Leila Houghteling, *The Income and Standards of Living of Unskilled Laborers in Chicago* (Chicago: University of Chicago Press, 1927), 24, 186–217.

13. Ibid., 57–58.

14. Ibid., 56.

15. Galush, "Journeys of Spirit and Space," 11.

16. Angela Mischke Papers, 9.

17. Ibid., 9–10.

18. Chester Parks, *Life in the Old Neighborhood . . . and Beyond* (Henderson, NV: Mystic Publishers, 2006), 60.

19. *Dziennik Chicagoski*, April 27, 1892.

20. *Dziennik Związkowy*, February 14, 1918.

21. Pacyga, *Polish Immigrants in Industrial Chicago*, 67.

22. Ibid., 58.

23. *Naród Polski*, January 8, 1897.

24. Angela Mischke Papers, 3–4. Her father's wages as a presser appear to be average for the industry at the time. See *Wages and Hours of Labor in the Men's Clothing Industry, 1911 to 1924* (Washington, DC: GPO, 1925), 7.

25. Ibid., 7.

26. John J. Bukowczyk, "The Transformation of Working Class Ethnicity: Corporate Control, Americanization, and the Polish Immigrant Middle Class in Bayonne, New Jersey, 1915–1925," *Labor History* 25, no. 1 (1984): 53.

27. "Yesterday's Proletarian Riot," *Chicago Tribune*, May 9, 1876.

28. *Dziennik Chicagoski*, May 10, 1895.

29. *Dziennik Chicagoski*, January 19, 1904.

30. *Dziennik Chicagoski*, July 27, 1893.

31. *Dziennik Chicagoski*, June 10, 1893.

32. "First Blood: A Collision between Strikers and Militia at Lemont," *Bloomington (IL) Weekly Leader*, May 7, 1885; "Two Strikers Killed," *Ogdensburg (NY) Journal*, May 5, 1885, p. 1.

33. Thaddeus C. Radzialowski, "The Competition for Jobs and Racial Stereotypes: Poles and Blacks in Chicago," *Polish American Studies* 33, no. 2 (Autumn 1976): 5–18. Radzialowski's account is based on Polish newspapers, *Kuryer Polski* and *Dziennik Chicagoski*, as well as the *Chicago Tribune* and *New York Times*.

34. Ibid., 10–11; *Dziennik Chicagoski*, June 16, 1893. Both Polish and English newspapers carried differing numbers of casualties in the days that followed, and some of the injured, like Kluga, died later from their wounds.

35. *Dziennik Chicagoski*, July 9, 1894.

36. *Zgoda*, December 26, 1894.

37. Dominic A. Pacyga, "Crisis and Community: Back of the Yards, 1921," *Chicago History* 6, no. 2 (1977): 167–76.

38. Quoted in Radzilowski, "Immigrant Women and their Daughters," 19–20.

39. *Dziennik Zjednoczenia*, February 3, 1922.

40. John Radzilowski, "Fr. Wincenty Barzyński and a Polish Catholic Response to Industrial Capitalism," *Polish American Studies* 58, no. 2 (Autumn 2001): 23–32.

41. See Adam Walaszek, "Polish Wobblies and their Press, 1905–1917," *Znanstvena Revija* [Maribor, Slovenia] Humanities 3, no. 2 (1991): 465–73.

## 4. Wiara: Faith and Religious Life

1. This can be confirmed by a close comparison of census figures by nativity and mother tongue in the early century. For Chicago, see John Radzilowski, "Conflict

between Poles and Jews in Chicago, 1900–1930," *Polin: Studies in Polish Jewry* 19 (2007): 117–33, esp. table 1.

2. See F. Niklewicz, *Historja Polaków w Stanie Illinois* (Green Bay, WI: n.p., 1938), 4, 33.

3. Kruszka, *History of Poles in America to 1908,* 2:239.

4. Radzilowski, *Eagle and the Cross,* 37–40.

5. "Krótka Historya Parafii św. Walentego w Peru, Illinois," 1916, scanned copy of twenty-fifth-anniversary parish history book provided by Mr. John Krolak of Peru, Illinois.

6. *History of the Joliet Diocese Presented on the Occasion of the Dedication of the Cathedral of St. Raymond Nonnatus, May 26, 1955* (Joliet, IL: n.p., 1955), 73.

7. *Dziennik Chicagoski,* February 29, 1892.

8. Parks, *Life in the Old Neighborhood,* 46; Parish offering book, 1930–66, Anna Procanin Papers, Immigration History Research Center, University of Minnesota.

9. *St. James Apostle Parish, Chicago, Illinois, Golden Anniversary* (Chicago: n.p., [1964]). 29.

10. *Zgoda,* April 16, 1890.

11. *Polonia,* February 13, 1936.

12. See *Dziennik Chicagoski,* April 25, 1896.

13. Parot, *Polish Catholics in Chicago,* 74.

14. Ibid.

15. Charles Shanabruch, *Chicago's Catholics: The Evolution of an American Identity* (Notre Dame, IN: Notre Dame University Press, 1981), 215ff.

16. Golec, *Polonia in St. Clair County,* 73–74.

17. *St. Mary of Czestochowa Parish, Cicero, Illinois, 1895–1995* (Chicago, 1995), 23.

18. The estimate is drawn from Reverend Francis Bolek, *The Polish American School System* (New York: Columbia Press Corp., 1948).

19. Sister Mary Feliciana, "The Chicago Province of the Felician Sisters," *Polish American Studies* 18, no. 2 (July–December 1961): 100–106; *Sacrum Poloniae Millennium,* vol. 6, *The Contribution of the Poles to the Growth of Catholicism in the United States* (Rome, 1959), 412–44; Raphael Middeke and Stanley J. Konieczny, *Profiles from Our Heritage: Stories of Catholics who Helped Shape the Church of Southern Illinois* (St. Louis: The Patrice Press, 1987), 220–23.

20. Shanabruch, *Chicago's Catholics,* 95–96.

21. Middeke and Konieczny, *Profiles from Our Heritage,* 114.

22. Kruszka, *History of Poles in America to 1908,* 2:257.

23. *Goniec Polski* [South Bend], February 2, 1901.

24. See for example *Goniec Polski* [South Bend], January 5, 1901.

25. *Pamiętnik Parafii Świętej Trójcy w Chicago, Ill., 1893–1918* (Chicago: n.p., 1918), 7–15.

26. Parot, *Polish Catholics in Chicago,* 102–4.

27. "An Open Letter from Reverend Vincent Barzynski, C. R., to the People of St. Hedwig Parish," *Dziennik Chicagoski*, January 19, 1895.

28. Parot, *Polish Catholics in Chicago*, 110–19.

29. James S. Pula, *Polish Americans: An Ethnic Community* (New York: Twayne, 1995), 42–44.

30. "Facts about the National Church," *Przebudzenie*, December 25, 1927; Paul Fox, *The Polish National Catholic Church* (Scranton, PA: School of Christian Living, 1953).

31. Adeline Szymaniak Kozak, *The History of All Saints Cathedral of the Polish National Catholic Church, Chicago, Illinois* (Chicago: All Saints Cathedral, 1996), 7–9.

32. Details of the history of many of these parishes remain sketchy at best, and standard histories of the PNCC are often vague on many basic details of parish founding. See Fox, *Polish National Catholic Church*, 139–41; Stephen Wlodarski, *The Origin and Growth of the Polish National Catholic Church* (Scranton, PA: PNCC, 1974), 110. At this writing, two of the remaining six PNCC parishes in Illinois serve Spanish-speaking congregations

33. Anna D. Jaroszyńska-Kirchmann, ed., *Letters from Readers in the Polish American Press, 1902–1969: A Corner for Everybody* (Lanham, MD: Lexington Books, 2014), 91.

34. Ibid., 82.

35. *Bicz Bózy*, April 12, 1912.

36. "First Polish Bishop in America," *Dziennik Chicagoski*, June 20, 1908.

## 5. Polonia: Polish Community Life in Illinois

1. *Pamiętnik Jubileuszowy 25-cio lecia Parafii Matki Boskiej Częstochowskiej w Hawthorne, Cicero, Ill., 1895–1920* (Cicero, IL: n.p., 1920), 28ff.

2. Franciszek Barć, "Na Koralowy Jubileusz Naszej Parafii," *Coralline Jubilee Ascension of Our Lord Parish, 1912–1947* (Evanston, IL: n.p., 1947).

3. Figures are taken from Bolek, *Polish American School System* (see appendix 2).

4. Mischke Papers, 6–7.

5. Parks, *Life in the Old Neighborhood*, 46–47.

6. *Dzeinnik Chicagoski*, June 25, 1890, quoted in *St. Stanislaus College—Weber High School, 1890–1940* (Chicago: n.p., 1942), 13

7. Ibid., 14–21; *Poles of Chicago, 1837–1937*, 128–30; *Chicago Polonia Directory* (Chicago: n.p., 1987), 8–9; Ray Quintanilla, "Weber High School to Close after 109 Years," *Chicago Tribune*, April 1, 1999. The school was renamed in honor of Bishop Józef Weber, C.R., an auxiliary bishop of Lwów between 1901 and 1906.

8. *Złota Księga Fundatorów* (Chicago: n.p., 1928); *Blue and Gold* Holy Trinity High School Yearbook, 1951, Central Archives of Polonia, Orchard Lake Michigan.

9. *Dziennik Chicagoski*, December 15, 1893; *Dziennik Związkowy*, October 8, 1910.

10. Frederick J. Augustyn Jr., "Together and Apart: Lithuanian and Polish Immigrant Adult Literacy Programs in Chicago, 1890–1930," *Polish American Studies* 57, no. 2 (Autumn 2000): 31–44.

11. *Poles of Chicago, 1837–1937*, 135; Mary Cygan, "Political and Cultural Leadership in an Immigrant Community: Polish American Socialism, 1880–1950," PhD diss. Northwestern University, 1989, 61.

12. See Karen Majewski, *Traitors and True Poles: Narrating a Polish-American Identity, 1880–1939* (Athens: Ohio University Press, 2003); Anna D. Jaroszyńska-Kirchmann, *The Polish Hearst: Ameryka-Echo and the Public Role of the Immigrant Press* (Champaign: University of Illinois Press, 2015).

13. Helena Chrzanowska, "Polish Book Publishing in Chicago," *Polish American Studies* 4, no. 1–2 (1947): 37–39.

14. Janusz Albin and Iwona Marciniak, "Chicagowski 'Tygodnik Powieściowo--Naukowy' na tle Działalności Księgarskiej i Wydawniczej Władysława Dyniewicza," *Ze Skarbca Kultury*, no. 42 (1986): 83–161.

15. See for example *Dziennik Chicagoski*, February 14, 1985.

16. Mischke Papers, 4–5.

17. See *A Guide to Polish American Newspapers and Periodicals in Microform* (Minneapolis: Immigration History Research Center, University of Minnesota, 1988).

18. Radzilowski, *Eagle and the Cross*, 47–57.

19. Pula, *Polish Americans*, 34–35.

20. Thaddeus C. Radzialowski, "Immigrant Nationalism and Feminism: *Glos Polek* and the Polish Women's Alliance in America, 1898–1917," *Review Journal of Philosophy and Social Science* [Meerut, India] 2, no. 2 (Winter 1977): 183–203.

21. See *Dzień Macierzy Polskiej: Pamiętnik 16 lipca 1939 r.* (Chicago, 1939) and *29th Convention Polish Alma Mater of America, 1897–1972* (Chicago, 1972) found in Central Archives of American Polonia, Orchard Lake, Mich.

22. *Ustawy Towarzystwa Bratniej Pomocy sw. Michala Archaniola w Radomiu, Ill.*, 1898, Booklet, Central Archives of Polonia, Orchard Lake, Mich., file box 56 Diocese of Belleville, Ill.

23. Ledger book, PNA Group 760—Towarzystwo Bratniej Pomocy Artylerii Polskiej, 1905–1975, Central Archives of Polonia, Orchard Lake, Mich.

24. Radzilowski, *Eagle and the Cross*, 87–114.

25. *The Healing Touch: Jubilee Memoir, St. Mary of Nazareth Hospital, Chicago, 1894–1944* (Chicago, 1944). A Polish version appears under the title *Bo Cierpią: Wspomnienia Jubileuszowe Szpital Matki Bożej z Nazaretu, Chicago, 1894–1944*.

26. Ibid.; "St. Mary of Nazareth Hospital Center," http://pgsa.org/research-directory /archdiocese-of-chicago-polish-parishes/other-institutions/st-mary-of-nazareth-hospital -center/ (accessed October 17, 2016).

27. *Pamiętnik Jubileuszowy ku czci Ks. Ludwika Grudzińskiego, 1903–1928* (Chicago: n.p., 1928), 63.

28. *Poles in Chicago*, 116–17.

29. Ibid., 117–18.

30. William Galush, "The Unremembered Movement: Abstinence among Polish Americans," *Polish American Studies* 63, no. 2 (Autumn 2006): 13–22.

31. *Poles in Chicago*, 116–17; *Dziennik Chicagoski*, January 22, 1921, and February 8, 1921; "The Polish Welfare Association—A Meritorious Organization," *Chicago Society News*, undated report [1921] in Chicago Foreign Language Press Survey; https://www.polish.org/en/home/our-history (accessed October 19, 2016).

32. "Polish Society for the Protection of Women," *Dziennik Związkowy*, March 28, 1917.

33. Ibid.

34. Thaddeus Gromada, "Goral Regionalism and Polish Immigration to America," in *Pastor of the Poles*, ed. Stanislaus Blejwas and Mieczysław Biskupski (New Britain, CT: Polish Studies Program Monograph, 1982), 105–11.

35. For a short history of the organization, see zppa.org (accessed on October 7, 2016).

36. *Golden Jubilee, Alliance of Polish Clubs: Związek Klubów Małopolskich, Chicago, Illinois, 1928–1978* (Chicago: n.p., 1978).

37. Jubilee books of Club Łęczan, Anna Procanin Papers, IHRC; "W trosce o Małą Ojczyznę," *Dziennik Związkowy*, February 24, 2012, http://dziennikzwiazkowy.com/sprawy-polonijne/przed-jubileuszem-90-lecia-klubu-czan/ (accessed October 3, 2016).

38. James S. Pula, ed. *The Polish American Encyclopedia* (Jefferson, NC: McFarland, 2011), 285–86, 562.

39. Radzilowski, *Eagle and the Cross*, 182–84.

40. Ibid., 184–88; Lori A. Matten, "Scouting for Identity: Recruiting Daughters to Save the Traditional Polish Family during the Interwar Years," *Polish American Studies* 71, no. 1 (Spring 2014): 5–36.

41. See John Radzilowski, "Conflict between Poles and Jews in Chicago, 1900–1930," *Polin: Studies in Polish Jewry* 19 (2007): 117–34.

42. *The Second Largest Polish City in the World*, 2.

43. See Victoria Granicki, *Chicago's Polish Downtown* (Charleston, SC: Arcadia, 2004).

44. *Dziennik Związkowy*, August 11, 1917.

45. Golec, *Polonia in St. Clair County*, 11–63.

## 6. Czykago: Capital of Polonia

1. See for example a Polish business directory, *The Second Largest Polish City in the World* (Chicago: Alliance Daily Zgoda, 1930), in the collection of the Immigration History Research Center Archives, University of Minnesota.

2. Jacob Kaplan et al., *Avondale and Chicago's Polish Village* (Charleston, SC: Arcadia, 2014), 6–8.

3. John Radzilowski, "Fecund Newcomers or Dying Ethnics? Demographic Approaches to the History of Italian and Polish Immigrants and their Children in the

United States, 1880 to 1980," *Journal of American Ethnic History* 27, no. 1 (Fall 2007): 60–74.

4. See Edward Kantowicz, *Polish-American Politics in Chicago, 1888–1940* (Chicago: University of Chicago Press, 1975); idem, "The Limitations of Ethnic Politics: Polish Americans in Chicago," in *Ethnic Politics in Urban America,* Angela Pienkos, ed. (Chicago: Polish American Historical Association, 1978), 92–105.

5. *Dziennik Chicagoski,* Oct. 7, 1892.

6. Quoted in Kantowicz, *Polish-American Politics in Chicago,* 50–51.

7. Cygan, "Political and Cultural Leadership," 16, 21.

8. Ibid., 34, 48–50.

9. Adam Walaszek, "Polish Wobblies and Their Press, 1905–1917," *Znanstvene Revija* [Maribor, SL], Humanities 3, no. 2 (1991): 465–73.

10. These numbers are a very rough estimate as scholars have been unable to establish precise numbers of Polish socialists. See Cygan, "Political and Cultural Leadership," 65.

11. Kantowicz, *Polish Politics in Chicago,* 121–24, 140–45.

12. Ibid., 95.

13. Walaszek, "Polish Wobblies and their Press," 465–73.

14. Donald Pienkos, *For Your Freedom through Ours: Polish American Efforts on Poland's Behalf, 1863–1991* (Boulder, CO: East European Monographs, 1991), 252–56.

15. *Dziennik Związkowy,* February 1, 1908.

16. Pienkos, *For Your Freedom through Ours,* 54–57.

17. *Dziennik Związkowy,* December 9, 1914; Radzilowski, *Eagle and the Cross,* 149–51.

18. *Naród Polski,* April 25, 1917.

19. *Dziennik Związkowy,* October 6, 1917.

20. *Naród Polski,* July 3, 1918, p. 7; Dominic Pacyga, *Chicago: A Biography* (Chicago: University of Chicago Press, 2011), 201.

21. *Polonia,* January 3, 1918.

22. *Dziennik Związkowy,* April 26, 1918.

23. Pula, *Polish Americans,* 60.

24. "St Adalbert Parish, East St. Louis, IL" typescript ca. 1949, collected by Fr. Francis Bolek, CAP Orchard Lake, Mich. See also *Jakubowo: Souvenir Silver Jubilee, 1914–1939, St. James Church, Hanson Park, Chicago, Illinois* (Chicago: n.p., 1939 [1940]), 32–36.

25. Radzilowski, *Eagle and the Cross,* 159.

26. *Naród Polski,* January 8, 1913.

27. *Naród Polski,* August 7, 1912.

28. Jack Lait and Lee Mortimer, *Chicago Confidential!* (New York: Crown, 1950), 80.

29. John Radzilowski, "Crime, Deviance, Delinquency and Reform in Polish Chicago, 1890s to 1940s," *Fiedorczyk Lecture in Polish American Studies,* Central Connecticut State University, no. 17, 2002 [2008], 12–13.

30. Ibid., 22–23 (quote from Frederick Thrasher, *The Gang* [Chicago: University of Chicago Press, 1929], 198–99).

31. Ibid., 15–19. There were also gangsters of Polish-Jewish origin, such as Jake "Greasy Thumb" Guzik, but these are outside the scope of this book.

32. *Naród Polski,* December 20, 1911.

33. Radzilowski, "Crime, Deviance, Delinquency and Reform," 35.

34. Kenneth Jackson, *The Ku Klux Klan in the City, 1915–1930* (Oxford: Oxford University Press, 1967), 95–96.

35. *Dziennik Zjednoczenia,* September 3, 1927.

36. Radzilowski, *Eagle and the Cross,* 236.

## 7. Kultura: Polish and Polish American Culture in Illinois

1. *Poles of Chicago,* 29–39; http://www.illinoisart.org/no-24-walter-krawiec (accessed November 14, 2016). Walter Krawiec was also a noted cartoonist for the *Polish Daily News.*

2. Ibid., 56–57.

3. Stanislaus Blejwas, *Choral Patriotism: The Polish Singers Alliance of America* (Rochester, NY: University of Rochester Press, 2005).

4. Polish Arts Club of Chicago, www.pacchicago.org (accessed March 17, 2017); Pula, *Polish American Encyclopedia,* 248–49.

5. See "News from K. Jasinski School of Music," *Dziennik Zjednoczenia,* October 19, 1927.

6. Sheet music collections at the Polish Museum of America include printed songbooks from the twentieth century from Polish publishers and shops such as W. H. Sajewski, Boleslaw J. Zalewski, Jan. R. Hibner, John Jasinski, Chart Music Publishing, Vitak-Elsnic Co., Goergi & Vitak Music Co., Gralak Music Co, and Jay Publishing.

7. See *Fire in the Mountains: Polish Mountain Fiddle Music,* vol. 1, *The Karol Stoch Band,* music CD, liner notes by T. Cooley and R. Spottswood, ([Minneapolis]: Shanachie Entertainment, 1997).

8. Robert Crease, "In Praise of the Polka," *The Atlantic,* August 1989: 73–83.

9. See the Lira Ensemble's website, www.liraensemble.org/.

10. See the Paderewski Symphony Orchestra's website, http://www.pasochicago.org/.

11. Stanley J. Konieczny, "Emergence of a Polish-American Community in St. Clair Country," in Middeke and Konieczny, *Profiles from Our Heritage.* On the history of Polish theater in America, see Emil Orzechowski, *Teatr polonijny w Stanach Zjednoczonych* (Wrocław: Ossolineum, 1989).

12. *Dziennik Chicagoski,* July 6, 1891.

13. See for example "The Fern Flower" or "A Night of Enchantment," *Dziennik Chicagoski,* August 30, 1892; "Jasnogóra," *Dziennik Chicagoski,* June 26, 1892; "Children of Israel," *Dziennik Chicagoski,* February 29, 1892; "Wnuka Piastów Czyli Perła Cyllejska,"

*Dziennik Chicagoski,* January 29, 1893. For a brief biography of Zahajkiewicz, see his obituary in *Naród Polski,* October 24, 1917; Pula, *Polish American Encyclopedia,* 559.

14. See *Dziennik Chicagoski,* October 12, 1892.

15. Mary Cygan, "Political and Cultural Leadership in an Immigrant Community: Polish American Socialism, 1880–1950," PhD diss., Northwestern University, 1989, 56.

16. Victoria Granicki, *Chicago's Polish Downtown* (Charleston, SC: Arcadia, 2004), 93.

17. Mary Cygan, "A 'New Art' for Polonia: Polish American Radio Comedy during the 1930s," Polish American Studies 45, no. 2 (Autumn 1988): 5–22.

18. *Dziennik Chicagoski,* May 11, 1896.

19. *Dziennik Zjednoczenia,* January 6, 1927; ibid., January 7, 1927.; ibid., January 17, 1927.

20. *Dziennik Chicagoski,* January 6, 1928.

21. Golec, *Polonia in St. Clair County,* 97. See also Józef Migała, *Polish Radio Broadcasting in the United States* (Boulder, CO: East European Monographs, 1987).

22. Cygan, "'New Art' for Polonia," 11.

23. Ibid., 11–22.

24. Lillian Cwik, interview transcript, Oral History Archives of Chicago Polonia, Box 2, fl. Cwi-072, Chicago History Museum, p. 33.

25. Edmund J. Dehnert, "From Neighborhood Tavern to Parish Hall: An Evolution of Polish-American Folklife," *Great Lakes Review* 11, no. 2 (Fall 1985): 3–21.

26. Radzilowski, "Crime, Delinquency, Deviance, and Reform," 27–28.

27. *Dziennik Związkowy,* August 11, 1917; *Poles of Chicago,* 190, 207.

28. *Poles of Chicago,* 202, 212.

29. Ibid., 218; http://www.atkfoods.com/our-brands/slotkowski.

30. *Poles of Chicago,* 227, 245.

31. Leah Zeldes, "How Do Local Polish Butchers Elevate Sausage to an Art Form? With Generous Use of Spices and More," *Chicago Sun Times,* October 22, 2008; http://www.jimsoriginal.com/jimsoriginal/Welcome/.

32. *Dziennik Chicagoski,* Oct. 10, 1893.

33. See http://www.smosparish.com/stations-of-the-cross.html (accessed December 3, 2016).

### 8. Po Wojnie: Poles in Illinois during the Cold War Era

1. Rae Bielakawski, "Polish Americans," *Ethnic and Racial Minorities in the U.S. Military: An Encyclopedia,* ed. Alexander Bielakawski (New York: ABC-CLIO, 2013).

2. Radzilowski, *Eagle and the Cross,* 211.

3. Anna Jaroszyńska-Kirchmann, *The Exile Mission: The Polish Political Diaspora and Polish Americans, 1939–1956* (Athens: Ohio University Press, 2004), 41.

4. Radzilowski, "Fecund Newcomers or Dying Ethnics?" 69–70; idem, "American Polonia in World War II: Toward a Social History," *Polish American Studies* 58, no. 2

(Spring 2001): 63–80. The 1944 survey data from Illinois apparently did not survive, but there is no reason to believe that Illinois would differ from other states with large Polish populations. Nationally, the U.S. Census in 1980 and 1990 showed unusually high rates of World War II–era veterans among Polish Americans. The survey data cards are now in the collections of the Polish Museum of America archives.

5. Radzilowski, *Eagle and the Cross*, 220–22.

6. *Chicago Tribune*, October 10, 1942, p. 13.

7. See http://www.history.army.mil/html/moh/wwII-m-s.html#MOSKALA and http://www.ww2research.com/frank-p-witek/ (both accessed November 25, 2016).

8. Liam T. A. Ford, *Soldier Field: A Stadium and Its City* (Chicago: University of Chicago Press, 2009), 138–39. In 1945, Nora Witek also christened a U.S. Navy destroyer, USS *Witek* named after her son.

9. *St. James Apostle Parish, Chicago, Illinois, Golden Anniversary* (Chicago: n.p., 1964), 25. Strank was born very close to the Polish border, adjacent to an area from which many of the parish's families had originated.

10. See *Five Holy Martyrs Church and School, 1909–1959: Golden Jubilee* (Chicago: n.p., 1959); *Golden Jubilee, 1893–1943: St. Stanislaus Bishop and Martyr Church* (Chicago: n.p., 1943); *Pamiętnik Złotego Jubileuszu Parafii Matki Boskiej Częstochowskiej, Cicero, Illinois* (Cicero: n.p., 1945), 48–50.

11. See Joanna Wojdon, *Red and White Umbrella: The Polish American Congress in the Cold War Era* (Budapest: Helena History Press, 2015).

12. Later, the PAC did allow individual memberships, but their position remained ambiguous.

13. On range of lobbying conducted by the PAC, see Donald Pienkos, *For Your Freedom through Ours: Polish American Efforts on Poland's Behalf, 1863–1991* (New York: Columbia University Press/EEM, 1991).

14. Tadeusz Piotrowski, ed., *Polish Deportees of World War II: Recollections of Removal to the Soviet Union and Dispersal throughout the World* (Jefferson, NC: McFarland, 2004), 196.

15. Ibid., 195, 197; Jaroszyńszka-Kirchmann, *Exile Mission*, 46.

16. Jaroszyńszka-Kirchmann, *Exile Mission*, 281n28.

17. Ibid., 121.

18. Wesley Adamczyk, *When God Looked the Other Way: An Odyssey of War, Exile, and Redemption* (Chicago: University of Chicago Press, 2004), 211–17.

19. Antonette Brusik Metelski, *Memories* (Chicago: n.p., 2004), 83–84.

20. John Z. Guzlowski, *Echoes of Tattered Tongues: Memory Unfolded* (Los Angeles: Aquila Polonica, 2016), xvii.

21. For the biography of a Siberian refugee who joined the Polish American Felician Sisters, see Sister Marie Irene Petrykowski CSSF, *Lucia's Journey: The Life Story of Sister Mary Lucia Skalka, C.S.S.F.* (Chicago: Felician Sisters, 2003).

22. *25 Lecie Hacerstwa Polskiego w Chicago, 1949–1974* (Chicago: n.p., 1974).

23. Helena Ziolkowska and Richard Lysakowski, "Polish Saturday Schools in the Chicago Area: Their Growth and Development." Chicago: Polish Teachers Association in America, October 1982. Typescript. Immigration History Research Center Archives, University of Minnesota.

24. Jaroszyńszka-Kirchmann, *Exile Mission,* 145.

25. Mary Janka, interview transcript, Oral History Archives of Chicago Polonia, Box 3, fl. Jan-116, Chicago History Museum, p. 9.

26. Ewa Bielański et al., *Kościół Świętej Trójcy, 1906–2006* (Chicago: Polish Pastoral Mission, 2006).

27. Illinois survey sheets, "Preliminary Study of the Use of Polish, Orchard Lake Center for Polish Studies and Culture, Orchard Lake, Mich." Central Archives of Polonia, Orchard Lake Schools, Orchard Lake, Mich.

28. *Diamond Anniversary, St. Josephat Church, 1884–1959* (Chicago: n.p., 1959), 38.

29. *St. Hedwig Parish: 85th Year, 1888–1973* (Chicago: n.p., 1973), 21.

30. *125th Anniversary, St. Boniface Church,* 6.

31. Nicholas Leffner, interview transcript, Oral History Archives of Chicago Polonia, Box 5, fl. Lef-085, Chicago History Museum, p. 17.

32. Golec, *Polonia in St. Clair County,* 99–100.

33. See for example, *Naród Polski,* August 6, 1919. On the lack of Poles in the 1947 Pullman race riot, see Janice L. Reiff, "Rethinking Pullman: Urban Space and Working Class Activism," *Social Science History* 24, no. 1 (Spring 2000): 7–32. More generally on this topic, see Radzialowski, "Competition for Jobs."

34. William M. Tuttle, "Labor Conflict and Racial Violence: The Black Worker in Chicago, 1894–1919," *Labor History* 10 (Summer 1969): 432.

35. Quintard Taylor, "The Chicago Political Machine and Black-Ethnic Conflict and Accommodation," *Polish American Studies* 29, no. 1–2 (Spring–Autumn 1972): 40–66.

36. Joseph Parot, "The Racial Dilemma in Chicago's Polish Neighborhoods, 1920–1970," *Polish American Studies* 32, no. 2 (Autumn 1975): 27–37.

37. Kirchmann, *Letters from Readers,* 448–50.

38. Joseph Parot, "Ethnic versus Black Metropolis: The Origins of Polish-Black Housing Tensions in Chicago," *Polish American Studies* 29, no. 1–2 (Spring–Autumn 1972): 7–33.

39. Cited in *Congressional Record,* 93rd Congress, 2nd sess., vol. 120, pt. 2 (May 9, 1974 to May 16, 1974), p. 15197–201 (Washington: GPO, 1974).

40. Thomas Napierkowski, "A Stepchild of America: My Polish-American Literary Odyssey," *Forkroads: A Journal of Ethnic American Literature* 1, no. 2 (Winter 1995): 57–68.

41. Thaddeus C. Radzialowski, "View from a Polish Ghetto: Reflections on the First Hundred Years in Detroit," *Ethnicity* 1, no. 2 (1974): 125–50.

42. Pula, *Polish Americans,* 119–21.

43. Mary Patrice Erdmans, *Opposite Poles: Immigrants and Ethnics in Polish Chicago, 1976–1990* (University Park, PA: Penn State University Press, 1998), 61.

44. Mary Patrice Erdmans, "Poland," in *The New Americans: A Guide to Immigration since 1965,* ed. Mary C. Waters and Reed Ueda (Cambridge, MA: Harvard University Press, 2007), 570–78.

45. Mary Patrice Erdmans, "Portraits of Immigration: Sour Milk and Honey in the Promised Land," *Sociological Inquiry* 69, no. 3 (August 1999): 337–64.

46. Erdmans, "Poland," 575. See also Alicja Kuklińska, "40 lat Polskiej Szkoły Sobotniej im. Mikołaja Kopernika w Niles," *Zgoda* 146, no. 1 (January–March 2016): 23.

47. Erdmans, *Opposite Poles,* 45, 114–17.

48. Ibid., 125–28.

## 9. Dziś i wczoraj: Poles in Illinois, Today and Yesterday

1. Jarosław Rokicki, "Polish Ancestry and Multiethnic Identity: A Case Study of Students in Wisconsin and Illinois," *Polish American Studies* 57, no. 2 (Autumn 2000): 67–91.

2. Rob Paral et al., "The Polish Population of Metro Chicago: A Community Profile of Strengths and Needs," Polish American Association, June 2004.

3. Ewa Bielański et al., *Kościół Świętej Trójcy, 1906–2006* (Chicago: Polish Pastoral Mission, 2006).

4. See "4 Officers Charged in Shakedowns," *Chicago Tribune,* November 22, 2000, http://articles.chicagotribune.com/2000-11-22/news/0011220397_1_official-misconduct -police-powers-police-veteran (accessed May 3, 2017).

5. John Radzilowski, "Polska Diaspora w Stanach Zjednoczonych, 1989–2000," in *Polska Diaspora,* ed. Adam Walaszek (Kraków: Wyd. Literackie, 2001), 112–17.

6. See http://www.canons-regular.org/.

# FURTHER READING

Bukowczyk, John. *And My Children Did Not Know Me: A History of the Polish Americans*. Bloomington: Indiana University Press, 1987.

Erdmans, Mary Patrice. *Opposite Poles: Immigrants and Ethnics in Polish Chicago, 1976–1990*. University Park, PA: Penn State University Press, 1998.

Gunkel, Ann Hetzel. "The Polka Alternative: Polish American Polka as Resistant Ethnic Practice." The Fiedorczyk Lecture in Polish American Studies. New Britain: Central Connecticut State University, 2005.

Jaroszyńska-Kirchmann, Anna D. *The Exile Mission: The Polish Political Diaspora and Polish Americans, 1939–1956*. Athens: Ohio University Press, 2004.

———, ed. *Letter from Readers in the Polish American Press, 1920–1969: A Corner for Everybody*. Translated by Anna D. Jaroszyńska-Kirchmann and Theodore Zaiwstowski. Lanham, MD: Lexington Press, 2014.

Kantowicz, Edward. *Polish Politics in Chicago, 1880–1940*. Chicago: Chicago University Press, 1975.

Kruszka, Wacław. *A History of Poles in America to 1908*. Part 2: *Poles in Illinois*. Edited by James S. Pula. Washington, DC: Catholic University of America Press, 1994.

Pacyga, Dominic A. *Polish Immigrants and Industrial Chicago: Workers on the South Side, 1880–1922*. Columbus: Ohio State University Press, 1991.

Parot, Joseph John. *Polish Catholics in Chicago, 1850–1920*. De Kalb: Northern Illinois University Press, 1981.

Pula, James S. *Polish Americans: An Ethnic Community*. New York: Twayne, 1995.

———, ed. *The Polish American Encyclopedia*. Jefferson, NC: McFarland, 2011.

Radzilowski, John. *The Eagle and the Cross: A History of the Polish Roman Catholic Union of America, 1873–2000*. New York: EEM/Columbia University Press, 2003.

———. *Traveller's History of Poland*. Boston: Interlink, 2007, 2012.

Zurawski, Joseph. *Polish Chicago: Our History, Our Recipes*. St. Louis, MO: G. Bradley, 2007.

# INDEX

Page numbers in italics indicate illustrations.

JOHN RADZILOWSKI is an associate professor of history at the University of Alaska Southeast. He is the author, a coauthor, or the editor of numerous books and articles on immigration and ethnic history and the history of Poland and east-central Europe, including *American Immigration: An Encyclopedia of Political, Social, and Cultural Change* (2013) and *A Traveller's History of Poland* (2007, 2011).

ANN HETZEL GUNKEL is an associate professor of cultural studies and humanities at Columbia College Chicago and a past director of the college's cultural studies program. A winner of multiple major grants, she is a two-time Fulbright recipient for both research (Germany, 1992) and teaching (Poland, 2011) and has won the Harmonia Research Grant from the Polish National Science Center (2012). A leading expert on ethnic music in America, Gunkel is also an award-winning designer of educational multimedia and a published documentary photographer.